MAKING

THE PROGRESSIVE CASE

MAKING

THE PROGRESSIVE CASE

Towards a Stronger U.S. Economy

DAVID COATES

continuum

2011

The Continuum International Publishing Group
80 Maiden Lane, New York, NY 10038
The Tower Building, 11 York Road, London SE1 7NX

www.continuumbooks.com

Library of Congress Cataloging-in-Publication Data
A catalog record for this book is available from the Library of Congress.

ISBN: 978-1-4411-8650-8 (PB)
978-1-4411-9103-8 (HB)

Typeset by Newgen Imaging Systems Pvt Ltd, Chennai, India
Printed and bound in the United States of America

For Eileen

"If it is to be taken seriously again, the Left must find its voice."

(Tony Judt, *Ill Fares the Land*)

Contents

Preface		ix
Introduction		1
Chapter 1	The Financial Meltdown and the Obama Response	12
Chapter 2	Making the Case for Regulated Markets	34
Chapter 3	Making the Case for Managed Trade	60
Chapter 4	Making the Case for a Green Economy	89
Chapter 5	Making the Case for a Reform of the American Model	114
Chapter 6	The Politics of Winning	141
Appendix 1	The Causes of the Meltdown: An Update on the Debate	160
Appendix 2	The Economics in Play	179
Notes		189
Author Index		243
Subject Index		246

Associated website: www.davidcoates.net

Preface

Making the Progressive Case attempts to be two things at once. It attempts to be a "living book," one that is constantly updated on the website that supports it; and it attempts in that way also to be a "one-stop shop" for busy but politically active readers—a single place where they can find most/all of what they need to settle a particular issue or concern of the day. We live, after all, not simply in an age of contentious politics and the 24-hour news cycle. We live also in the age of the Internet and the iPhone. Because the politics is contentious, understanding and comparing divergent political positions is a vital democratic necessity. Because political events change rapidly while basic political positions do not, understanding the unchanging positions that shape dominant responses to the changing events is now more important than ever. And because modern readers draw their information from a multiplicity of new technologies, the presentation of political arguments, to be effective, requires that the gap be bridged between traditional methods of communication and new ones.

As a book and as an argument, *Making the Progressive Case* was designed from the outset as a mixture of the old and the new. The old is what you now have in your hand—a text written in what is hopefully an accessible and easy reading style, bringing into one place the core general arguments that progressives should find of value when attempting to counter conservative assertions on politics, economics and society. The text is solidly grounded in the best research that my support team and I could find. Its arguments are laid out in what we believe to be a carefully structured and clearly labeled way; and its material has been so organized that it can be read as a whole, or in sections, depending on your particular needs. The new is the linking of the text to a regularly updated website—www.davidcoates.net—where the immediate relevance of the general arguments is consistently re-established by linking them to the on-going daily political debate. The website will have, at the very least, the latest data sets, opinion pieces, video clips, and links to other sites—all designed to keep the arguments in *Making the Progressive Case* immediately applicable. The website will also take you to the earlier and companion volume to this one, *Answering Back: Liberal Responses to Conservative Arguments*. The books and the website together should give you most of what you need to handle immediate issues, but they will also point you to further reading, and other sources, to enable you to deepen your knowledge of the arguments in play if you so choose. I hope that you will settle into the habit of mixing books and website on a regular basis, and feel free to comment, on the website, on what you find there.

The material in *Making the Progressive Case* has another important characteristic, one first developed in *Answering Back*. In both volumes I have tried, as far as is possible, to lay out the strongest and more intellectual as well as the weaker and more popular conservative arguments, and to fully source those as well, in that way making it easy for you, the reader, to explore both sides of any political debate with which you are concerned, the better to come to your own view on the basis of that exploration. There is a politics in this approach as well as a pedagogy—an insistence that democracies flourish best when political opponents understand and respect the views of those with whom they disagree, and that democracies weaken if ignorance and intolerance trump the day. The quality of civil discourse is a vital democratic safeguard in a modern society, and one that is locally threatened by the enhanced stridency of much recent political debate in the United States. The manner in which the progressive case is made, as well as the content of that case, matters; which is why so much space is given, in the italicized sections of the chapters that follow, to arguments that are not progressive at all.

Preparing and writing a volume of this kind, and maintaining a website to constantly update the data sets and arguments it contains, is only possible with help. I have received much help, for all of which I am immensely grateful. A remarkable team of Wake Forest undergraduates has generated what often seemed endless quantities of high-quality data, filling my office with boxes and boxes of reports, press cuttings, government papers, and transcripts of programs and speeches. Kara Dickstein, Caitlin O'Connell, Benjamin Hunt, Nirali Parikh, Scott Gillespie, Jonathan Coates, Bradley Harper, and Ashley Smith are not responsible for what is written here, but they are responsible for making much of that writing possible. Will Clarke and Audrey Fannin designed the website, Ellen Sedeno and Carol Lanham publicized it, Wake Forest University granted me the resources that made the research and website possible, and endless kindred souls (friends all) tolerated hours of debate and discussion as I struggled to get the arguments into the appropriate shape. Don Frey and Mike Lawlor, John Leurini and Ian Taplin, Peter Siavelis and Katy Harriger have been more important in that role than even they probably realize; so while responsibility for what follows is mine and mine alone, the debt is theirs and deserves full public honor.

This volume is dedicated to my great partner and the love of my life. Every day I wake by her, it is bright morning.

David Coates
Winston-Salem, North Carolina
Thanksgiving 2010

Introduction

> *Two months into the presidency, approval ratings for the new president were still in the high 60's and for his Republican opponents in the mid 20s, with four Americans in five believing that the economic downturn was Bush's legacy rather than Obama's fault. But time will narrow those gaps. Conservative fortunes will rise again; and the Republican Party can be relied upon to do everything possible to slow liberal initiatives and to rewrite history in ways that place the blame for our contemporary ills on the politics of the center-left rather than on the politics of the center-right . . . So on one set of things at least we can be clear. If this liberal moment is to be consolidated, that consolidation will have to be won, and once won it will have to be defended. It will have to be won and defended by the adequacy of the policies emerging from the White House; and it will have to be won and defended by the quality of the arguments used to deflate and deflect an inevitable and well-orchestrated conservative push-back.*
>
> *(Answering Back, 2–3)*

What a difference two years make in times as serious as these. In November 2008, all was hope and glory on the center-left in American politics, all was despair and despondency on the center-right. But by November 2010, that was no longer the case. By then, a Democratic president swept to office on the promise of changing the polarized politics of Washington had hit the buffers created by that very polarization. He and his supporters had discovered just how difficult it was to effect bipartisan change when the party on the other side of the aisle was determined regularly to say "no." And a president elected on the assertion that "yes we can" had discovered the critical difference between campaigning in poetry and governing in prose. Saying and doing are very different things in American politics, and the discovery of that perennial truth drained the enthusiasm out of the Democratic base just as effectively as it re-galvanized the Republican one. In consequence, in what Paul Starr rightly calls "America's 20-year tug of war,"[1] political momentum shifted back—and shifted back very rapidly—into the hands of the very conservative forces whose future looked so bleak when Barack Obama first entered the White House. Since those conservative forces are now not simply back on the offensive, but are also significantly *more* conservative in policy and ideology than were their defeated predecessors, this shift in momentum is both critical and potentially dangerous for those of us committed to progressive change. If unchecked, the rise of the new conservatism will move the whole agenda of American politics even further to the right than it was in the Bush years: it will effect a genuine "moving right show" unless it is stopped. Stopping it requires a clear understanding of why the tidal wave of progressive enthusiasm that swept Obama to the presidency has now dissipated. Stopping it also requires that that tidal wave be rapidly reconstituted. Quite how to meet those urgent requirements is the central issue underlying all that follows here.

I

It is fairly clear why the tidal wave of enthusiasm that carried Obama to the presidency has now lost much of its force. From the very outset, it was a tidal wave that created expectations way beyond anything envisaged by the political actors it lifted to power; so that, even in easier political and economic times than those which beset us now, a level of disillusionment was presumably inevitable. Out of executive power for so long, progressive opinion poured all its hopes and dreams into the Obama campaign, ignoring as it did so the necessary limits on presidential capacity in a political system as constitutionally divided as this one. Moreover, what many of us missed on the night, but which now is all too evident, is that the Obama campaign put together a winning electoral coalition but it did not bring a governing coalition with it into Washington. On the contrary, the Democratic Party too often in 2008 picked up Congressional seats in traditionally Republican areas only by running ultra-conservative candidates under the Democratic banner. Voter alienation from the Bush administration was deep enough in that election to tip the balance in favor of such candidates, but that voter alienation proved quickly (and predictably) volatile, as likely as not the next time round (in 2010) to swing away from the new incumbents as (in 2008) it had swung away from the old ones. As was evident in similar political circumstances long ago, "support won by such methods is a reed shaken by every wind;"[2] in this instance, able to be retained only so long as vulnerable incumbent Democrats opposed the liberal elements in the Obama program.

Barack Obama came to Washington, that is, not simply with a supporting cast of liberal legislators but also with blue-dog Democrats in his camp. Keeping such a diverse coalition together then slowed the pace of reform and blunted its effectiveness, so helping to undermine the confidence of independent voters in the reform capacity of the new administration. It was a confidence that was also quickly eroded by the willingness and ability of the Republican Party to use every procedural device—and especially the senatorial filibuster—to slow this administration down. Two years of procedural wrangling and Democratic Party infighting later, and the Obama promise of a new politics looked particularly empty.[3] The irony of this, of course, is that when faced with that gap between promise and performance, the American electorate at midterm chose to punish more heavily, not the conservatives of either party who were responsible for it, but the liberals who had pushed so hard for reform. Obama came to Washington promising an end to gridlock. His failure immediately to meet that promise has left Washington now more gridlocked than ever.

II

In addition, there is the small matter of the legacy that the Obama administration inherited. It is a feature of democratic politics in predominantly conservative societies like this one that center-left governments are invariably called into existence only when severe circumstances have discredited the more normal governments of the center-right. Progressive administrations invariably enter office with much to prove and many promises to deliver, only to find themselves battling sets of problems that would test the mettle of any government, liberal or otherwise. Certainly the Obama administration entered office in just such an environment—one described by Frank Rich in his characteristically colorful way:

> His achievements so far have been accomplished in spite of obstacles that would fell most mortals—the almost unaccountable messes he inherited from Bush-Cheney, a cratered economy, a sclerotic Congress in thrall to lobbyists and special-interest money, and a rabid opposition underwritten by a media empire that owns both America's most-watched cable news channel and its most highly circulated newspaper.[4]

The scale of those problems, widely recognized as they were, initially induced many of Obama's liberal supporters to cut his administration a large amount of slack.[5] It was not the scale of the problem that eventually wore that support so thin. What wore it thin was the cautious nature of the administration's response to that scale. Obama the president proved as wobbly on the issue of the federal deficit as famously, two generations earlier, had FDR.[6] Obama the president proved way too dependent—in the eyes of many of his liberal supporters—on the caution of a Larry Summers or a Timothy Geitner, appearing to remain as close to the Wall Street orthodoxy and power-brokers as had the Bush administration before him. And Obama the president regularly under-performed as an orator in ways that shocked supporters dazzled by the oratory of Obama the candidate. Teachable moments were missed with alarming regularity. They were missed in the February 2009 launch of the administration's housing policy. They were missed in the 2010 State of the Union Address.[7] They were missed when the president first launched, and later defended, his escalation of U.S. troop numbers in Afghanistan. The result for progressives was that "just when they thought they'd finally found a president they could love with a full heart, they wind up as conflicted as they'd felt about every other Democratic politician."[8]

III

This is not to deny that much *was* achieved by the Obama administration in its first two years in office—not least, a large stimulus package, a comprehensive health care reform, and new and tighter regulation of the financial sector. Indeed, the scale of that activism was a major cause of the conservative revival—the Republican Party and its allies had much to fight against, and they did.[9] It was rather that the compromises necessary to the achievement of those landmark pieces of legislation dulled the fire in Obama's more liberal supporters, so creating the enthusiasm gap evident in the midterm polls. The lack of enthusiasm among both progressive and independent voters was not just caused by liberal pique, however. It was also a response to another gap—that between the scale of the recession inherited by the Obama administration and the limited impact of policies designed to abate it. As one of his most loyal grassroots supporters put it to the president at a town hall meeting in September 2010:

> I am tired of defending you, defending your administration, defending the mantle of change that I voted for and deeply disappointed with where we are now. I have been told that I voted for a man who said he was going to change things in a meaningful way for the middle class. I'm one of those people, and I'm waiting, sir, I'm waiting. I don't feel it yet.[10]

So if the political paradox of Obama's first midterm elections was that gridlock triggered gridlock, the economic paradox was that a recession released by inadequately regulated money markets ultimately strengthened the political hand of those favoring even less regulation of market forces. The very recession whose immediate impact had carried Obama over the line to power had persisted long enough by November 2010 to blunt the capacity of his administration to make the economic and social difference that his election had promised. Obama defeated McCain for the presidency in no small measure because the financial tsunami occurred on George Bush's watch, discrediting the entire Republican ticket as it did so. Obama's governing majority in the House is now gone because the economic hardships triggered by that crisis are occurring on *his* watch and are having a similar discrediting effect.

IV

There would be sadness enough in progressive circles if this were where the story stopped; but if it did, the solution would be immediately and obviously to hand. To rekindle the tidal wave of progressive enthusiasm, all that the Obama team would have to do would be to step back from their proclivity to compromise with Republicans who are visibly closed off to any form of bipartisanship, and to proceed as those Republicans would themselves proceed were they in full control: by pursuing an explicitly partisan agenda. That indeed is one of the requirements for Democratic Party success in 2012—the repositioning of the Obama administration as an unambiguously progressive force, governing in the same manner between now and 2012 as (prior to 2008) its leading figures campaigned; which is why the nuts and bolts of how to fight Republican fire with Democratic fire will be a central concern of Chapter 6. But to be in a position to do that effectively, Democrats will have to something else as well. They will have to find answers to the claims and programs of the new conservatism now gripping the Republican Party base. The task for 2012 is not the same as the one for 2008, because unlike last time, next time progressives will face a new and more dangerous political opponent. Currently it is Tea Party activists who are driving the U.S. political agenda and debate on the right, and because they are, the space for progressive politics will not return on any significant scale until the Tea Party Movement itself is stopped in its tracks.

Is this to overstate the importance of Tea Party activists? Possibly, but I don't think so. It is true that we have seen versions of this activism before, and that whenever the Democratic Party wins the White House, the Republican Party (and particularly its base) does have a tendency to become briefly apoplectic. It did so in 1964 with Goldwater, angry at the prospect of Lyndon Johnson's

Great Society. It did so in 1992, angry with the Clintons' commitment to universal health care: and again in 1996, angry with Bill Clinton and his sexual peccadilloes. It is also true that, on the extreme fringe of right-wing politics in the United States, it has long been possible to find a litany of deeply unattractive libertarian, white supremacist and evangelical conservative groupings and individuals. So, in that sense, the Tea Party is not that unusual. What makes it unusual, however, is the appeal of Tea Party libertarianism to core Republican activists. The typical Tea Party identifier is not some fringe nut. The 18 percent of Americans who so identified when polled in April 2010 turned out to be overwhelmingly white, male, married, and over 45. Most were reasonably affluent and even content with their current level of taxation. Most sent their children to public schools. There were long-standing conservative extremists among their number, but most of those polled were mainstream Republicans suddenly agitated to genuine anger by the drift of public policy. More than half of those polled thought that the policies of the Obama administration excessively favored the poor. A quarter thought those policies favored blacks more than whites. Most were angry about "the recent health overhaul, government spending, and a feeling that [their] opinions were not represented in Washington." Most "wanted their country back," though from quite whom was less clear.[11]

So the Tea Party Movement—new as it is[12]—is not safely dismissed by its liberal critics as yet another right-wing fringe phenomenon. On the contrary, the Tea Partiers are now what Mark Lilla correctly labeled "the new Jacobins," standing center stage and already well funded by the usual billionaire backers of conservative activism:[13]

> The new Jacobins have two classic American traits that have grown much more pronounced in recent decades: blanket distrust of institutions and an astonishing—and unwarranted—confidence in the self. They are apocalyptic pessimists about public life and childlike optimists swaddled in self-esteem when it comes to their own powers.[14]

As of September 2010, "more than 5 million Americans [had] participated in Tea Party events or given money to Tea Party organizations" and "71 percent of Republicans counted themselves Tea Party supporters."[15] Little wonder, then, that after the midterm election, the Republican Party in Congress should have found itself with a significant Tea Party presence in both the House and the Senate. The Tea Party Movement is also the catalyst to a new form of mainstream conservatism—one that is particularly hysterical, extreme and ideologically intolerant when set against conservative positions of the immediate past. To win back a sizeable progressive space, saner people will need to challenge the hype, the libertarianism and the anger of this new form of conservatism—and will need to do it quickly, and do it well. Because if we do not, the danger is that Tea Party activism, having tasted electoral blood in 2010, will carry all before it in 2012.

V

So, let us deal first with the hysteria. There is a lot of it about in the base of the Republican Party these days, and most of it is pretty unattractive stuff that needs to be challenged and dismissed out of court as entirely without factual foundation.

- As soon as Barack Obama was elected president, there was the whole birther movement—the claim that the new president was not an American, that he was born in Kenya, and that his birth certificate in Hawaii was a fake. There was a double irony in this particular set of nonsense—in that the president *was* born in Hawaii and that it was not he, but his opponent John McCain, who had actually been born outside the territorial boundaries of the United States. Irony, therefore, but still impact: for as late as August 2010, two in every five Republican supporters polled believed that the president was not a genuine American.[16]
- Then there was—and there remains—the claim that Barack Obama is a secret Muslim, a claim reinforced by the propensity of right-wing talk-show hosts to refer to him with deliberate regularity as Barack *Hussein* Obama, laying the emphasis, as they do so, on the second name, not the first. The irony here, of course, is again a double one: Barack Obama *is* a practicing and committed Christian, well able to talk about his faith and its impact on his politics; which is just as well, given that he had to do so on a regular basis as a candidate when criticized by his Republican opponents for his choice of the Reverend Jeremiah Wright as his *Christian* pastor! Yet, as late as August 2010, 43 percent of Americans polled still remained uncertain on the president's religion, and another 18 percent (*up* from 11 percent in March 2010) remained convinced that their president was a Muslim.[17]
- Throughout these last two years, we have heard over and over again the parallel claim that Barack Obama is the most partisan of recent U.S. presidents. Here the irony has been, if anything, thicker still: irony because he (unlike his immediate predecessor) has proved to be a great enthusiast for triangulation, one whose failure to effectively triangulate has been primarily the product not of any defect on his part, but rather the inevitable consequence of the intransigent partisanship of his Republican detractors. Partisan Republicans criticizing a centrist Democrat for not reaching across the aisle—it would be priceless were it not also so frustrating to the project of good government!

But for now at least, the prize for recently whipping up hysteria out of nothing but nonsense has to go to the former Republican House speaker Newt Gingrich, who in a string of comments on the president has reinforced the view, apparently widespread in conservative circles, that Barack Obama is determined to weaken America's standing in the world because of his possession of an anti-colonist mindset inherited from his father.[18] The thesis was Dinesh D'Souza's, in his *The Roots of Obama's Rage*,[19] but the endorsement was the former Speaker's: "the most profound insight I have read in the last six years" was apparently how he put it. Obama driven by "Kenyan, anti-colonial behavior" is profound—really? Whatever next!

VI

Much of this could and should be laughed away, were it not for the fact that a significant core of Republican activists believe some or all of these hysterical claims, and have them regularly reinforced by the emphases (and the silences) that surround the news media to which they adhere—most notably *Fox News* (with Bill O'Reilly,[20] Sean Hannity and Glenn Beck[21]) and conservative talk radio (from Rush Limbaugh[22] to Michael Savage). Perhaps it would be discountable even then, were it not also for the fact that the militant Republicans who hold these views now dominate the internal politics of candidate selection within the Republican Party, and have proved capable of defeating—in party primaries—Republicans more moderate than themselves. Among the casualties of that process were individuals with impeccable conservative credentials like Representative Bob Inglis (South Carolina), or Senators Robert Bennett (Utah) and Lisa Murkowski (Alaska): replaced in competition with the Democrats by extremely conservative Republicans such as Rand Paul, Sharron Angle, Christine O'Donnell and Joe Miller. The views of that quartet contained some pretty remarkable stuff, even for conservatives. Rand Paul, for example, wondered out loud early in his election campaign about the appropriateness of passing certain parts of the 1964 Civil Rights Act; and Sharron Angle went on record as favoring the complete phasing out of Social Security and Medicare. She, Joe Miller, and Christine O'Donnell all believed that abortions should be illegal, even in instances of rape and incest, while Rand Paul supported a Human Life Amendment to the U.S. Constitution. Rand Paul is now a member of the U.S. Senate, and two of the other three came terrifyingly close to joining him. So, although the Tea Party Movement may be primarily motivated by immediate economic concerns, and currently be overshadowing the Religious Right that was so influential in Republican politics in the Bush years, it is still clear that the Tea Partiers remain a happy hunting ground for extreme social conservatives as well as for economic libertarians. If you get one, you also get the other.

Even more mainstream Republican leaders like Paul Ryan, people not obviously connected to the Tea Party Movement directly, would commit the party in power to the widespread deconstruction of the already—by international comparative standards—thin U.S. welfare net. The House Republicans' *Pledge to America*, published in the run-up to the midterm elections and highly reflective of Ryan's views, was short on detail but clear on message. A Republican-controlled House will do its upmost to roll back the health care reform, financial market regulation, and stimulus acts introduced by the Obama administration. It will endeavor to enshrine as permanent the Bush tax cuts that were adding to a federal deficit that Republicans will attempt to cut in other ways—in total, taking us back to the failed economic programs of the Bush years. Of course, those programs did not fail everybody, which is presumably why—freed to pour limitless money into lobbying activities by the Supreme Court ruling on *Citizens United*—conservative lobbyists did just that: spending a reported $70 million in support of midterm campaigns by conservative candidates, and outspending Democrats in the ratio of 7:1.[23] Little wonder then that the Obama White House campaigned hard and long in the fall of 2010 in defense of vulnerable Democrats; and little wonder, too, that so much of that campaigning proved ineffective. It was ineffective not just because of the imbalance of money. Democrats spent heavily, too. It was also ineffective because so much of that White House campaigning came so late, and because so much of it was delivered against a background of job loss, job insecurity, and home foreclosures that the administration had by then had two years to solve—but had failed to do so.

VII

To see the true scale of the danger now before us, we need to add to this lethal conservative cocktail just one extra ingredient—namely the level of intolerance in much of this right-wing presentation of their counter case. Partly, that intolerance has manifested itself in the form of pejorative labeling: a disliked health care reform package became "Obamacare," the phasing out the Bush tax cuts for the very rich became "job-killing," and so on. Partly, the intolerance has manifested itself in the form of an under-current of racism—the president being depicted on Tea Party banners with a Hitler moustache or as a monkey—excesses denounced by mainstream Republicans, but denounced normally only mildly and with due qualification. And partly, the intolerance has been rooted in paranoia and xenophobia—both visible in the denunciation of the building of an Islamic community center close to Ground Zero, and in the regularly repeated claims (by leading conservative politicians and commentators) that Obama is taking the U.S. towards socialism, towards global weakness, and towards defeat at the hands of the infidel. There is anger out there, not just opposition, a genuine feeling that because liberals are in power, some of the rules of civilized democratic discourse can and must be discarded. Take, for example, this description of a new book by David Limbaugh, a description circulated by the Conservative Book Club. It is typical of much of the literature and arguments readily available in conservative circles these days:

> In *Crimes Against Liberty,* Limbaugh shows that everything about Barack Obama's radical background signals his visceral contempt for America—our culture, our values, and our political and economic systems. He demonstrates that Obama's unmistakable goal is to bring America down to size . . . Limbaugh, a practicing lawyer, builds a devastating case against Obama, detailing how his policies encroach upon our inalienable rights as Americans, and all too often strip us of those rights altogether . . . his crimes against the private sector, his crimes against American industry, his crimes against the public interest, his crimes against our posterity, his crimes against America's ally Israel, and his crimes against national security. From exploiting the financial crisis for political gain, to restricting our personal freedoms through invasive healthcare and "green" policies, to endangering America with his feckless diplomacy and reckless dismantlement of our national security systems, Limbaugh proves—beyond a reasonable doubt—that Obama is guilty of crimes against liberty.[24]

Such a view of an administration that is in truth more centrist than liberal, labels as unacceptable a broad swath of policies on economic reconstruction and welfare provision that are the stock-in-trade of conservatives elsewhere in the industrial world, and re-catalogues as evil the policies of the center-left everywhere. The Southern Poverty Law Center released *Rage on the Right* in the spring of 2010, reporting "an explosion of new extremist groups and activism across the nation." It found at least 1,000 hate groups in existence, an 80 percent increase in anti-immigrant groups (up from 173 to 309 in just one year), and an even more dramatic rise in the number of Patriot Groups—149 in 2008 but 512 a year later—groups arming themselves against the federal government as their primary enemy.[25] There is an underlying and intense anger in the center of this new conservatism that is truly terrifying.[26]

VIII

All of which makes the politics of the moment all the more pressing and vital. As Adele Stan has argued, "to halt the destruction that would follow in the wake of a successful Tea Party Movement, progressives need to do two big things: thwart the growth of the Tea Party Movement, and organize as a counter-force."[27] Each, of course, is easier said than done, but both require a clear sense of what the Obama administration has so far achieved, and where it has fallen short, and a progressive audit of the things still remaining to be completed. Both make essential the dissemination of powerful coherent refutations of the libertarian economics now again being proselytized by a resurgent Republicanism; and both necessitate the creation of a clear set of immediate and long-term policy goals around which to rebuild a strong and self-confident progressive movement. This book has been written to help that rebuilding. The audit of Obama in power is the business of Chapter 1. The creation of powerful arguments in defense of a progressive economics is the business of Chapters 2–5, and the mapping of a way forward is the agenda for Chapter 6. Two appendices have been added to help refute the more complex of the conservative economic arguments now in play, both designed to be of use to those challenging more-informed conservative debaters. We have an administration to shape and an electorate to win back; and we don't have much time to do either. I simply hope that reading what follows will in some small measure strengthen your hand in this—the most important political struggle of our lifetime.

CHAPTER 1

The Financial Meltdown and the Obama Response[1]

The economic crisis to which the incoming Obama administration was immediately obliged to respond was both severe and inherited. It was *severe*: the administration began its watch facing the deepest crisis in American capitalism since the onset of the Great Depression, one in which an indeterminate number of major financial institutions were potentially insolvent, credit markets were effectively frozen, Gross Domestic Product (GDP) was in freefall and unemployment was racing to a post-war high. The crisis was also *inherited*: its first stages had occurred entirely during George W. Bush's tenure as president, those stages breaking largely without warning on an administration which proved ideologically and programmatically ill-equipped to address them.

In defense of the Bush administration, the 2008 financial meltdown came without major warning. As late as October 2007, the U.S. economy was still creating jobs at a rate of more than 150,000 a month, and as late as November 2007, the prime concern of the Federal Reserve was reportedly the danger of inflation—not deflation—inflation linked to rising oil prices and a weakening dollar.[2] When the first isolated signs of financial instability were then spotted, their general and systemic implications were not. "At this point the troubles in the subprime sector seem unlikely to seriously spill over to the broader economy or the financial system" was Fed Chairman Ben Bernanke's public position as late as June 2008.[3] The initial Bush administration response to difficulties in the U.S. housing market was therefore to allow market forces to play themselves out. To householders facing negative equity as house prices fell in 2007, or foreclosure as subprime "teaser" rates gave way to real ones, the administration's initial argument was this: that "a federal bailout of lenders would only encourage a recurrence of the problem. It is not the government's job," President Bush told American homeowners in September 2007, "to bail out speculators or those who made the decision to buy a home they knew they could never afford."[4]

In an important sense, that unwillingness to bail out the unsuccessful remained the Bush administration's underlying philosophy to the end. "It would be a terrible mistake," the outgoing president told world leaders weeks before leaving office, "to allow a few months of crisis to undermine faith in free markets. While reforms in the financial sector are essential, the long-term solution to today's problems is sustained economic growth, and the surest path to that growth is free markets and free people."[5] And even when the administration did reluctantly change its mind, Republicans in the House of Representatives initially did not change with it. It is often now quietly forgotten—and it should not be—that Henry Paulson's first Troubled Asset Relief Program (TARP) attempt was originally *defeated* in the House by a 228–205 vote that was overwhelmingly organized on party lines.

So initially, all that the Bush administration was prepared to do, in the face of growing evidence of problems in U.S. housing and financial markets, was quietly (behind the scenes) to orchestrate private-sector rescues designed to contain the spreading fire. When in mid-2007 Countrywide Financial could no longer meet its short-term debts, its purchase by JPMorgan Chase was orchestrated by a U.S. Treasury which initially looked to the two Government-Sponsored Enterprises (GSEs)—Fannie Mae and Freddie Mac—to so expand their liabilities as to fill the resulting mortgage gap.[6] When in 2008 the bankruptcy of Bear Stearns could no longer be avoided, the initial Paulson response was again to have JPMorgan Chase (and now also the Federal Reserve) be the key player: this time extending credit to the struggling investment bank with the Fed underwriting the $30 billion loan—and when that was not enough, to trigger a "yard sale" of the investment bank to JPMorgan Chase at the rock-bottom price of $2 a share. Even that federally orchestrated sale was treated by the administration at the time as a regrettable intervention not likely to be repeated—the moral hazard issues involved were too serious to replicate—which helps explains why when six months later Lehman Brothers found themselves similarly strapped for cash and credit, that company was allowed to fail. Indeed, on the very day that Lehman Brothers filed for bankruptcy, Bank of America was strong-armed by Paulson's Treasury to swallow Merrill Lynch at $29 a share, twice its market value, in a deal that a year later (amid shareholder fury) cost Bank of America's CEO Ken Lewis his job.

However, reality eventually dawned even on an administration as wedded to free market principles as was that of George W. Bush; and when it did so, it produced one of the greatest *volte-faces* in recent Republican Party history. At the eleventh hour, the Bush administration saw the need for unprecedented public intervention directly into the heart of the U.S. financial system, and went in for bailouts on the grandest of scales:

- The GSEs were already in federal hands by the time Lehman Brothers fell. Finding it increasing difficult in 2008 to raise loans on U.S. money markets as their share of mortgage debt moved towards 50 percent, Fannie and Freddie were initially "rescued" by a federal intervention in July 2008. Overnight, they were given a flexible government credit line and allowed access to emergency funds from the Federal Reserve.[7] By September 7, 2008, with losses mounting, even access to Fed funds was not enough to enable Fannie and Freddie to borrow short-term in the market, and both were taken into full "conservatorship" (that is, effectively nationalized) by a hitherto entirely blue-chip, free-market Republican administration. And just in time, because a week later, Lehman Brothers filed for bankruptcy, and the resulting panic—with suddenly no financial institution certain of the viability of any other–brought interbank lending to a screeching halt and, with it, the entire credit-creating system.
- The initial Poulson response to that credit crisis was a $700 billion rescue package (contained in a three-page document giving the Treasury unprecedented powers and freedom from Congressional oversight) aimed at locating and absorbing mortgage-backed securities whose value was in free fall—the so-called toxic assets. It was this Treasury power grab that Republicans in the House initially rejected, and it was a plan that Poulson himself abandoned within weeks of its legislative enshrinement. (The bill passed early in October 2008 was 450 pages long rather than three, and included Congressionally imposed $150 billion of tax breaks, limits on executive pay in bailed out companies, and powers to ease mortgage terms to prevent foreclosure). Poulson used the resulting TARP money in the last months of the Bush administration not to buy toxic assets (finding and valuing them proved too difficult), but to recapitalize commercial and investment banks, and the largest of the insurance and hedge funds, hoping in that way to restore interbank confidence and the large-scale flow of credit again.
- In that process, key financial institutions received huge sums of public money. Manufacturing companies, by contrast, did not. By the time the Obama administration came to power, the U.S. Treasury had made

available $125 billion in aid to nine major banks (including $25 billion each to Wells Fargo and Citigroup), an additional $125 billion to smaller banks and an extra $40 billion to AIG; but had refused to give even a paltry $14 billion to Detroit without the formulation of major plans for industrial restructuring (Washington talk for plant closures, reduced wages and benefits for car workers, and much new unemployment). Bankers and their bonuses survived, but car workers and their jobs were not so fortunate.[8]

- Alongside the moves to ease fiscal policy, monetary policy, too, continued quietly to change. Huge quantities of Fed largesse were directed at a financial sector in structural crisis. There was much talk of eventual bank re-regulation. Even Paulson himself went on the record for that. But more immediately, there were Fed-financed injections of yet more credit guarantees, and central bank-orchestrated expansion programs for the financial industry worldwide. Some $900 billion in loans to banks were made available by the Federal Reserve as early as December 2007, followed by a further $250 billion in March 2008 to encourage mortgage lending, $29 billion to smooth the sale of Bear Stearns to JPMorgan Chase in March 2008, eventually $123.8 billion to bail out AIG, $620 billion in October 2008 to help foreign central banks trade foreign currency for dollars, $1.8 trillion to buy commercial paper, and $540 billion to buy assets from money market mutual funds short of cash—theses last two again in October 2008. In the last 15 months of the Bush presidency, breathtaking amounts of money were poured into the financial system on a regular basis by the Federal Reserve to keep institutions viable and credit-creation intact.[9]

One final feature of the crisis that the Obama administration inherited is also worth noting before we close in on its response—*the depth of the crisis, and the associated width of the policy agenda that its resolution required.* This was a crisis whose origins lay in two different sectors of the economy and in the relationship between them—the U.S. housing market and the U.S. financial sector. It was also, as we all know to our cost, a crisis with a huge impact on the rest of the U.S. economy (Main Street as well as Wall Street, in the popular idiom) and on the rest of the world. The policy response required had, therefore, to be as many-sided as the crisis itself. The Obama administration entered office required, as a matter of overwhelming urgency, to resolve a foreclosure crisis, a credit freeze, a full-scale domestic recession, and the danger of global economic meltdown. Doing one thing at once was not an option. The administration had to act across the board, and to do so in ways that were consistent one with another. We can at least say that they tried.

The Obama response

The Obama administration came in to office with a very different attitude to the role of the federal government than that prevalent in George W. Bush's White House. They came in determined to act, and to act quickly and across the full spectrum of the crisis: in the following manner.

1. *Moving to alleviate the housing crisis*

The Obama administration moved quickly to help American families remortgage their houses and avoid foreclosure. It did so within parameters set out explicitly by the president in his February 2009 announcement of the plan.[10] *He said this:*

> *I want to be very clear about what this plan will not do. It will not rescue the unscrupulous or irresponsible by throwing good taxpayer money after bad loans. It will not help speculators who took risky bets on a rising market and bought homes not to live in but to sell. It will not help dishonest lenders who distorted the facts . . . and it will not reward folks who bought homes they knew from the beginning they would never be able to afford . . . This plan will not save every home.*

- *Even so, and sharply reversing the Paulson policy of not using TARP money to directly help struggling mortgage holders, within a month of being in office the Obama administration put aside $75 billion of the bank bailout fund to help up to 4 million homeowners renegotiate their primary mortgages. Under the Obama Home Affordable Modification Program (HAMP) plan, TARP money was not to be used to reduce the size of the mortgage loan (the principal) or to share ownership of the house with the recipients of public funds. It was to be used instead to provide financial incentives to lenders to modify loan terms, and to subsidize the borrowers' interest payments over a five-year period. Borrowers with mortgages of up to $729,750 could see their interest cuts temporarily cut to as low as 2 percent: the target here was to get mortgage payments down first to 38 percent of monthly income, and then to 31 percent. To encourage bank participation, the administration backed a legal change allowing courts to modify mortgage terms if voluntary agreement failed.*
- *The Obama plan also allowed mortgage holders whose mortgages were backed by the GSEs—roughly one mortgage in two—to refinance at lower rates even if the mortgage holders had less than 20 percent equity in their property, but only if their mortgages were no more than 105 percent of their property's value. (That was said potentially to aid another 5 million mortgage holders.) By July, the administration's instructions to the 2 GSEs had been reset, to allow refinancing of mortgages that were up to 25 percent higher than the current value of the property mortgaged, and banks were put under increasing pressure by administration officials to include principal modification in their negotiations with overstretched mortgage holders. Following*

Congressional pressure, Fannie Mae announced in November 2009 that homeowners facing foreclosure on mortgages it underwrote would now be able to stay in their homes and rent them for up to a year. And in September 2010, with one in five U.S. houses (some 11 million in total) being valued now at less than the amount of the mortgage outstanding on them, the administration set aside a further $14 billion of TARP money to finance the renegotiation downwards of Federal Housing Administration (FHA) loans that were in this sense "under water."

- *In February 2009, the administration also put an extra $200 billion into Fannie Mae and Freddie Mac, to enable them to increase credit for mortgages generally. It was a plan built on the recognition that Fannie and Freddie would probably stack up losses of $65 billion from the $200 billion given them in September 2008—hence the doubling of the amount federal authorities would reimburse. On Christmas Eve 2009, the Treasury then quietly announced that it would provide unlimited financial assistance to both Fannie Mae and Freddie Mac, effectively removing the $400 billion cap on emergency aid. By August 2010, Fannie and Freddie together had received $148.3 billion of taxpayer aid, well within the ceilings allowed but way beyond the levels of public subsidization normal before the September 2008 crash.*
- *To support funds flowing back into mortgage creation through Fannie and Freddie, the Fed (with administration support) purchased from them hundreds of millions of dollars of mortgage-backed securities, with the aim of ultimately owning $1.25 trillion worth. The Treasury ran a similar, smaller program. Likewise, the FHA increased the number of home loans it insured (giving it maybe 18 percent of all new mortgages) and the Department of Veteran Affairs also provided mortgage guarantees. By early 2010, in a determined effort to keep mortgage provision buoyant and interest rates low, the government was underwriting, through one agency or another, 86 percent of all new home loans. In 2005, that figure had been just 30 percent.*[11] *It left leading figures in the Obama administration urging caution on any quick wind-down of the portfolios of the two GSEs, proposals on which were accordingly delayed throughout 2010.*[12]

2. Recapitalizing and regulating financial institutions

Housing wasn't the only sector, of course, in turmoil as the Obama administration began: finance was, too. The administration moved quickly to stabilize financial institutions, address public outrage about banking excess, and—more slowly—address the issue of how best to avoid a repetition of the crisis.[13]

- *Keeping major financial institutions afloat and get credit flowing again was a major concern. (As Obama became president, it was estimated that maybe half of all the credit flowing in 2007, before the recession struck, had been sucked out of the system, so that there was still a huge task of credit regeneration to be successfully completed.)*[14] *The administration inherited a set of TARP loans given to both major and minor banks, and continued that policy: in March, taking up to a 36 percent stake in Citigroup and making a fourth injection of capital into AIG—this time taking the total injection into that single company to a remarkable $180 billion; in May, putting TARP money into six major insurance companies, including Prudential Financial, Allstate, and the Hartford. Given the weakness of some of the major financial institutions—as late as October 2009, the FDIC was reporting that the number of "problem banks" had risen to 552, its highest level in 16 years*[15]*—it is also perhaps not surprising that further TARP money was still being distributed, to GMAC among others, as late as December 2009, and that the Treasury then decided to extend TARP into 2010. (Other temporary support measures—including the temporary Treasury underwriting of the money market mutual fund industry—were, however, allowed to expire on schedule in late 2009.) Federal guarantees of $30 billion or more were still being given to the nation's wholesale credit unions as late as September 2010, as U.S. financial institutions continued to struggle with the legacy of the subprime mortgage collapse.*

- *Individual bailouts were supplemented during the early months of the Obama administration by a three month-long stress test to establish the financial viability of 19 major U.S. banks. (The test found ten of them needing to raise a total of $75 billion in extra capital, and gave the rest a clean bill of health. Among those ordered to strengthen their asset base were Bank of America, Wells Fargo, Citigroup and GMAC, the financing arm of General Motors.) Alongside the stress test, the new administration announced in February 2009 a new Fed-financed (and Treasury-underwritten) lending initiative to kick-start financing of student, auto, and credit card loans, and the outline of a scheme to purchase toxic assets from banks—with a total price tag of $2.5 trillion. The details of that toxic assets plan came a month later, and had the Treasury partially financing a series of public–private investment funds to buy up unwanted mortgage-based securities, with federal authorities lending as much as 85 percent of the purchase price, plus a matching dollar-for-dollar contribution to cover the remaining 15 percent.*
- *By as early as April 2009, major financial institutions were already attempting to return their TARP money, while quietly retaining other forms of public subsidy that had come with fewer strings attached. A major reason for the keenness of many bank CEOs to do that were the constraints on senior salaries and bonuses that had come with the original injection of federal aid. Initially denying them that right, the new Obama administration made clear its disgust at excessive bank remuneration, particularly for senior figures in banks which had required taxpayer money to survive. It even created a "compensation czar" to restrain top salaries in*

companies in receipt of TARP money. But by June 2009, permission was given to ten stronger institutions (JPMorgan Chase, Goldman Sachs, and Morgan Stanley, in particular) to begin repaying a combined $68 billion, so splitting major U.S. financial institutions effectively into winners and losers, and freeing the winners from direct government direction and control.[16] *Permission for Citigroup and Wells Fargo to begin paying back TARP money was followed in December 2009 by a similar statement of intent for Bank of America.*[17] *As the stronger financial institutions returned their TARP money, they returned to old practices, as well. Profitability came back, and so did bonuses. The* Wall Street Journal *estimated in January 2010 that the top 30 major U.S. banks and securities firms were on target to award staff $145 billion in bonuses in 2009, up 18 percent from the previous year.*[18] *With unemployment outside the financial sector still high, the contrast between such Wall Street largesse and Main Street recession prompted the president in January 2010 to condemn the planned bonuses as "obscene," and to propose a $90 billion bank tax over a ten-year period to dent excess profit taking, particularly by the largest financial institutions.*[19]

- *The Obama administration's proposals on the regulation of financial markets were published in May 2009, part of an avalanche of legislative proposals then emerging on how best to tighten supervision. The Geitner regulatory plan initially proposed the establishment of a single regulatory agency (he reportedly favored the Fed for this role), more conservative capital requirements for major institutions, the forcing of large hedge funds and private equity firms to register with the SEC, new regulation of derivative markets, and strengthened requirements for money market funds. New limits on the marketing and charging of credit cards were signed into law late the same month. By early summer 2009, the administration had retreated from its initial enthusiasm for a single regulator, preferring instead to add new levels of regulation on top of the existing structure as it discovered the defensive political power and propensities for turf war of first one existing regulatory body and then another. The revised plan gave the Federal Reserve greater supervisory authority over large financial institutions whose problems pose potential risks to the economic system. It expanded the reach of the FIDC to seize and break up troubled financial institutions. It proposed both a council of regulators, led by the Treasury Secretary, to fill in regulatory gaps, and a Consumer Financial Protection Agency charged to live up to its name. It was these proposals that eventually formed the core of the Dodd-Frank Wall Street Reform and Consumer Protection Act passed in July 2010.*[20]

3. Stimulating the economy, searching for jobs

Then, of course there was the small matter of Main Street, and its concerns. The drying up of bank credit threatened generalized recession; and generalized recession would not only compound the problem of home foreclosures, it also threatened the tax base on which the Obama administration's wider social agenda depended for finance. Unemployment, and the fear of unemployment, was the major legacy of the 2008 financial crisis inherited by the Obama people as they entered office: a legacy they sought to defuse not just by bank recapitalization but also by ambitious programs of public spending. An ambitious budget and an immediate stimulus package were the Obama administration's main weapons as they fought to raise the economy's growth rate—and slow the rate of job loss—during their first two years in office.

- *The first Obama budget, announced in February 2009, reversed Bush tax policy by increasing tax rates for wealthier Americans—some $637 billion over ten years—to help finance a ten-year $634 billion reserve fund to finance health care reform, $150 billion over a decade on clean air technologies, $576 billion to fix the alternative minimum tax, and (now on, rather than off, the books) $75.5 billion additional Pentagon spending. The resulting budget deficit was projected by the CBO to run at $1.67 trillion, or 11.9 percent of U.S. GPD in 2009, the vast majority of which derived from Bush policies (tax cuts and war spending) and the downturn in the U.S. economy.[21] The overall deficit was targeted in the first budget to come down to just $533 billion in four years. As early as January 16, 2009, the incoming president announced an "entitlements summit" to consider how best to control the cost of entitlement programs, and in May 2009 the Obama administration proposed cuts of $17 billion by ending or reducing 121 federal programs. The Obama administration, that is, unlike its predecessor, did openly recognize the important role of federal deficit spending as a trigger to private sector growth and employment in the depth of a recession, but also publicly subscribed to the view that, as that growth returned, a phasing-out of the deficit was both politically and economically necessary.*
- *The stimulus package, created alongside the first budget, was signed into law in late February 2009. Costing in total $787 billion, the American Recovery and Reinvestment Act (ARRA) contained $276 billion in tax cuts for low- and middle-income Americans and for small businesses, and over $500 billion in a series of spending programs, including: $39 billion of direct aid to states struggling to cover particularly education costs, $5.5 billion to make federal buildings more energy efficient, and $7.4 billion on immediate infrastructure projects. The initial stimulus package was followed later by moves to speed up the distribution of stimulus funds, and in December 2009 by a jobs summit called because of the limited initial impact of the stimulus on rates of unemployment. All through 2009, unemployment remained stubbornly high, and the dispersal of ARRA money stubbornly slow: maybe only $81 billion in total dispersed by the third quarter of 2009,* [22] *certainly less than a quarter of the total available.*[23] *In*

January 2010, the president used his first full State of the Union Address to call for a new jobs bill that would ignite "the true engine of job creation in this country . . . America's businesses."[24] He proposed directing TARP money to community banks (and through them to small businesses), a small business tax credit for companies hiring new workers or raising wages, and funds for high-speed rail links and a clean energy economy. He followed that in the fall of 2010 with proposals for a new round of infrastructure spending—$50 billion—distributed through a public-private infrastructure bank, and a plan to allow companies to write-off against tax 100 percent of their new investment in plant and equipment for the whole of 2011.

- *Specific assistance was also rendered directly to the U.S. auto-industry early in this administration. The Obama White House inherited a reluctantly provided $17.4 billion lifeline provided to General Motors (GM) and Chrysler by the Bush administration, and entered office insisting on major industrial restructuring as the price of further aid. Aware that the total collapse of the Detroit-based car industry would have significant ripple effects through the entire North American supply chain, the administration initially threatened both companies with bankruptcy proceedings, giving them only 60 (GM) and 30 (Chrysler) days to redesign their survival strategies and, in the end, had both companies file for Chapter 11 bankruptcy protection. Both emerged from bankruptcy only after extensive plant closures, heavy job losses, the extensive termination of dealerships (800 in the case of Chrysler, 2,600 in the larger GM network) and, in the end, new owners: the UAW and Fiat in the case of Chrysler, the federal government and the Canadian government in the case of GM. By the end of 2009, the federal government owed 70 percent of the now-leaner GM franchise, having committed $50 billion over a five-year period. A temporary "clunkers for cash" program stimulated car sales in the summer of 2009. Its termination slowed car sales in the fall of the same year.*

4. *Working with America's global partners to reactivate global economic growth*

A final element in the Obama response to the financial crisis was an enhanced willingness to work in an international setting both to alleviate its consequences and to prevent its reoccurrence. That international cooperation was well underway in the last months of the Bush administration, with repeated coordinated central bank initiatives to lower interest rates and make capital available on easy terms to financial institutions in difficulty. What Obama added was support for a continuation of this unprecedented degree of international monetary cooperation, a willingness to rethink the rules and governing structure of world growth and trade, and—eventually—a willingness to see strengthened international regulation of banks and other financial institutions.

- *The cooperation between central banks, and between the U.S. Treasury and other key finance ministers, was a feature of Obama's opening year. Relations between the U.S. and UK continued to be close: those between both of them and the institutions and governments of the Eurozone were less so. Larry Summers, Tim Geitner, and Ben Bernanke led the charge for continued fiscal and monetary stimuli in a series of international meetings through 2009, but met degrees of resistance from the chairman of the European Central Bank, and from the German Chancellor, Angela Merkel, who even took the unusual step of publicly criticizing Fed policy as unconventional. The route to long-term stability for the Germans lay through bank regulation rather than demand stimulation—and initially that was not the route that the Obama administration chose to prioritize.*
- *The split between the U.S. and the EU did not prevent agreement at the G20 summit in London in April 2009 on a series on enlarged funding pledges: $750 billion for the International Monetary Fund (IMF) to lend to struggling economies, $250 billion to boost world trade, and $100 billion for international banks to lend to the world's poorest countries. Nor did it prevent agreement in principle on the creation of new global institutions of financial regulation and tighter and more-comprehensive coverage of all forms of financial institution and instruments. The agreement marked a significant change in the U.S. attitude to external review, with the president explicitly conceding in London that the Washington consensus on unfettered globalization and deregulation was now outmoded, and needed replacing by a more balanced approach to the regulation of markets.*
- *Behind it all, the Federal Reserve continued to be in the vanguard of central banks, urging the use of quantitative easing to maintain the flow of money into the banking system and out into the wider economy. The UK central bank was similarly active, and yet both economies continued to teeter throughout 2010 on the brink of a return to recession. The U.S. recession officially ended in June 2009, but more than a year later unemployment remained high and consumer confidence low, so that as the 2010 midterm elections approached, the Federal Reserve chairman was publicly pondering again whether further quantitative easing was appropriate. His problem by then was that, with interest rates so low and with the Fed's balance sheet already so large, the techniques available to a central bank keen on such a move were increasingly losing their potency.[25] This did not prevent Bernanke, however, from announcing in November 2010 the Fed's intention to pump an additional $600 billion into the U.S. economy over the first half of 2011, an announcement widely criticized by other G20 finance ministers and central bankers.*

Evaluating the Obama performance

1. Disappointing results

When in November 2010 Theda Skocpol and Lawrence Jacobs made their assessment of the first two years of the Obama administration for the Russell Sage Foundation's working group on *Obama's Agenda and the Dynamics of U.S. Politics,* their view was that "Obama's early presidency had indeed reached for another New Deal, and much of the ambitious agenda had been furthered." But as they conceded, what progress had been made was less than fully "visible to many citizens and analysts." "An ambitious presidency that seemed to have strong winds at its back has run into such fierce blowback," they wrote, with "the immediate political results, certainly . . . not what anyone could have anticipated"[26] at the moment of Obama's election. Nowhere was that invisibility of progress more in play—as we will now see—than in the Obama administration's handling of the home foreclosure crisis.

Housing

The housing crisis deepened rather than eased in the first two years of the Obama presidency, his solutions at best having only a very limited impact on the problems facing more and more U.S. house-owners, and at worst compounding the problems that his policies were supposed to redress. As late as September 2009, fewer than 5 percent of the borrowers participating in the administration's foreclosure prevention program—just 31,000 people—had received permanent loan modifications: that in a national housing market in which house prices were by then down 40 percent on average from their 2006 peak, in which 23 percent (10.7 million) households had negative equity, more than 7 million households were behind on mortgage payments or facing foreclosure (one in eight borrowers), and a further 2.4 million foreclosures were expected in 2010 among households already more than 90 days behind on their payments. A year later, with fewer than 400,000 loans modified, foreclosures were still running at a rate of more than 300,000 a month and house sales were at a 15-year low. The share of mortgages that were seriously delinquent did fall in the second quarter of 2010 (and the rate of foreclosure briefly eased with the moratorium called by financial institutions unsure again of the adequacy of their paperwork), but the share of newly delinquent mortgages actually rose, leaving just over 4 million American homes in/on the edge of foreclosure by the fall of 2010.[27] For by then, involuntary unemployment, not subprime excess, had taken over as the main cause of people's inability to maintain their mortgage payments. And if that was not bad enough, job loss and falling house prices were by 2010 pushing more and more Americans into personal bankruptcy. Rates of personal bankruptcy, up 32 percent nationally in 2009 over 2008, were up by twice that rate in states hardest hit by the falling value of their housing stock. The figure for Arizona, for example, for 2009 was a 79.6 percent rise in personal bankruptcies in just one year. The 398,198 people permanently helped to modify their loans was literally a drop in the ocean, as the threat of a second foreclosure spike left 2 million American families ejected from their homes in 2009 and a further 1.9 million in 2010 facing an equivalent fate.

Banking

The banking bailout was enormously expensive, but did not immediately generate the flows of credit to Main Street that the TARP architects had promised. Here, as elsewhere, one main claim for the program was that it prevented something significantly worse—a deeper and longer generalized recession—and that claim, though difficult to prove, does seem intuitively right.[28] But the bailout was from the outset riddled with double standards and beset with insider dealing: generous to financial institutions that had often been big players themselves in the mortgage-lending and speculative fever that had created the crisis, while tough to the point of parsimony on industrial firms whose competitive difficulties were compounded by the financially induced recession.[29] The bailout proved particularly beneficial to financial institutions closely linked to key policymakers—top personal from Goldman Sachs, in particular. Indeed, it quickly turned into a safety net for favored bank-holding companies—companies whose profits (and bonuses) came racing back, but whose willingness to pass the bailout money on to smaller firms (or even to the banks within their networks) remained frustratingly low. In the third quarter of 2009, with a year of TARP money behind them, the total loan balances of U.S. lenders actually *fell*—by $210.4 billion, or 3 percent—"the biggest decline since data collection began in 1984,"[30] with the large banks owned by the bank-holding companies that had received the greater share of bailout funds responsible for a full 75 percent of that fall.[31] Taxpayer money, that is, bailed out the banks more effectively on Obama's watch than the banks bailed out the taxpayers, and it did so without removing the underlying causes of the crisis. "It is hard to see," the TARP administrator reported as late as January 2010, "how any of the fundamental problems in our financial system have been addressed to date. Even if TARP saved our financial system from driving off a cliff in 2008 . . . we are still driving on the same winding mountain road, but this time in a faster car."[32] By the third quarter of 2010, bank profits were back to their 2007 levels, but bank lending was not: and 15 million Americans remained involuntarily idle, unemployed in a credit-starved economy.[33]

Employment and the recession

The stimulus package may have saved jobs and staved off even deeper recession—Blinder and Zandi certainly thought so. They calculated in 2010 that "without the government's response, GDP in 2010 would be about 11.5% lower, payroll employment would be less by some 8.5 million jobs, and the nation would now be experiencing inflation."[34] Tim Geitner, for one, hailed the official end of recession in June 2009, writing a celebratory piece for *The New York Times* entitled "Welcome to the Recovery,"[35] and in September 2010 the vice-president's team issued a very upbeat report of ARRA's impact on employment and growth.[36] But the president, at least, was aware that the recovery from recession "had been painfully slow," that much stimulus money remained unspent,[37] that some of that spending was anyway poised to run out if not renewed, and that unemployment remained too high and might even begin to grow again. Unemployment certainly remained unprecedentedly high throughout Obama's first two years in office: the rate was still officially 9.6 percent (14.8 million Americans) as the midterm elections loomed, with 4.2 million jobs lost in 2009 alone. Moreover, the broad numbers hid even more serious unemployment pockets in key areas of the economy: throughout 2010, unemployment totals remained particularly acute, for example, in classic blue-collar sectors, with employment down 18 percent since 2007 in industries like construction, maintenance and repair, machine operation and transportation.[38] At 6.7 million in June 2010, or 46 percent of the unemployed labor force, long-term unemployment within the total became a significant feature of the U.S. labor market for the first time in any major recession since the 1930s, and public sector employment levels proved increasingly vulnerable to falling tax revenues at the level of the states.[39] Christine Romer, Obama's first chair of the Council of Economic Advisers, had predicted unemployment as peaking at 8.5 percent with the stimulus package in play: but no such luck—it peaked at more than 10 percent on her watch, as the economy continued to shed jobs, even in the context of ARRA spending. The result: "between November 2008 and April 2010 about 39 percent of households had either been unemployed, had negative equity in their house or had been arrears in their house payments."[40] TARP may have saved the banking system during its two-year existence, but TARP and ARRA together did not lift the rest of the U.S. into any equivalent generalized recovery during that same period. Hence the call, from both Left and Right, for a change in policy-direction as soon as the midterm elections were over.

2. Conservative condemnation

The Republican Party took a while to find its voice, but the more the administration sought to increase public spending, tighten regulations, and bail out economic losers, the more that voice became coherent, strident, and self-confident. Obama's policies on housing, finance, and economic recovery were critiqued as follows.

Housing

According to his critics on the Right, Obama relied too heavily for the resolution of the housing crisis on the GSEs that had created it, and by seeking short-term cover for feckless borrowers only extended the period of recovery that the housing market required. Writing regularly in *The Wall Street Journal* and from his vantage point as a member of the Financial Crisis Inquiry Commission, the AEI's Peter J. Wallison was one important conservative voice keeping the spotlight firmly focused in 2009 and 2010 on the two GSEs and on their use by the Obama administration. "Barney Frank's decision to 'roll the dice' on subsidized housing is becoming an epic disaster for taxpayers," he told *Wall Street Journal* readers in December 2009, as "the price for Fannie and Freddie keeps going up."[41] The Cato Institute's Jeffrey Miron was one of many libertarians agreeing with him, believing that if redistribution to low-income families was to be public policy, it should be done directly, not indirectly through subsidized mortgage credit, and that "adjusting policy to incorporate this [was] relatively easy. It require[d merely the] elimination of specific pre-existing policies such as Fannie Mae, Freddie Mac, the Federal Housing Administration, and so on!"[42] The great mistake that Democrats had made, and had made ever since 1992 according to their conservative critics, was to confuse housing policy with social policy, interfering with the first to effect the second. The better solution would be to separate the two, and let the housing market operate like any other. "When the private securitization market revives," Wallison wrote in August 2010, "Fannie and Freddie can gradually be eased out of their secondary market role," eventually being "liquidated or privatized, leaving a private market for well underwritten mortgages and a government insurer for those mortgages that can't meet market tests."[43]

Banking

From Ron Paul and the more libertarian wing of the Republican coalition, a parallel critique emerged in 2009, focused primarily on the way the Obama administration was extending the already excessive role and largesse of the Federal Reserve—exactly the wrong thing to do, in the libertarian view, since they held that it was Fed policies, and the Fed's prolonged interference with money markets, that had created the financial bubble in the first place. And because that was so, having the Federal Reserve monitor systemic risk, as the Obama administration proposed, was "like asking a thief to police himself."[44] Neither TARP nor the Dodd-Frank Act won many Republican supporters once Obama was in office. Jeffrey Miron was one of many critics arguing that "instead of bailing out banks, U.S. policymakers should have allowed the standard process of bankruptcy to operate . . . and that going forward, [they] should abandon the goal of expanded home ownership."[45] And not just libertarians: mainstream Republican leaders like Richard Shelby gave the incoming administration similar advice—no bailing out of failing banks, however large; rather, "close them down, get them out of business. If they're dead, they ought to be buried."[46] For the lack of burials was what was wrong with the Dodd-Frank Act: "The competitiveness, innovativeness and risk taking that have always characterized U.S. financial firms will, under this new structure, inevitably be subordinated to supervisory judgments about what these firms can safely be allowed to do." The result, "Creative destruction, destroyed."[47] Alan Greenspan was one voice among many warning that Obama policies were laying the groundwork for financial crises to come: criticizing the Obama administration for stacking up a burden of federal debt that was bound to delay the much-needed economic recovery.[48] "Exploding debt threatens America," John Taylor wrote in May 2009. "The risk posed by this debt is systemic and could do more damage to the economy than the recent financial crisis."[49] Desmond Lachman called the debt "the fiscal road to serfdom."[50]

Employment and the recession

All those specifics were invariably presented by conservative commentators as part of a generalized critique of federal interference with private markets. As North Carolina's Virginia Foxx put it, "[M]assive government intervention into America's economy . . . will fundamentally change our marketplace by rewarding financial companies that made bad decisions and placing those who exercised prudence at a serious disadvantage."[51] Likewise, Peter J. Wallison:

> Barney Frank was right. The signature initiatives of the Obama administration were very much in the mold of the old New Deal—the heedless spending, a stimulus plan focused on government employment, a health-care program that brought one-sixth of the economy under government control, and now the financial regulatory bill that would control another sixth. It will be years before the damage can be undone.[52]

Certainly, the Fed should now start to back off, not least because a further round of quantitative easing, according to Harvard's Niall Ferguson, could trigger "a debt spiral of rising interest rates, widening deficits, crumbling credibility and yet more rising rates."[53] Even the well-intentioned subsidization of weak industries, and burdensome new taxes (especially linked to health care) were presented by many conservatives as barriers to business recovery and as the key source of prolonged unemployment.[54] The case for tough love towards the victims of recession appeared regularly in the conservative media. Really tough love: even extending unemployment benefit was held up as an extra incentive for people to remain unemployed, and certainly support for comprehensive immigration reform was ridiculed for adding to the number of people seeking a falling number of jobs. "My calculations suggest," Robert Barro wrote in *The Wall Street Journal* just ahead of Labor Day 2010, "the jobless rate could be as low as 6.8% instead of 9.5% if jobless benefits hadn't been extended to 99 weeks." That was "the folly of subsidizing unemployment."[55] More generally, William White wrote, "some fires are best left to burn out."[56] The many economists who in February 2009 signed the Cato Institute's document opposing the Obama stimulus plan clearly agreed with him.

This kind of argumentation need not delay us long here. Its general characteristics and deficiencies have already been fully explored in Chapter 10 of *Answering Back* and will be again in the chapters that follow. But what is new, and worth briefly commenting upon before we turn to those, is the overwhelming parochialism of the conservative case as it is constructed here in the United States. From the intensity and certainty with which that case is currently being disseminated, you could be forgiven for thinking that conservatism globally was in favor of deregulated markets. The truth, however, is otherwise. Major center-right governments across the industrial world have normally adopted a *tougher* stance on bank regulation than the Obama administration has yet proposed. For conservative leaders like Angela Merkel of Germany and Nicholas Sarkozy of France, the financial meltdown of 2008 was evidence of the flawed nature of the American model, not a testimony to its strength, one whose toxic weaknesses infected the entire global system and against which now they are demanding the construction of strong regulatory firewalls. Even David Cameron, leading a British Conservative Party imbued with the spirit of Margaret Thatcher and facing just the same economic agenda as Obama and the Republicans, could appear before his party conference as the newly minted prime minister and tell them, "I don't believe in *laissez-faire*. Government has a role not just to fire up ambition but to help give it flight." And in any cuts in welfare spending, "it's fair that those with broader shoulders should bear a greater load."[57]

So you have to ask, on what planet do libertarians actually live, when as august a body as the Organization for Economic Co-operation and Development (OECD) can rightly congratulate the central banks of the major industrialized nations for their coordinated and large-scale interventions into frozen global credit markets in 2008 and 2009, attributing to that intervention a successful softening of the resulting recessionary blow.[58] Right-wing fantasy lands are just that, fantasies—whose pursuit could only deepen the economic downturn against whose management they now rail. Indeed, there was something particularly galling in the internal U.S. debate in 2009 and 2010 about the speed and enthusiasm with which main architects of the crisis the Obama administration had inherited—Alan Greenspan among them—pointed the finger of responsibility at liberals attempting to solve problems left behind by their critics.[59] The new president was well within his rights (and within the terrain of truth) when, in his first full State of the Union Address in January 2010, he stressed the degree to which the federal deficit then accruing was largely *not* of his making:

> Let me start the discussion of government spending by setting the record straight. At the beginning of the last decade, the year 2000, America had a budget surplus of over $200 billion. By the time I took office, we had a one-year deficit of over $1 trillion and projected deficits of $8 trillion over the next decade. Most of this was the result of not paying for two wars, two tax cuts, and an expensive prescription drug program. On top of that, the effects of the recession put a $3 trillion hole in our budget. All this was before I walked in the door. Now—just stating the facts. Now, if we had taken office in ordinary times, I would have liked nothing more than to start bringing down the deficit. But we took office amid a crisis. And our efforts to prevent a second depression have added another $1 trillion to our national debt. That, too, is a fact.

3. Liberal frustration

The groundswell of criticism that built slowly from the liberal wing of the Democratic coalition was entirely otherwise, of course. It charged the president not with doing too much but with doing too little, or with doing what was needed too late. From its liberal supporters, the Obama administration found itself increasingly criticized for not meeting the biggest economic crisis since the Great Depression with policies sufficiently radical to match the severity of the problem. So, on . . .

. . . the housing crisis

Obama's concern to avoid moral hazard issues initially restricted his capacity to get fully to grips with the scale of the foreclosure crisis. The February 2009 plan that focused on the funding of temporary interest rate reductions and the incentivizing of loan term restructuring did nothing to save millions of American homeowners from the reality of negative equity and a new round of foreclosures. Things that could have been done were not done. America's bankruptcy laws were not reformed. The use of federal dollars to create temporary co-ownership of housing—to parallel the co-ownership of financial institutions and car firms—was not contemplated. Instead, the very architecture of U.S. housing finance that had created the crisis was left intact to guarantee further rounds of housing misery. As Robert Reich observed in 2009, "American bankruptcy law does not allow homeowners to declare bankruptcy and have their mortgages reorganized. If it did, homeowners would have more bargaining power to renegotiate with banks"[60]—which is presumably why Wall Street has been so set against it, and the Obama administration so inert. The administration was at least advised to go the co-ownership route—no less a body than the Federal Reserve Bank of Boston, among others, arguing in June 2009 for direct action to reduce the principal owed on mortgages with negative equity, plus a temporary program of loans and grants to help unemployed workers stay in the their homes.[61] Unfortunately, it was advice that in 2009 the Obama administration chose not to take.

So the foreclosure pipeline was temporarily slowed by the Obama initiative, but his reforms did nothing to seal it. At best, because of it, people were left temporarily in houses that ultimately they would not be able to afford to retain.[62] As the Congressional Budget Office concluded as early as October 2009, the Obama reforms would "in the best case, prevent fewer than half of the predicted foreclosures," not least because the administration's plans seem "targeted at the housing crisis as it existed six months ago, rather than as it exists now."[63] The intention behind HAMP may well have been laudable, but its implementation was less so. Policy designed to deal with a housing crisis that was initially anchored in the *voluntary* purchase of subprime mortgages was literally drowned by a housing crisis that by 2010 had become rooted in the *involuntary* unemployment of so many Americans; in consequence, the Obama housing policy was forever running behind events. As Elizabeth Warren, one of its sternest critics close to the administration, put it: "[I]t's as if we had a boat that's taking on gallons of water, and they're trying to bail it out with a teaspoon."[64]

The banking crisis

According to his liberal critics, an opportunity to fundamentally reform the banking system was missed in 2009, partly because of what Daniel Carpenter rightly called "institutional strangulation,"[65] partly perhaps because the architects of his policy were too involved in either denying or benefiting from the excesses in the banking system that policies were supposed to resolve. As James Galbraith put it:

> Up to a point, one can defend the decisions taken in September–October 2008 under the stress of a rapidly collapsing financial system. The Bush administration was, by that time, nearly defunct. Panic was in the air, as was political blackmail—with the threat that the October through January months might be irreparably brutal. Stopgaps were needed, they were concocted, and they held the line. But one cannot defend the actions of Team Obama on taking office. Law, policy and politics all pointed in one direction: turn the systemically dangerous banks over to Sheila Bair and the Federal Deposit Insurance Corporation. Insure the depositors, replace the management, fire the lobbyists, audit the books, prosecute the frauds, and restructure and downsize the institutions. The financial system would have

> been cleaned up. And the big bankers would have been beaten as a political force. Team Obama did none of these things.[66]

On this argument, Tim Geitner, Larry Summers, and Ben Bernanke[67] were all part of the problem rather than part of the solution. They had all been significant players in the deregulatory regime headed by Alan Greenspan which had laid the foundation for the financial tsunami; and Geitner, in particular, played an important role in moderating administration policies on regulatory reform.[68] It took Obama a whole year—and the critical loss of a Senate seat in Massachusetts—to listen to Paul Volker rather than to Geitner, and even then he spent critical political capital retaining the Republican-adviser Bernanke as head of the Fed, in the process missing a critical opportunity to place a more active and progressive chairman in that key role: no Paul Krugman,[69] no Elizabeth Warren, no Joseph Stiglitz,[70] just Ben Bernanke again! There was "no economic team of rivals on Obama's staff," Steve Clemons spotted very early on: instead "Rubin's Manic Neoliberals dominate."[71] "The problem here," according to Arianna Huffington, was "the Obama economic team's flawed cosmology: still believing the world revolves around the banks," and so engaging in "mission shrink," moving "from saving Wall Street to Save Main Street, to just saving Wall Street."[72] Obama should have taken on the banks[73]—nationalized them in the moment of weakness[74]—but he did not: a failure of political courage that let private finance off the hook, hit ordinary American workers hard, and left his administration vulnerable to a populist backlash.[75]

Employment and the recession

Moreover, in the eyes of many critics sympathetic to the president and his overall project, insufficient FDR-type policies were implemented during Obama's first two years in office, in part because of a misplaced search for bipartisanship. Paul Krugman put the counter-case best, responding to the midterm election results by noting that:

> In retrospect, the roots of current Democratic despond go all the way back to the way Mr. Obama ran for president. Again and again, he defined America's problem as one of process not substance—we were in trouble not because we were governed by people with the wrong ideas but because partisan divisions and politics as usual had prevented men and women of good will from coming together to solve our problems. And he promised to transcend those partisan divisions. This . . . may have been good general election politics . . . but the real question was whether Mr. Obama could change his tune when he ran into the partisan firestorm everyone who remembered the 1990s knew was coming. He could do uplift—but could he fight? So far the answer has been no.[76]

Frustration with the moderate nature, and the moderate impact, of the stimulus package was palpable in many of the center-left critiques floating round the blogosphere within even the first 12 months of the new administration, as was increasing anger at the double standard visible in the treatment of financial and non-financial institutions. Liberal commentators struggled to comprehend why the original stimulus package was so small.[77] They also struggled to comprehend why banks should be given money to bail out overseas creditors and car companies financed to export manufacturing jobs, while those same banks were not compelled to lend to small American businesses and when the large companies saved were not required to expand their American operations.[78] By late 2010, it was very clear that many big corporations were borrowing heavily but sitting on their cash—not hiring, not expanding output as the administration required—and as they stalled, so too did liberal support for Obama. Coming into power as the champion of those excluded from power, Obama quickly found himself criticized for tolerating the immiserization of Main Street by Wall Street, for the absence of direct work creation programs by federal and state authorities, and for his slowness in generating a further stimulus package when the modest impact of the original one became clear.[79] Time and again, liberal commentators and activists called for more federal spending, for direct job creation on New Deal lines,[80] and for direct federal aid to state budgets, all designed to protect existing employment and to generate faster job growth;[81] but time and again, the search for bipartisanship remained dominant and administration initiatives were consequently too conservative for liberal tastes. Stimulus measures proved to be both too little and too late. "There never was a big expansion in government spending," Paul Krugman later complained. "In fact, that has been the key problem . . . we never had the kind of fiscal expansion that might have created the millions of jobs we need."[82] Little wonder then that, by November 2010, a Republican Party with its confidence renewed should have been able to make such inroads into the Democrats' temporary grip on Congressional power, or that disillusionment should have spread among Obama's more liberal supporters. "The real story of this election," Krugman wrote ahead of the midterms, "is that of an economic policy that failed to deliver. Why? Because it was greatly inadequate to the task." [83] Watching from a distance, Martin Wolf put it this way, and spoke for many of those supporters as he did so: "Obama's mistake was being too cautious in fearful times."[84]

Going beyond the immediate debate

The Obama proposal in January 2010 to freeze discretionary federal spending from 2011 was particularly resented by his liberal allies: resented for playing into the Republican songbook (that all public spending is bad, all private spending is good)[85] and resented for hamstringing him and them down the line, blocking the route to further stimulus bills if unemployment persisted. When a progressive president can go before the American people and say that because "families across the country are tightening their belts . . . the federal government should do the same,"[86] the case for counter-cyclical public spending has been entirely given away! For progressive politics to flourish in this country, the Keynesian case needs to be reclaimed and widely understood, which is why the building of that understanding is such a key task for the chapters that follows.

It is not the only task, however; for what progressive politics needs right now is more than some familiarity with the writings of John Maynard Keynes. What progressive politics needs right now—and what the Obama administration is not delivering—is a compelling overarching narrative and a body of *general* arguments on which it (and we) can draw to deal in a consistent way with the daily *detail* of American politics. Conservatism in America is so effective on a day-to-day basis—conservatism has a consistent message to send and a standardized response to make to any progressive initiative—because it has such a narrative, one built around a general argument that asserts the socially desirable outcomes of unregulated markets. We all know that story. We hear it all the time. It is a story that links freedom to free markets, and ties both to the Republican Party through a canonization of Ronald Reagan. Progressives need an equivalent and superior counter-story, one that links freedom to managed markets and—if canonization is appropriate—reminds people of FDR and the New Deal. Debunking FDR and the New Deal is so vital to conservatives—their intellectuals do that debunking regularly—because they see the progressive potential of that alternative story. If conservatives can see it and fear it, then progressives should see it too, and take heart.

So here is our task: to build an effective progressive narrative again, and to build it on the basis of the case for regulated markets. How? This way . . . beginning with Chapter 2.

CHAPTER 2

Making the Case for Regulated Markets

What people take for granted, what you might call the "common sense" of the age, gathers its force precisely by appearing both natural and timeless. Yet the ideas that bind us together invariably have long and complex histories of their own, and rarely if ever have been a permanent presence in human life. Rather, certain ideas, certain ways of understanding the world, come to occupy central places in our minds only because—in earlier generations—they were advocated, and eventually advocated successfully, in fierce competition with other ideas that are now lost in the mists of time. When, after two or more centuries of market capitalism, bread is in short supply, we expect its price to rise. When bread supplies fell in earlier centuries and prices rose, people rioted—and even hung the odd baker—because taking advantage of other people's hunger caused them moral outrage.[1] It has taken centuries of ideological (and political) struggle to flush that morality out of our system. It has taken centuries to sink the idea of *the market* deep into the collective consciousness of all of us: but it is there now. It is there in our consciousness. It is there even in our language. When governments regulate markets these days, there are invariably said to "intervene," even to "interfere." It is unregulated markets that are given linguistic priority in a popular culture that, in the first decades of the twenty-first century, largely takes for granted the economic and moral superiority of competitive struggles for economic advantage. In such a culture, regulating markets runs counter to the common sense of the age.

John Maynard Keynes once wrote that "the ideas of economists and political philosophers, both when they are right and when they are wrong, are more powerful than is commonly understood. Indeed, the world is ruled by little else. Practical men, who believe themselves to be quite exempt from any intellectual influence, are usually the slaves of some defunct economist."[2] He was writing of Europe in the 1930s but he could with equal force have been writing of the United States in the 2010s: and, in both cases, among the defunct economists that would have been in his sights was the eighteenth-century moral philosopher Adam Smith. For it was his *Wealth of Nations*, published in the same year as the Declaration of Independence, which has provided down the ages much of the intellectual ammunition used by those who would have markets left largely/entirely unregulated. Their case goes something like this.[3]

The Case for Deregulated Markets

1. Capitalist markets are the great drivers of human progress

Unregulated markets are a defining feature of a successful capitalist economy. Capitalism as a way of organizing economic life has proven its superiority to all forms of economic organization, and continues to do so.

- *Capitalism's own success is indisputable. Living standards in pre-capitalist Europe, or in contemporary societies in which capitalism does not flourish, cannot compare to the generalized affluence created by a fully organized and liberated capitalist economy. Living standards in North America, Western Europe, and Japan have doubled in a generation, in the process leaving far behind living standards in under-developed capitalisms, no matter what part of the world they are in.*[4] *Capitalism's superiority as a vehicle of mass prosperity is not just evidenced by contemporary comparative data. It is also evidenced by its own track record over time. Early capitalism did not raise generalized living standards, but contemporary capitalism has. Try to imagine any other form of economic organization with this internal capacity for reform and improvement. You will not be able to, because no such alternative exists.*[5]
- *If there was any doubt about the desirability and superiority of capitalism as a way of organizing economic life, that doubt was completely put to rest by the collapse of the Berlin Wall. By 1989, living standards in Eastern Europe had fallen to no more than 15 percent of those then prevalent in the capitalist West,*[6] *in the process creating a gap in performance so wide and so visible that popular uprisings brought Soviet communism to its knees. Though governing parties in other major communist countries (most notably China, but also Vietnam and even Cuba) have so far avoided the fate of the Communist Party of the Soviet Union, they have done*

so only by incrementally transforming themselves into capitalist classes, so releasing the entrepreneurial capacity of an emerging middle class that is everywhere the driver of capitalist success. In the great twentieth-century clash of capitalism and communism, there is no doubt which system decisively won. Capitalism did.

- *Of course it did, because centrally planned economies of the communist kind simply cannot hope to compete with the dynamism of free-market capitalism. Central planning cannot oversee the vast complexity of modern economic systems without seriously blunting industrial efficiency and individual freedom of choice. Central planning, communist or otherwise, is inherently vulnerable to bureaucratic stagnation and to the erosion of personal rights, and invariably generates alongside it a privately run black economy into which the irrepressible energy of the entrepreneurial spirit invariably pours.*[7] *You can ban the capitalist spirit but you cannot keep it down; which is why, as Robert Degan has it, "There is today widespread recognition that capitalism is the socio-economic system of choice."*[8]

2. Unregulated markets are optimal allocators of resources

Markets left to themselves do effectively three things that regulated markets can do at best only imperfectly. They transmit myriad information to an endless list of economic actors. They so shape the incentive structures of those actors that the collective result is an optimum allocation of scarce economic resources; in the process, they generate a distribution of rewards that is reflective of the usefulness and capacity of each and every market participant. Moreover, they do all those things without any central direction of any kind.

- *If goods and services are left to find their own price in an unregulated market, that price tells both buyers and sellers everything they need to know about the relative value of the good and service in question. The differing demands of consumers, and the differing intensity of their preferences for a particular purchase, give each commodity its own demand schedule. The costs of producing that good, and the likelihood that producing it will or will not be profitable, fixes the equivalent schedule of supply; and the interaction of the two schedules fixes that price point at which an optimum allocation of scarce resources is obtained. Artificially alter the price by some kind of ruling or subsidy, and the whole economy is pulled away from that optimum point: the immediate consumer or supplier may be the beneficiary of that arbitrary change, but the society as a whole is not. There would be temporary individual benefit, but long-term general loss.*[9]
- *Unregulated prices in open competitive markets draw the entrepreneurial into economic action. The market rewards the skillful, the brave, and the enterprising. It punishes the inefficient, the incompetent, and the cautious. Unregulated market competition produces winners as well as losers in a fair competition in which the criteria for success are economic efficiency and innovation. The long-term systemic*

consequence of unregulated price competition is, therefore, technological advancement, increased factor productivity, and enlarged total output: in other words, economic growth and prosperity. By rewarding the successful and penalizing the unsuccessful, unregulated price competition necessarily generates a meritocratic society, which then feeds upon itself. People see that merit is rewarded. They become achievement oriented and, collectively, they raise the efficiency bar.

- *The beauty of unregulated price competition is that these wider benefits flow automatically and to everyone. Adam Smith said it first, and he was right. In a free capitalist economy, the entrepreneur "is, in this as in many other cases, led by an invisible hand to promote an end that was no part of his intention." That the positive consequence of the single-minded pursuit of individual self-interest is unintentional is an additional gain. Smith again: "Nor is it always the worse for the society that it was not part of it. By pursuing his own interest he frequently promotes that of the society more effectively than when he really intends to promote it."[10] What could be more efficient and better than that?*

3. Unregulated markets guarantee freedom in ways that even democratic politics cannot

Advocates of the market as the dominant mode of economic coordination do more than emphasize its capacity to stimulate efficiency and innovation in production. They also stress its ability to coordinate without conscious human intervention, the literally millions of individual decisions made in a complex economy and, accordingly, point to the greater equality and freedom enjoyed within capitalist markets by individual producers and consumers, when set against the degrees of equality and freedom possible under either feudalism or communism.

- *As a historical phenomenon capitalism rose as the middle class rose; and that middle class consistently played a progressive political role, demanding that state institutions be representative in character and having them operate in line with the wishes of the represented. Free entry into product markets by new firms, and free entry into labor markets by freed peasantries, were the building blocs on which Western democratic institutions were subsequently build. Capitalism and freedom have been, in that basic sense, intimately connected since birth, and capitalism deserves at least one cheer for its "peculiar congenial[ity] to a large measure of personal liberty."[11]*
- *Free markets give consumers power. In free markets, consumers rule; and they rule not simply through the volume of their preferences, but also though the varying intensity of those preferences. Give a consumer a dollar, and they will spend it to achieve a set of personal ends that no central authority can know ahead of time, and spend it with a sensitivity to the marginal value of the last thing bought,*

which no central authority is capable of anticipating or measuring. Money, in the hands of free consumers, brings an unbeatable level of rationality to the demand side of the capitalist economic equation, and by its deployment triggers an equally unbeatable level of rationality in the supply side response. The opportunity cost of each purchase is known, and known at the instance of purchase, by each consumer in turn. Try to imagine a welfare state or a central plan with that level of knowledge and nuance. You won't be able to, because "nobody spends somebody else's money as carefully as he spends his own."[12]

- *Even the democratic vote is not as sensitive to opportunity costs as is private consumption. Government spending is inherently flawed in this regard. "The fundamental difference between the political market and the economic market in that in the political market there is very little relation between what you vote for and what you get. In the economic market, you get what you vote for."*[13] *When voters chose between policies, the immediate benefits of those policies are visible to all—put there by their advocates—but the long-term costs are not. No advocate exists to bring them into sight. When private consumers forgo one purchase by making another, they immediately and individually experience the cost of the loss of that alternative. When voters chose to forego one policy by choosing another, no such immediate awareness of loss comes into view; which is why—when the alternatives are government expenditure or private expenditure—private expenditure is always to be preferred. As Milton Friedman famously put it, in relation to the size of state spending, there is always "a line we dare not cross."*

4. Markets and morality go together

The great strength of free-market capitalism is not simply that it generates great products for people to buy and sell. It also generates great people. Its modes of operation develop and reward virtue, and the affluence is generates makes possible a civilized and compassionate society.

- *In pre-capitalist societies, dominant moral codes were established by the major religions and transmitted between generations primarily by church and family. In early capitalism, certain forms of Protestantism were particularly empathetic to the work ethic and frugality required for capital accumulation, and to this day, there is an intimate and mutually reinforcing connection between the best of modern morality and the requirements for successful market performance. Capitalism reinforces an ethic of personal responsibility. Its reward systems privilege hard work, self-discipline, sobriety, the conservation of resources, and the honoring of contracts. Individual capitalists may lapse on occasion—human nature is not perfect and a rule-governed society always attracts those who seek to profit by breaking rules—but the mass and generality of business owners and workers find their own high levels of personal morality reinforced and rewarded by the rigors of market competition.*

- *The bounty of capitalism brings into being economies with a considerable social surplus. People make more than they need, and that productivity is the base on which generous systems of provision can be, and are, created for those unable to work. It is capitalist societies that have the finest education and health systems. It is capitalist societies that now sustain, for the first time in human history, generous pension provision, and aid for the physically disabled and the mentally ill. It is capitalism, through the centrality of its market competition, that alone generates the corporate and individual winners who are then free to pay back part of their success in extensive charity giving; and it is the developed capitalist world—unlike any developed world before it—that now extensively aids the development of economies and societies poorer than itself. People might criticize wealthy and successful capitalists for not giving back enough, but those critics need to recognize that capitalist economies are the first ones ever to make that giving back possible on any large scale.*[14]
- *Capitalism has been a great force generating higher and higher standards of personal morality over time. In advanced market economies, "people care deeply about eliminating pain and injustice and ensuring the welfare of fellow humans"; and so they should, for "life is no longer nasty, brutish and short; rather it is gentle, kind and long, and more precious than before." As Martin Wolf put it, "The market economy rests on and encourages valuable moral qualities . . . it is the most inherently just economic system that humankind has ever devised."*[15]

5. The regulation of markets by governments necessarily impairs their performance

So why spoil a thing by interfering with it? Unregulated market capitalism has been the wellspring of modern prosperity and success, so why now—with that success in place and still ongoing—mess about with the very market forces that have brought us to this place?

- *Regulation of markets necessarily distorts the workings of the price mechanism, so pulling the whole economy away from its optimal distribution of resources. Regulate and over-tax a company, and you weaken its capacity for innovation,*[16] *its ability to compete, and the incentives of its senior management to take necessary economic risks. Regulate a labor market and you undermine the capacity of managers to manage. You price labor out of employment*[17] *and you leave both company and workers vulnerable to competition from less-regulated economies and states. By all means, intervene to break up monopolies, but then get out of the way, out of the market, and let market actors interact freely without fear of later public intervention.*[18]

- *Whatever you do, do not follow the maxims of John Maynard Keynes. Governments cannot manufacture economic growth. Nor can they create genuine demand. All they can do is redistribute resources from the economically successful to the economically unsuccessful, so raising a whole string of moral hazard issues and eating away at key structures of individual and corporate incentives.*[19] *Yes, governments can print money and build big spending programs, but the financing of that spending, if real, takes money away from private investment growth, and if it is not real—if the enhanced money supply has no commensurate collateral in greater output—government spending fuels inflation, not growth.*[20] *The realities of market competition cannot be wished away by over-active and ultra-liberal state actors. It is true that not all market outcomes are immediately ideal—markets generate losers as well as winners—but the long-term conditions of the losers will not be improved by excessive government spending. On the contrary, any short-term adverse consequences of unregulated market competition will only be made worse and more permanent by government expenditures designed to alleviate them. FDR's New Deal did not solve the Depression. It actually extended it. It made it Great; and Obama's Keynesianism is likely to be equally disastrous.*[21]
- *This is not to say that government has no role to play. For most free marketeers, the role of government is necessary but limited. It is true that there are powerful libertarian voices in the conservative coalition, advocating the abolition of the Federal Reserve and of income tax,*[22] *but more normally the advocates of free markets stay loyal to Adam Smith's "three duties" of the "sovereign": the provision by the state of goods that free markets find difficult to generate—national defense, the administration of justice, and public goods such as education and road systems. This third "duty" remains, in Milton Friedman's words, "troublesome" for free marketeers, and they, like Smith, tend to give it "a narrow application."*[23] *The job of government, they say, is simply to remove "impediments to work, saving, investment and production," and accordingly "lower tax rates and a reduction in the burden of government are the best ways of using fiscal policy to boost growth."*[24]

6. Free markets are the American way: disturb them at your peril

America is not Europe and does not need to be recast in a European mold. On the contrary, America has been, and remains, the bastion of liberty and freedom precisely because it has eschewed European ways of organizing its economy and society.[25]

- *Unregulated markets are as American as apple pie. Unlike Europe, America had no feudal past. It inherited no aristocratic tradition of strong state leadership and noblesse oblige. American was a capitalist society from its inception, and it drew the best of Europe to it for that reason. No strong labor movement emerged here to hamstring American business with rigid collective agreements and over-developed welfare nets; and in the space created by the absence of anti-capitalist and pro-socialist political formations, American business flourished as never before. Once what was good for General Motors was also good for America; and though the car company has recently faltered, the general point still holds. Free markets and American prosperity go hand in hand. You cannot undermine one without undermining the other.*

- *And why should you want to? The American business model is the envy of the world. America is a mecca for the world's poor—the ultimate immigration success story. People don't emigrate to economies and societies that don't work, but they emigrate to here. There was a time, roughly from 1948 to 1973, when the Japanese and Western European welfare economies were growing faster than was the U.S.—but they were doing that only by aping established American corporate practices. It was "catch up growth" which, once over, could not be replicated; and if there is now convergence between models of capitalism, in this new age of globalized trade, it is a convergence towards American ways of doing business. The future is still American, and will remain so just so long as we don't over-regulate our economy into the kind of "institutional sclerosis"[26] now besetting the economies of the European Union.*
- *The equation of free markets with American prosperity is a regular theme in the Republican Party's presentation of itself, and rightly so. The Democratic Party would do well to follow the Republican example. As recently as November 2005, the then-Treasury Secretary John Snow told a radio audience that "we have adopted, on a scale beyond that of any other country, a reliance on market forces . . . Markets work. We let markets work. The market is a marvelous mechanism for high GDP growth, high job creation and high wages." Which was why the Bush administration was so keen, Snow said, to "put in place a low tax-rate environment": it is only that kind of environment that "encourages capital investment and job creation . . . by giving incentives . . . to people to invest, and to establish new businesses and to take risks."[27] His boss agreed. "I'm optimistic," the then-president told reporters later, "that we have good policy in place that will encourage the entrepreneurial spirit. And I firmly believe, so long as this is an entrepreneurial-oriented country, America will remain the economic leader we want it to be."[28]*

7. *The Obama administration is a disaster waiting to happen*

Not surprisingly, therefore, free-market conservatives have greeted the Obama administration with a steady mixture of condemnation, rejection, and, at times, hysteria. They have seen his mild Keynesianism as exactly the wrong response to the financial meltdown, and as a "cure" that was as capable of destroying as of restoring the prosperity of American capitalism.[29] In their darkest moments, American conservatives paint a picture of an America poised to be reset into a "quasi-socialist" economy and society, Western European or worse.[30] *The worst is sometimes described like this:*

1. *IT WILL BE AN AMERICA where a majority of citizens receive lavish government handouts and benefits but pay no income taxes, meanwhile voting themselves still more benefits from the shrinking minority who do pay taxes—at ever more "progressive" rates.*
2. *IT WILL BE AN AMERICA where "universal health care" means waiting months, even years, for urgently needed treatment—unless you happen to be politically powerful or connected—and where all your private medical information is on a governmental database.*
3. *IT WILL BE AN AMERICA where "green" ideologues and other nanny-staters dictate what we drive, what we eat, home energy usage, the size of our houses, and even how many children we can have.*
4. *IT WILL BE AN AMERICA where our major industries, crippled by government mandates, taxes, and regulations end up becoming taxpayer-supported dinosaurs that can no longer complete in the global marketplace.*
5. *IT WILL BE AN AMERICA where all employers will be forced to hire and promote not according to ability but according to race, gender, and ethnicity—all in the name of "diversity."*
6. *IT WILL BE AN AMERICA where our once great centers of finance, industry, culture, and innovation—from New York to Silicon Valley—will have gone to seed, while only Washington, DC, and its environs prosper.*
7. *IT WILL BE AN AMERICA, in short, where only politicians, government bureaucrats, and their favored constituencies are able to thrive—and where the only "liberty" that remains is the government's unlimited freedom to control every aspect of your life.*[31]

A liberal response

So what should the liberal response be: this much, at least:

1. The choice here is not one between capitalism and socialism, but between unregulated and regulated capitalism

Free marketeers are often way too quick to label any proposal for market regulation as "socialist" in impact or intent. When they do, their thinking is sloppy and their vocabulary is misleading.[32] Very few people on the Left are proposing to abolish private property, or indeed even seriously to diminish the freedom of Americans to dispose of that property as they see fit, and certainly the Obama administration is not.[33] The case made by progressives against unregulated markets is far less draconian that that. It is, in the first instance, one built on the critique of the quality and relevance of much of the free marketeers' claim. That claim—that unregulated markets automatically generate an optimum distribution of resources through the workings of some invisible hand—assumes a state of perfect competition among both buyers and sellers in those markets. Those advocating the absence of state regulation invariably paint for us—and invite us to adopt as our understanding of the world—a picture of fully informed, fully rational, and fully empowered consumers and investors engaged in calm economic interaction with an equally substantial, rational, and informed set of small companies. In such a picture, all those involved are price-takers rather than price-setters, because none is large enough alone to influence market prices by the manipulation of demand or supply. This picture is misleading in at least the following ways:

- *The Invisibility of the Invisible Hand.* The "invisible hand" is not a perfect mechanism for optimal resource allocation, even under the extremely rare circumstances of perfect competition, as Adam Smith himself was well aware. Smith wrote of the "invisible hand" on only two major occasions in his work—once in *The Wealth of Nations*, once in his earlier *Theory of Moral Sentiments*.[34] It was never his central thesis, no matter how regularly contemporary free marketeers try to make it so. We do well to remember that the passage in *The Wealth of Nations* "containing the invisible hand metaphor came only late in the book and was not about general equilibrium theory: its purpose [was] to explain why merchants would continue to buy British products even if tariffs were removed."[35] We also do well to remember that as a moral philosopher—and Smith was primarily that—he gave as much weight to the passions, to social interests, and to justice as he did to unbridled egotism in his exploration of the human condition. So that, taken in the round, "his analysis question[ed] many of the theses [now conventionally attributed to him], that human beings are primarily self-interested rational utility maximizers, that we are social atoms, and that a perfectly competitive market is either 'free from morality' or an 'exemplar of rational morality.'"[36] ("For Smith, individuals commit grave injustice when in the pursuit of their interests they cause even the least harm to others,"[37] not that you would know that from the way his work is presented to us by many of his modern-day acolytes.[38]) And even on their narrow reading of *The Wealth of Nations,* it is clear that the invisible hand argument rests on three linked propositions, only two of which are without controversy. It is true that actions can have unintended consequences, and that those consequences can, "given the right circumstances [spontaneously] result in an order that is understandable to the human mind and appear as if it were the product of some intelligent planner."[39] But what is less true is that the resulting pattern of resource allocation is inevitably and automatically optimal. That claim relies on a judgment on desirable outcomes that rational people have a right—indeed a duty—to discuss. The outcome of unfettered market competition may well be optimal, for example, if you do not happen to care about income inequality, but not optimal if you do. Markets serve purposes. The question we have always to ask (and answer) is whose purposes do unregulated markets actually serve?

- *Markets as Constructs.* We do well to remember, too, that the notion of a market is just that—a notion. It is a mental construction we place on complex human interactions in order to understand their character. In doing so, we illuminate the interaction by obscuring its parameters and preconditions. Conservatives often talk of markets as alternatives to state action, when in truth markets and states necessarily go together. Well-functioning markets only exist where governments both create and enforce the rules that make market exchange possible—rules of property, rules of competition, rules of contract. We do well to remember, too, that the scope of markets is socially decided. The scope is not fixed by the character of the human condition but by the value choices of each generation of humanity.[40] There are things that should not be for sale, and there are things that have a use value quite different from their exchange value.[41] What those things are varies over time. There were once slave markets. Even today there are third world labor markets that are wholly focused on the employment of children. Many advocates of "unregulated markets" in advanced industrial societies such as ours draw the line at child labor. All of them, I assume, draw the line at slavery; but that makes the point. The scope of unregulated markets is necessarily set by regulation, and it is an entirely legitimate area of political discussion to resolve how wide or narrow that scope should be.[42]

- *Perfect and Imperfect Competition.* Moreover, idealized versions of perfectly competitive markets are exactly that. They are idealized. They are abstract conceptual devices and, as such, they mislead us when offered as more than they are: when offered as concrete and complete descriptions of underlying economic realities. Modern economies are dominated by large firms, not by small ones—and inevitably so. Precisely because market competition generates winners as well as losers, the size of companies must increasingly diverge over time; and with size come economies of scale that then preclude the easy entry of new firms into well-established competitive sectors. The "optimal resource allocation" claim for perfect competition does not, and cannot, apply to situations of imperfect competition and oligopoly, as leading economists of many intellectual persuasions have long conceded.[43] In conditions of imperfect competition, it is the economic theories of Joseph Schumpeter, not those of Adam Smith, that operate.[44] In the world of imperfect competition, public policy has to be geared to the generation of dynamic efficiencies over time, not to static efficiency in one abstract moment of thought. Those dynamic efficiencies are as likely to be guaranteed by carefully regulated large companies, and by publicly subsidized research and development, as they are by the unregulated clash of small and ill-equipped small firms. There was a time when the underlying character of the U.S. economy was best captured by a model of perfect competition between small companies: but no longer. To continue to analyze twenty-first century American business through the lens of free market competition is to remain forever trapped in the mental furniture of the nineteenth century. The American economy has moved on, but in certain conservative circles it would appear that patterns of thought have not.[45]

- *The Limits of Rationality.* The rationality of investment markets is currently a matter of huge debate—so huge and important, in fact, that it warrants its own appendix in this volume. What is similarly debated, though currently in a less intense fashion, is whether contemporary consumers are always as rational or as knowledgeable as the free market model of perfect competition requires. The evidence would suggest that in general they are not. Consumers fall short of how theories of perfect competition would have them act, in part because of the market power of big companies with their capacity to sustain large advertising budgets geared to the construction of demand. We buy things because we are persuaded that we need them, even when in truth we don't. Consumers also fall short of perfect rationality because there are thought processes in all of us that do not match the free marketeers' requirement of fully informed individuals rationally calculating their immediate self-interest. That is not how most of us structure our consumption decisions. Our sense of self is often wider than merely us alone, stretching out to family and friends, to neighbors, to fellow citizens, even to fellow members of the human race. We often value things that cannot be achieved by the purchase of commodities alone—things like security, happiness, social respect, and mutual trust. We occasionally act irrationally, consuming by following our whim—and even in more measured moments invariably lack full information about either the commodities we buy or those we forgo.[46] Consumer sovereignty is neither as total, as informed or as rational as free market advocates would have us believe, and because it is not—because it is constructed from a myriad of social influences over which individually we have little control—it is legitimate for public policy to be one of those shaping forces.

2. There are downsides to unregulated markets that Milton Friedman systematically ignored

Very few people on the left these days favor central planning. In the debate between planning and the market, the market clearly won. But it "won" in spite of a set of recognized deficiencies in the workings of unregulated markets that has left a huge political space for the advocates of market regulation. European Social Democracy, European Christian Democracy, and sections of the American Democratic Party occupy that political space, and properly so, because they are aware of things that markets do that require correction: at least these.

- *Inequality*. Markets respond to the purchasing power of the consumers within them rather than directly to the perceived needs of the consumers themselves. If purchasing power is equally distributed between all consumers within the market, then markets are indeed ideal mechanisms for the meeting of those needs;[47] but in capitalist economies unregulated markets do not generate income equality. Even if markets begin on level playing fields, their internal competitive dynamic steadily undermines that equality as winners move ahead and losers fall behind. Unregulated markets in capitalist economies are great mechanisms for the generation of *inequalities* between individuals, inequalities that are invariably cumulative.[48] Unregulated markets and deepening socio-economic differences go together. In general, the children of the poor stay poor. At the very least, those who would leave markets unregulated have therefore to explain how they square their passion for individual freedom and equality with the inequality and differences in social empowerment that divide the children of the rich from the children of the poor. Children are is not something that free marketeers talk about often, but they are something that we need to talk about all the time.

- *Monopolies and Externalities*. Markets also generate inequalities between companies as well as between individuals, and in a capitalist economy market competition obliges companies to protect their internal processes from exposure to those who would do them down. Markets that start on a level playing field of competitive companies do not stay there. Nor do they of themselves generate institutions capable of balancing the private needs of individual companies with the public needs of companies and consumers in general. On the contrary, unregulated markets generate both monopolies and externalities—big companies able to set rather than receive prices, and companies whose adverse impact on the physical and social environment in which they operate does not automatically appear in the internal structure of their costs. At the very least, those who would leave markets unregulated have therefore to explain how they square their antipathy to public regulation of private corporate practices with this propensity of unregulated markets to undermine themselves internally and to degrade the wider commons as they do so.

- *Hidden Losers.* That degradation is not merely environmental, though pollution is clearly one major externality that unregulated markets have difficulty in addressing.[49] It is also social. The companies that fail leave non-economic casualties—workers without jobs, towns without companies, local authorities without adequate tax bases, local children without hope. Markets may well be excellent at bringing demand and supply together, but they only do so *ex post* and only by leaving human resources periodically under utilized. Even on a good day, and no matter how regulated, market competition breeds insecurity and stress in all the human elements involved in its economic equations. The other side of immediate competitive success is the possibility of later economic failure; and in truth, lightly regulated markets do more than simply raise the anxiety stakes. They also contain no mechanism capable of tying failure to personal performance. They appear to do so, but in reality they don't. The advocates of unregulated markets tell us with great frequency about the fate of entrepreneurs who innovate and those who don't; but what they trumpet far less often is the fate of the many workers employed by each non-innovator. Those workers have invariably labored diligently at the tasks set for them, but still lose the entirety of their employment, income, and potential. Where is the justice—or, indeed, the freedom—in that?

3. The general case for big government

American conservatives seem preoccupied these days with maintaining their distance on all things European, but they need not worry. That distance is largely one of their own making and maintenance. Unlike major conservative political traditions in Western Europe, American conservatism has a propensity for *anti-statism* that sets the United States apart. In France, in Germany, in Japan, even in the United Kingdom, political parties of the center-right have long understood that state policy can *aid* their national business community, if properly directed. The political dispute abroad is largely focused on the scale and kind of public management of private businesses required for the competitive health of those businesses. But not here: here it is virtually axiomatic on the Right that governments govern best that govern least, and it is so in spite of the fact that, on a daily basis, the U.S. Federal Government and large American business corporations are heavily engaged with each other. Too often, conservatives paint a picture of government-industry relations in the United States that leaves out defense procurement by the Pentagon and farm subsidies from the Department of Agriculture, to mention but two of many possible examples.[50] Key sectors of American business flourish because of state aid rather than in spite of it, but you would never know that if all you read were the "anti-socialist" tirades of the libertarian Right.

Their principled *anti-statism* is vulnerable to the following general arguments in favor of market regulation and state support.

- *The Supporting State.* The adverse economic and social consequences of unregulated market competition provide fertile ground for those who see a *positive* role for the state in the management of a successful private economy. At the very least, governments have the job of establishing and implementing legal codes protecting the rights of private corporations and of maintaining a high degree of competition between them. Periodic trust-busting is a key role for public policy.[51] So, too, is the regulation and reduction of a string of negative externalities created by unregulated market competition. There is a positive case to be made for taxation, to offset the negative one provided by conservatives—a progressive case advocating taxation as *the* fairest collective way to finance the long-term upkeep of society.[52] There is a key role for public policy in the protection of the environment, in the maintenance of minimum standards of consumer protection, and in preventing the raiding of corporate funds for illicit private gain. There is also a key role for public policy in offsetting the adverse social consequences of unregulated market competition—creating a welfare net for those unable to work and a retraining net for discarded workers. It is even possible—liberals would say desirable—for the state to go the extra mile and develop an *active* industrial policy: policy to increase general skill levels in the labor force, to support high-risk, high-return research and development, and to create new and complex infrastructures. The state may even have a role in aiding the takeoff of new industries, and in setting the bar on labor rights so high as to block off sweatshop routes to corporate profitability. There is a strong case, that is, for big government as a *supplement* to private enterprise and as a *facilitator* of its long-term competitive success.[53]

- *The Keynesian State.* This is particularly so because of another feature of unregulated markets that tends to go unnoticed by those who advocate their continued deregulation, and that is the propensity of such markets to clear (to find their equilibrium) at levels of employment that leave many out of work. Unregulated markets and full employment do not automatically go together, no matter how often free marketeers assert that they do. Cutting wages (to generate jobs) also cuts demand (to generate unemployment). Uncertainties endemic in economies that work in the medium of time can, on occasion, induce liquidity preferences that keep money out of circulation when it is needed most. There is, therefore, a major role for a Keynesian-inspired state in a modern economy, particularly at moments of crisis. Public spending does not automatically squeeze out private investment, and certainly does not do so at times of deep recession—both in the 1930s[54] and again in 2008[55]—when private investment had ground to a halt for want of secure demand. In such circumstances, and in line with Keynesian thinking, public spending then generates the wages that can rekindle that demand, public infrastructure projects generate that demand directly, and both public investment and public expenditure have a profound and pervasive multiplier effect on the economy as a whole. A dollar initially spent by the federal government passes from hand to hand, generating income at each stage of its journey, in the process creating the tax base from which that initial dollar can eventually be retrieved. To base the revival of private investment on stock market recovery alone is to place undue faith in the workings of a private casino—a gamble that can be avoided by the prudent use of the public purse.[56]

- *The Democratic State.* And let no one tell us that votes and money are equivalents, and that markets work better than democracies because consumers with money can better calculate the costs and benefits of resource choices than can those same consumers armed only with a vote. The "line we dare not cross"[57] argument is profoundly ideological and dangerous. Votes and money would be equivalents if—*but only if*—everyone in the market had the same amount of money, the same voting power. In contemporary markets, no such income equality exists, and because it does not, the economically privileged are able to buy disproportionate political influence, as Milton Friedman observed, and so fuel conservative *anti-statism* of the kind he so effectively articulated. But the money-based lobbying that so distorts the democratic process in the United States is itself a major political consequence of the inequalities created by unregulated markets.[58] Progressives should want money out of politics. To get that, we will need to regulate the markets that generate such uneven distributions of income and wealth in the first place. Leaving economic decision-making to the market is not some process of subordinating our free and rational selves to an impersonal and neutral force. It is rather a process of subordinating our powerless workers and consumers to the unchecked authority of the highly paid men (and, occasionally, women) who head our largest corporations. Market power means CEO power. We need to remember that. We need to remember, too, that state power can mean people power, because in the absence of income equality in the United States, the possession of the vote is *the* great social leveler. The rich and the poor have equal voting rights. They enjoy an equality politically that they do not possess economically; and so the public policies for which they vote (unless distorted by money-based lobbying)—including policies to regulate the adverse consequences of unregulated market competition—must hold the moral high ground. Democracy trumps unregulated markets every time, and we need to say so.

4. The particular features of labor markets

There is another critical distinction on which liberals need to insist when engaged in dialogue with conservatives about the desirability, or otherwise, of unregulated market competition: the distinction between markets for commodities (in which inanimate objects are bought and sold) and the markets for labor (places in which people's capacity to labor is bought and sold). In the latter camp, we should also include the market for health (places in which the needs of the human body are bought and sold). Health care should not be treated as a commodity in the way that a car or food can be treated;[59] and certainly people, as employees, are not car-equivalents. There are special features of labor markets that require higher levels of public regulation than those required for general commodity markets: special features of the following kind.

- *Labor as people.* Labor is not just any commodity, to be analyzed in abstracted models of labor market performance. It is a very special commodity, which, because it is highly perishable ("it cannot be stored, and if it is not used continuously it is wasted"[60]) and because it is highly active (with workers needing to be present at its delivery), requires managing in a very particular kind of way.

  This is especially the case in a capitalist mode of production, where there is a perpetual wage–effort bargain to be struck between managers and workers within the context of highly differentiated patterns of reward. Labor markets are inherently complex social systems, and have to be studied with sensitivity to the wider social universes in which they are inserted. At the very least, this means that the definitions, goals, motivations, and stocks of knowledge that individual laborers bring to the production process inevitably shape productive outcomes. It also means that the workings of labor markets are shaped by sets of social forces (institutions, histories, cultures, and practices) that lie beyond the immediate control of any one individual labor market actor (labor markets are quintessentially *not* the appropriate territory for forms of analysis based on the interaction of socially abstracted rational individuals.) And most important of all, it means that the settlements arrived at inside labor markets have outcomes and significances that stretch far beyond the boundaries of the labor market itself, such that nothing going on within the market can safely be treated in isolation from wider questions of status and power.[61]

In consequence, the free marketeers' enthusiasm for "factor flexibility" cannot be reduced in labor markets to a simple managerial capacity to hire and fire, without the resulting insecurity of employment corroding the capacity of labor—as a self-motivating factor of production—to function at full capacity. If the advocates of labor market deregulation genuinely want labor to be efficient—as distinct from just supine—they need to treat workers as people, not simply as commodities. Yet that is something that neither their theoretical systems nor their policy prescriptions encourage them to do.

- *Gradients of Power.* Nor is it the case that labor markets automatically "clear" at socially and economically optimal levels of employment and efficiency unless disturbed by trade union intervention, or that what we face without trade unionism is a level playing field between employer and worker, which trade unionism then distorts. We do not. Unregulated labor markets are stacked heavily against labor. There is a basic asymmetry of power between the individual worker and his or her employer that trade unionism attempts to address.[62] There is a power gradient running against labor in capitalist societies, unless unions act to pull it back. That retrenchment or redressing has never been more than partial, even when at its greatest (to date) in the labor codes of the Western European welfare states. If American conservatives work to widen the distance on labor rights between the United States and Europe, what they are actually arguing for is an intensification of the gradient *against* American labor. They are implying that rapid economic growth here requires an increase in already unprecedented levels of economic inequality, and a redress of even the modest worker rights enjoyed by organized workers in the United States. Given the existing imbalance of power between management and managed in the contemporary American economy, the call for labor market deregulation is not simply a technical issue. It is a blatant class project. Its purpose, and its consequence, can be nothing other than the amplification of the already excessive authority, wealth, and arrogance of American senior management, and needs to be rejected by progressives as such.[63]

- *Labor Power as Positive.* That rejection has ultimately to rest on a retelling of the post-war American growth story. Free marketeers like to place responsibility for economic growth on American entrepreneurs alone, and to write trade unions out of the story. But American entrepreneurial capacity did not free us of depression in the 1930s. Nor did it free us of global recession in 2008 and 2009, and the dates are significant ones. For the United States has enjoyed two periods of sustained economic growth in the post-war period—one long, one short—and in the long one, but not the short one, trade union strength played a major and a positive role. Between 1948 and 1973, the U.S. economy grew on the basis of a social compact negotiated between Northeastern and Midwestern manufacturing industry and powerful industrial unions. Productivity and wages rose together in those years, rising wages which then gave the entire U.S. economy a strong internal demand dynamic.[64] After 1992, growth came again, but this time to an economy in which trade unions had been seriously weakened by an employers' offensive and a hostile federal government.[65] Ronald Reagan, you may remember, liked Polish trade unions enormously but American unions not at all. Economic growth after 1992 did not rest on rising wages; real wages/hour in the U.S. economy for the mass and generality of American workers stayed broadly stagnant through this second brief growth period. Growth in that second period rested on an extension of the working week and an explosion of personal credit in a debt-based system that came crashing down in the financial meltdown of 2008–2009.[66] It was the first growth period, not the second, which provided the U.S. economy with a quarter-century of stable growth and rising living standards, at least for those workers fortunate enough to be in trade unions. Free marketeers invariably treat unions as monopolists who distort labor market outcomes. Progressives ought to see them in a more positive light: as potential partners with enlightened employers in the modernization of the U.S. economy, and as barriers to sweatshop routes to short-term and unstable corporate profitability.[67]

5. The immorality of unregulated capitalism

It is a striking feature of the claims made for the morality of capitalism as an economic system, and of unregulated markets as capitalism's defining element, that cherry-picking is not treated as a moral vice; for in the making of those claims, there is moral cherry-picking in abundance. On the downside of capitalism's moral account, we must include at least the following:

- *Capitalism and its Friends.* Free-market capitalism has long proved compatible with social orders of a highly exploitative kind and with labor (and labor market) practices and consequences that are hard to justify in moral terms. Combined and uneven economic development has been a feature of global capitalism from the outset: the bounty of capitalism in its core economies has never been matched by the generalization of that affluence in to the more peripheral economies drawn into capitalism's web. On the contrary, unequal exchange and the development of under-development have been key features of the trading relationships linking the first world to many economies in the third, in global political networks that were once explicitly colonial in character and now arguably are still neo-colonial.[68] Even within core capitalisms, income inequality and the persistence of poverty remain key features of the social landscape. The degree of inequality at home and of outsourcing abroad varies with the type of capitalism involved—the more deregulated the capitalism, the greater the scale of unemployment and external exploitation—but in all capitalist economies a distinct underclass of the economically and socially less privileged continue to constitute a blot on the overall moral adequacy of a form of economic organization praised by its adherents as morally superior to all others.

- *The Humanizing of Capitalism.* The central driving impulse of free-market capitalism is private capital accumulation. Success is measured by the capture and control of more and more common economic resource. Greed, rampant individualism, and the treatment of others as simply commodities are endemic to this form of economic organization. So, too, is salary excess.[69] Just think of the rigged way in which CEO compensation is currently determined in the United States—no unregulated labor markets there—rigged labor markets responsible for, among other things, the Wall Street bonus culture that so offended middle America in the wake of the 2008 financial crisis.[70] So, too, are the periodic corporate scams of the Enron and Worldcom kind.[71] Those central impulses for personal and corporate greed can—and often are—tempered by values and practices of a more socially responsible kind, but that tempering necessarily comes from value systems that sit in tension with the underlying need privately to accumulate capital.[72] They come from pre-capitalist modes of thought and living, often religious in nature.[73] They come from post-capitalist social movements, often those based in capitalist production itself (labor movements) but also those anchored in spheres of consumption and/or non-economic private life (the green and women's movements). They do not come from core capitalist classes themselves. In fact, the more "perfectly competitive" the capitalism, the *less* space free market competition allows for corporate beneficence.[74]

If capitalism is to some degree humanized, it is humanized from outside, not from within.

- *Capitalism and the Charity Illusion.* The main counterargument to that assertion is invariably one pointing to the scale of corporate giving, to the propensity of free market economies to generate a private and informal welfare net under the poor and dispossessed that is voluntarily financed by large and successful businesses. Yet part of that corporate giving is clearly instrumental in nature—put in place to improve the image of private corporations inside wider social cultures that are still shaped by these pre- and post-capitalist value systems, or to exploit tax concessions put in place by more center-left political formations. It is corporate giving, that is, that occurs in response to (and because of) anti-capitalist forces, not in response to (and because of) any core driving forces within capitalism itself. And any corporate giving which is not so instrumental in nature is normally sustained in spite of the free-market tendency to force companies in competition with each other to minimize *all* their costs, including those of charitable contributions. Companies operating within free-market capitalism in periods of easy economic growth may well give generously to charities of their choice, but that charity giving is invariably an early casualty of any major downturn in corporate profits. Whatever else 2009 turned out to be, it was not a good year for charities; and the fact that it was not demonstrates the fragile morality underpinning the largesse of the successful in market systems where private charity is steadily replacing progressive taxation as the way to fund assistance to the poor. If we genuinely want a morally sound and sustainable economic system, then the deregulation of markets is not the way forward.

6. Issues of freedom and happiness

There is an alarming degree of hubris and self-deception in many of the claims made by advocates of market deregulation about the connection between markets and freedom. Individual freedom is, of course, one of life's most precious possessions, and there is no doubt that a society of affluence offers a scale of individual freedom which a society bereft of resources and technologies can never hope to match. But that very truth serves to remind us of the narrowness of the notion of freedom deployed in many free-market defenses, and of the dangers of too materialistic an understanding of the determinants of freedoms, individual and collective.[75]

- *Negative and Positive Freedom.* If freedom is defined narrowly as "negative freedom," as freedom from tyranny, injustice, and want, then the workings of a free market in a democratic society are a far better way of achieving freedom than is any centrally planned economy in a dictatorial regime. But even in a free society, the capacity of individuals to enjoy the full reality of their formal freedoms depends on the ease of their access to the resources and skills commonplace in the society as a whole. Inherited inequalities and uneven access to social capital rob the least affluent among us of the true capacity to live freely alongside us. "The man who is hungry," Lyndon Johnson said, "who cannot find work or educate his children, who is bowed by want, that man is not fully free."[76] Advocates of market deregulation tend to

> . . . operate with a conception of negative liberty which is strict in two relevant senses. First, freedom is freedom from coercion. Secondly, coercion is the result of intentional interference by another individual or group of individuals. This idea of freedoms allows [them] to argue that the outcomes of markets are not coercive in relation to people who end up with least as a result of market transactions.[77]

But that will not do. Negative freedoms have to be supplemented by positive ones: by access to high quality education, to easily affordable health care and child support, to decent housing and security from crime and vandalism—by access to "a set of basic abilities and associated resources . . . needs, the failure to satisfy which would restrict freedom because they are related to the capacity for action itself."[78] Have all of those, and you will find yourself on a level playing field with the rest of your society, able to progress by your own industry and prosper by your own values. But lack them, and try as you will, your freedoms will not have the same substance as many around you. Unregulated markets do not bring equal access to the pre-requisites for freedom in a modern society. Regulated markets, if regulated properly, do. A society that is genuinely free combines negative and positive freedoms. Markets need to be regulated, not to reduce freedoms but to guarantee them.

- *Freedom and Happiness.* Societies need to be judged too by more than the formal freedoms they guarantee. They have to be judged additionally by the quality of life they make possible within them. Advocates of market deregulation tend to measure success by the volume and quality of the goods and services generated. They measure success in consumption terms, and consumption by its scale. But the evidence is clear that economic growth and human happiness go together only for so long. When people are desperately poor, a rise in living standards is an unambiguous boost to happiness; but after a certain level of material wealth, that relationship weakens. One television in the house is a blessing. Five may be additionally positive, but 19? Twenty-six? No, at some point, extra consumption becomes a fading pleasure, particularly if the money to make it possible can only be acquired by lengthening and intensifying the working day. As Peter Saunders had it, "in a world of bountiful commodities, we seemed to be locked into a spiral of ever increasing accumulation as we seek to attain an always elusive sense of final contentment."[79] Market societies have ultimately to be judged by the quality of life they make possible: the sense of security they give to people as they work and consume, the sense of worth people find from the work they do and the relationships they build, and the fit they experience between the things they hold important and the central thrust of daily life around them.[80] There is nothing in the insecurities and pressures of unregulated market competition that makes free markets necessarily the best delivery system for that wider sense of worth and happiness.[81] On the contrary, the reverse may actually be the case. Certainly the latest OECD study of "life satisfaction" in advanced industrial democracies found the highest levels of contentment among the populations of highly regulated economies (Denmark, Finland, and the Netherlands). The lightly regulated U.S. economy didn't even make the top ten.[82]

- *Freedom and Stress.* And that should not surprise us, given the evidence suggesting that, as the United States has moved deeper and deeper into its post-Reagan market deregulation phase, levels of personal happiness here have either stabilized or slightly declined.[83] If Robert Lane is correct, and the trend is downward, then the United States here is truly exceptional—levels of happiness have not fallen in the same way in the economies of Western Europe. But they have here. It is in the United States that the consumption of tranquilizers is at its greatest and the average hours worked per year is now highest—when set against the leading bloc of industrialized economies.[84] For since 1980, U.S. living standards have risen, for the vast majority of American families, only by more and more family members going out to work, working longing hours, and maxing out their credit cards. Work stress, debt-stress, stress about rising health costs, the stress associated with job loss that would bring a loss of key benefits, stress about the need to maintain rising standards of consumption to stay in line with neighbors . . . there are lots of stresses underneath the "bounty" of American capitalism.[85] They are stresses, moreover, that are born disproportionately by the poor: and poverty remains a lived reality for at least one American in seven (with significantly higher rates for minorities). It remains a proximate fear for almost one American in three. It is a little-mentioned feature of the last three decades of intensified deregulation of markets in the United States that the resulting distribution of income has left more than 90 million Americans living within one tranche of the poverty level: meaning nearly one American in three whose family income is barely *twice* that of the official poverty level for their size and composition of family.[86] In a society like ours—where the social wage is low and the welfare net is limited—the pressures on families to maintain a high personal wage to compensate for that thinness is enormous: but high personal wages are now the privilege of the few[87] in an economy and society which, since 1980 at least, has been on a Republican-inspired deregulation binge!

7. The contemporary crisis of unregulated capitalism

An American audience that remembers the initial response to Katrina may not be so sure of the veracity of any claim for the superiority of the public sector over the private. In that crisis, Wal-Mart got supplies into Louisiana faster than FEMA did, so reinforcing a view—widespread on the American Right—that public institutions are neither as efficient nor as compassionate as private ones. But what the response to Katrina really showed was that when the federal government is in the hands of people who are ideologically opposed to its growth and functions, the federal government does regularly under-perform.[88] Put the federal government in the hands of more progressive politicians and administrators however, and the reverse is likely to be the case.

- *The Price of Deregulation.* Certainly the case for the continued deregulation of American business and finance took a major hit in the financial crisis of 2008–2009. As we argued more fully in *Answering Back* and will again here in Appendix 1, at the core of that crisis was the systemic failure of regulation in an industry—finance—which most embodied the propensities of free markets to encourage speculation, greed, and personal excess. In the first decade of the new century, an industry which had been systematically denuded of tight public control, and allowed to trade across divisions (between commercial and investment banking) that had sustained financial stability for more than half a century, engaged in a frenzy of speculation and fee-taking (speculating with other people's money and paying itself unprecedentedly large bonuses in the process) which culminated in a credit collapse that cost at least 50 million innocent people their jobs world-wide, and wrote-off the hard-earning savings of a generation of baby-boomers. Apologists for free markets will (and do) point the finger of blame elsewhere—at feckless home owners, the urban poor, and a Federal Reserve too influenced by Keynesianism—but in the end, those players had, at most, a secondary responsibility for the debacle we have just experienced. The urban poor have long been with us, and Federal Reserve monetary management is nearly a century old. What was new in the run up to the foreclosure tsunami was extensive financial deregulation and excessive speculation in ever more complex financial instruments. Unfettered markets ultimately always create crises. This time the crisis created was of an unprecedented scale, and raised issues that are as much moral as they are economic.[89]

- *The Choice Before Us.* So the claims that the world is in awe of the American business model, and that business deregulation is the guaranteed way to a more prosperous and secure economic future, now lie in ruins, one piece of conservative self-delusional ideological wreckage left behind by a global financial meltdown that began in an inadequately regulated U.S. housing market. Tighter financial regulation on a global scale is clearly the order of the day; and with that tighter regulation will come the possibility of a steady weaning of the American consumer off a lifestyle based on the seemingly endless availability of credit. Before 2008, that credit was never cheap but it was plentiful. It is likely now to be more expensive still and in more limited supply. As we will argue in more detail in the chapter on "free or fair trade," the financial meltdown of 2008 has left the American economy at a crossroads. The economy faces increasing global competition both from economies in which labor standards are even lower than they are here, and from ones where labor standards are higher—the first outcompeting us on volume and costs, and the other on quality and productivity. The structural dependency of low-cost producers on high-cost affluent markets sets a limit to how long the low-cost (Chinese) route to global market dominance can survive; but if it is the key driver of global competition for the foreseeable future, we will all find ourselves engaged in a race to the bottom that will eventually produce—for lack of purchasing power—an even deeper general recession than the one we are currently experiencing. But if high-quality, high-productivity economies act together now to protect and deepen labor rights and welfare provision, the spread of global trading networks may yet generate a new virtuous cycle of global growth. That is the underlying choice now before us: either to deregulate our way to poverty or to regulate our way to wealth.[90] It is hardly much of a choice, except for those so ideologically blinkered as to believe that a blind faith in the superiority of unregulated markets is an adequate substitute for the managed development of renewed American prosperity. We saw earlier in this chapter how ideologically blinkered the more paranoid sections of the American Right currently are: let us simply hope that this time blind faith fails to win the day.

- *Paradigm Shift.* We seem to be at a genuine moment of paradigm shift. No longer is it obvious to all informed commentators that government

> spending is bad and that private companies can always be relied upon to know best. Even Alan Greenspan has admitted the error of his ways.[91] Like any moment of paradigm rupture, this is not an easy moment of transition—particularly for those politicians and political commentators who have so much personal capital invested in the defense of the old model, or for those CEOs whose personal pay packages have long been justified in the language of "trickle down economics." Moments of rupture are created by the visible failure of an old system, but that process alone does not guarantee the creation of a new paradigm. New paradigms have to be created and consolidated. They are created in part by arguments (such as those here) that point to the weakness of old modes of thought and advocate new ones, but they are consolidated only by the creation of new institutions (and new experiences for most people) that turn these new ideas into a lived reality, into a new common sense of the age. For those reasons, moments of paradigm realignment are always periods of intense intellectual stridency and partisan bickering, moments when the old guard understand there is so much at stake for them and the new guard (if they are wise) know that they have much to prove. The greatest danger, at such a moment, is that the new political forces catapulted into power so unexpectedly by the collapse of the old order lack the clarity of vision and determination of purpose to make the most of the crisis.

Let us be clear on the politics we now face. The old guard will demand "bipartisanship" to slow down the rate of change, to spread confusion in the public mind, and to generate half-hearted solutions to deep problems whose very timidity will help to discredit their new architects. But it is neither possible nor wise for progressives to pursue bipartisanship with the intransigent. Admittedly, it takes a very self-confident political leadership to point out to the previously dominant party that they were not so keen on bipartisanship when they held the reins of power: but we do need regularly to make that point. Market regulation is like pregnancy. You cannot be only a little pregnant. Let us hope that those now in the White House remember that, and give birth on their watch to a qualitatively superior order, and not to one which has one foot in the past and one dangling somewhere in midair. For if the Obama administration leaves us with the latter, then as the 2010 midterm elections made clear, the administration will not make it to a second term. But what will make it to that second term will be the underlying weakness of the U.S. economy that brought Barack Obama to power in the first place—and that would be tragic in the extreme.

CHAPTER 3

Making the Case for Managed Trade

It is hard to imagine a more firmly established "truth" in modern economic thought than that asserting the desirability—and indeed inevitability—of free trade. We hear it all the time and from all sides of the political spectrum: free trade is good for you. It is good for you if you live and work in an advanced industrial economy. It is good for you if you live and work in a developing economy. It is good for you if you are rich. It is good for you if you are poor. Indeed, if the conventional wisdom holds, free trade is essential both to make your wealth grow and your poverty disappear. It is the universal panacea. It is the one point of agreement between politicians of the center-left and those of the center-right. Free trade is the holy grail of the modern age.

It is strange then how resistant so many of us are to its automatic embrace.[1] It is strange, too, how often public policy falls short of the free trade standard.[2] For a universal panacea, free trade seems to lack the automatic legitimacy that panaceas might ordinarily expect. Certainly the advantages of free trade are not always obvious to those in the developed industrial world whose jobs are, or could be, outsourced, when even the threat of such a possibility immediately erodes their capacity to negotiate better wages and conditions for themselves. Nor are they always obvious to those in less-developed economies, particularly when the opening of protected markets lets in powerfully established and often extensively subsidized competitors, whose arrival destroys local employment options and helps to keep local workers poor. Could it be perhaps that global free trade is more in some people's interests than in others?

There is a debate. It is not one that divides conservatives and liberals as much as it should.[3] It is rather one that divides the bulk of the contemporary political class from a few radical outliers—on both the left and the right. The conventional case for global free trade is given below. The progressive case for managed trade will then follow.[4]

The case for global free trade

The case for global free trade is simultaneously theoretical and empirical, positive and negative. It is theoretical—based on a view of comparative advantage. It is empirical—based on a reading of global economic developments over time. It is positive—linking the spread of free trade directly to a list of desirable outcomes; and it is negative—linking the absence of those outcomes to the impact or persistence of protectionism. The general case is as follows.

1. Exploiting comparative advantage

The great advantage of free trade, according to its advocates, is that it encourages different national economies to specialize in the manufacture and export of those commodities in whose production they enjoy a comparative advantage, so automatically—and without any centralized direction—moving the global economy as a whole towards its point of optimal resource distribution. The emphasis here is on comparative, not absolute, advantage. One economy may be (and often is) so much more developed than another that it enjoys an absolute advantage (in cost terms) over the lesser economy in all commodity production, but still—for the system as a whole—it is preferable that the strong economy concentrate on producing that at which its advantage is most pronounced, leaving the weaker one to play to its (admittedly lesser) strengths by producing that at which it, too, is best. "What spurs trade and specialization," Robert Krol has written, "is not the absolute cost advantage that one country's producers have over their competitors in another country, but the relative advantage they have compared to other sectors within their own country."[5]

The original source of this argument was the writing of David Ricardo. In his model, premised on the notion of a single type of labor in both trading partners, there were no losers. All parties benefited from the trade between them being free of protective tariffs. Later models, like those of Hechscher and Ohlin, relaxed that original premise, and were obliged to concede the possibility that trade liberalization could have winners as well as losers. But the positive thrust of all the major free trade models remains the same: that "openness and economic integration have been pre-requisites for economic growth and prosperity," triggering specialization, increasing the variety of products available to consumers, spurring competition and technological innovation.[6] *So, too, the negative thrust: that there just is no truth in the counterclaim that free trade between developed and developing economies produces dependency in the latter. On the contrary, if countries fail to develop economically through the spread of global trade, that underdevelopment is entirely due to some internally generated shortage of vital pre-requisites for successful economic growth. It is not due to any externally imposed process of economic subordination. There is no development of under-development brought about by trading relationships between unequal economic partners. Free trade and universal development go together. They are two sides of the same coin.*[7]

2. The many benefits of untrammeled free trade

Why should that be so? Quite simply, because development and trade have been intimately interwoven since the very inception of modern capitalism. Go back to Italy in the fifteenth century. See how vital trade was to Venice, to Florence, to Genoa. It was the surplus earned in global trade that set the Western world on the path to its contemporary affluence, and the free exchange of goods and services across national boundaries remains central to the sustenance and ever-wider dissemination of that prosperity. Arguments we first saw deployed in the previous chapter against the public management of domestic markets reappear here as arguments against the public management of trade flows:

- *Trade and economic growth continue to go together. As trade patterns have thickened over the last two centuries, Western living standards stagnant for at least two millennia have at last broken free. Since 1820, average real income per head has increased ten-fold in a global population now six times larger than it was then. Increased international trade has certainly been one of the biggest drivers of economic growth in recent years, intimately linked—in the U.S. case—to the Bush administration's successful negotiation of seven new free trade agreements with 11 different countries. America has nothing to fear, and everything to gain, from this free trade expansion. As one of the world's largest exporters, what the American economy requires more than anything else are open markets for its commodities. With each new free trade agreement, exports rise, and with them profits, employment, and economies of scale.*
- *The competition triggered by the free exchange of goods and services across national boundaries is a critical spur to efficiency in production and innovation in technology.*[8] *With both comes rising productivity and falling unit costs—the source of the great and steady rise in generalized living standards that has been such a feature of the post-war American experience. Trade barriers cushion the*

inefficient and penalize the inventive: get rid of them, feel the fresh air of fierce competition, and the entire economy is obliged to reset itself to meet and exceed the productivity gains of its main rivals. Protected economies stagnate. Unprotected ones do not.

- *"Open markets lead to higher productivity by encouraging most if not all of [the] positive forces in the economy . . . efficiency, the spread of new ideas and technology, the more efficient allocation of capital, and a greater international division of labor." Because of this international specialization, "countries enjoy higher productivity and higher living standards than they would if they were not in trade." For consumers, this means "lower prices, better quality and wider variety, raising the real value of their wages." For domestic producers, "trade allows access to lower-cost inputs and more sophisticated machinery." For exporters, "trade expands markets abroad, making possible larger production runs and cost savings through economies of scale." Moreover "an open economy also provides additional capital from abroad, lowering domestic interest rates, expanding the nation's stock of capital, and raising the productivity of American workers."[9]*

3. *Any costs associated with free trade are temporary, slight, and focused, while its benefits are permanent, substantial, and general*

Part of the problem of selling free trade is that any job losses (however indirectly linked to its introduction) are immediately visible and opposed, while the longer term gains associated with it are less self-evidently linked to free trade alone.

- *In the perennial dispute between free trade and protectionism, there is a structural asymmetry between clear benefits and dispersed costs that always favor the opponents of fully opened markets. Those protected by tariffs and subsidies (normally producers) benefit enormously and immediately. Those hurt by them (normally consumers) suffer incrementally and over time. Agricultural subsidies are a major case in point, and very much of the moment. Food prices spiked dramatically in mid-2008, bringing the fear of starvation to the global poor and political unrest in countries as disparate as Mexico and Côte d'Ivoire. Agricultural subsidies and trade barriers in both the United States and the EU bear a heavy responsibility for that crisis,[10] but "northern" farmers are well entrenched politically, while the "southern" poor are not. Likewise, the "outsourcing" of low-skilled jobs by U.S. corporations invariably invites strong public condemnation—it certainly did from John Kerry in the 2004 presidential campaign—but such criticism was blind to the clear empirical data showing that overseas and domestic job creation by U.S. companies is normally complementary: low-skill jobs overseas triggering higher-paid headquarters and research jobs here at home.[11]*

- *So while the competition which free trade brings does impact the economically weak, only rarely and temporarily does it do so in adverse ways. Inefficient firms in developed economies do lose market share, and so their capacity to protect immediate employment, but these costs must not be exaggerated.*[12] *"While trade is responsible for destroying some jobs, it also creates new jobs. The result is not more or fewer jobs . . . but a better mix of jobs."*[13] *The Cato Institute's Daniel Griswold has recently estimated that "trade accounts for only about 3 percent of displaced workers," arguing that "technology and other domestic factors displace far more workers than does trade."*[14] *He has also argued that any shrinkage of employment in the manufacturing sector in the United States in the last decade has been more than offset by the creation of new jobs in sectors whose average wages are higher than in manufacturing. Ross Perot may have claimed that the passage of NAFTA would turn the United States into a nation of hamburger flippers, but he was wrong. Service employment has grown massively since 1994, but the bulk of that growth (80 percent, at least) has occurred in sectors where wages are at least five percentage points higher than the manufacturing average.*[15]
- *Open trade makes everyone richer and, if anything, actually lessens rather than widens income inequality*[16] *by triggering the redeployment of labor to more productive and/or less exposed sectors. Researchers as different in their politics as Paul Krugman and William Cline have concluded that international trade (the flow of goods) and immigration (the flow of people) "are unlikely to have been the dominant force in rising wage inequality."*[17] *The Cato academics remain unconvinced that wage stagnation has occurred in the United States of late—on this they hold a view much challenged elsewhere in the relevant literatures—but stagnant or simply rising more slowly than CEO pay, the claim remains the same: that free trade is an income generator, not a wage depressant. At the very least, the general consensus among economists working in the relevant fields appears to be that, at most, "greater trade played only a small role in the widening inequality of wages and virtually no role in the slow growth of wages overall."*[18] *With free trade, that is, living standards in advanced industrial societies do not fall: they systematically rise.*

4. Free trade is unambiguously good for America

To those who would argue that free trade is now a luxury that America cannot afford, the advocates of free rather than managed trade make both a historical and a contemporary argument.

- *Historically, the claim is this. True, the United States initially industrialized behind a tariff, but that was when the economy was largely internally focused and sustained. As productivity grew in key U.S. industries, export markets became vital to the sustenance of growth and prosperity at home. In the new post-war conditions of American global power, living standards in the United States came to depend heavily on the opening of more and more overseas markets to U.S. goods. Throughout the post-war period, "trade has been the backbone of the U.S. economy, contributing almost 30 percent of GDP by 2007."*[19] *From the Marshall Plan of the 1940s to the free trade agreements of the contemporary period, the spread of free trade and the growth of American prosperity have gone hand-in-hand.*[20] *"The big winners have been American families, who benefit from the lower prices, greater variety, and higher quality of products that international competition makes available."*[21] *The 2007 Economic Report of the President even put a figure on that benefit: post-1945 free trade, we are told, "has contributed an additional $10,000 to the typical American household of four."*[22] *The Petersen Institute had a grander figure still: gains from trade liberalization since 1947 of $1.4 trillion, equivalent by 2003 to roughly 10 percent of total U.S. GDP.*[23]

- *Contemporary job creation and real living standards in the United States remain heavily dependent on the openness of foreign markets to American goods and of American markets to goods made abroad.*[24] *The flow of cheap imports into the contemporary United States is vital to the maintenance of affluence here; and the competition which that flow brings—at home and abroad—is a key spur to rising U.S. productivity. "Rising imports need not and typically do not translate into a net loss of jobs. In fact, the growth of real good imports and manufacturing output tends to be positively correlated."*[25] *The fact that currently the U.S. imports more than it exports is not a sign that free trade is hurting us. On the contrary, that trade deficit speaks to the general global faith in the United States as the consumer of last resort and in American institutions as a store of wealth, and represents a significant transfer of real wealth from foreign producers to American consumers.*[26]*Record trade deficits are not a problem. They are "the benign consequence of foreign capital flowing into the United States," making "U.S. workers more productive, raising living standards above what they would be without it, and building the foundations for future growth."*[27]*Indeed a widely cited paper by Bradford, Grieco and Hufbauer speculated that "the potential additional gains from removing the rest of U.S. trade barriers range[d] from $400 billion to $1.3 trillion, or about $4,000 to $12,000 per household."*[28]
- *That is why Congress should "avoid using trade deficits and concerns about employment levels as excuses for imposing trade restrictions."*[29] *Any retreat to protectionism will have long-term adverse consequences for U.S. competitiveness and affluence. True, some workers lose out in the competitive flow of commodities in and out of the United States, but only temporarily, since the redeployment of labor in which they involuntarily participate leaves the American labor force as*

a whole better placed to generate rising productivity (and, hence, job security and rising wages)[30] *over time. If trade deficits worry politicians, they should recognize the role of their own spending, and correct them accordingly: cutting entitlement programs, not trade. If the outsourcing of jobs worries politicians, they should recognize that, for U.S.-based companies, "foreign and domestic operations tend to complement each other and expand together."*[31] *"Countries that run away from globalization in the 21st century," New York Mayor Michael Bloomberg has argued, "will pay a heavy price for decades to come." It is no good blaming China for taking American jobs. If China didn't take them, those jobs would still go somewhere else. "The U.S. government cannot keep them here through costly consumer-funded tariffs and taxpayer-funded subsidies." We tried that for the auto industry in the 1970s "when congressional protection of the automotive industry only hurt Detroit and helped its foreign competitors."*[32]

5. Free Trade is good for the "south" as well as for the "north"

Free trade is not just for the economically strong. It is also vital for the economically weak. Protective barriers may look an ideal solution for economies just beginning, but hiding infant industries behind powerful protective walls only stunts their growth and lowers already low third-world living standards.

- *We know that partly through the failed experiments of "import substitution industrialization [ISI]." ISI was very fashionable—particularly in Latin America—in the first decades of the post-war period, and was initially associated with rapidly rising levels of GDP. But not for long. ISI cut emerging economies off from vital sources of technological improvement. It kept domestic industrial productivity low, prices high, and competitive capacity weak—in the end obliging one ISI experiment after another to be set aside in favor of GATT/WTO membership and opened borders. Though the transition from ISI to free trade was invariably temporarily painful for the economies making the move, once made, full entry into global trade opened a route to rising employment and wages for "southern" workers previously trapped in deep rural poverty. Over time, free trade has brought more and more people into the global labor force, able to improve their own living conditions by their capacity to earn wages that rise (with their productivity) over time.*[33] *"Between 1965 and 1998," Johann Norberg has argued, "the average world citizen's income practically doubled," with the rate of rise greatest among the world's poor. The globally engaged labor force has quadrupled over the past two decades, lifting "three billion more people . . . above the poverty line. This is historically unique."*[34]

- *With those rising living standards come other things as well. Freedom from want, of course, and that is vital. "The existence from which globalization delivers people in the Third World really is intolerable. For the poor, existence means abject poverty, filth, ignorance, and powerlessness."*[35] *It is trade that has lengthened life expectancy, eroded infant mortality rates, eased levels of global hunger, reduced illiteracy levels, and set in train a whole list of other freedoms, too: freedom of thought and conscience, freedom of expression and diversity, freedom to support others less fortunate than oneself, freedom from violence, and tyranny, freedom from gender oppression.*[36] *It is blocked economic development that fuels the fires of terrorism, not economic growth.*[37] *Free trade is a key ingredient in the world-wide spread of democratic institutions and political pluralism. The surest way to defeat a terrorist, or to prevent war, is to thicken economic relationships between developed and developing economies. Prosperous societies do not fight each other; societies locked together by trade learn to understand and value each other's cultures in ways impossible in a world fragmented by trade barriers.*
- *So, forget the argument that free trade is a weapon of the "north" to hold the "south" in perpetual economic servitude. Not even direct colonialism did that. Colonialism was immoral on almost any basis, but its long-term economic impact was a positive one even for those who were colonized, laying the foundations for their own economic development once the political constraints of the colonial period were removed. It was imperial preference that blocked development in the global south, and free trade—as we see daily—that now is facilitating an explosion of economic growth in countries as disparate as China, Brazil, India, and Indonesia. By opening their markets to goods produced in Japan, South Korea, and Taiwan, advanced industrial economies triggered the Asian growth miracles of the Cold War era; and by opening their markets to the products of newly developing economies now, they can generalize that miracle again. And don't let anyone tell you that all this new industrial development is widening global inequality. It is not. Do the figures correctly, adjusting for purchasing power, and the evidence is clear: "inequality between countries has been continuously declining since the end of the 1970s."*[38]

6. Anyway, we have no choice: globalization is here to stay

Challenged mightily in the streets of Seattle in 1999, the advocates of free trade came back strongly in the first decades of the new century, defending their policy commitment under its new label—of globalization. The argument now was that we live in new times from which no retreat is possible: that "every year, global economic integration deepens. Inaction in promoting new agreements will not slow the growth of trade, only the acceleration of the growth of trade,"[39] *and even that would be undesirable.*

- *A key intellectual arguing this case has been Jagdish Bhagwati. His much-quoted "In Defense of Globalization" argued that greater free trade was both socially and economically benign. Distinguishing clearly between international flows of trade and international flows of capital, and conceding that the latter do need tight regulation, Bhagwati treats enhanced trade flows as key generators of reduced global poverty, expanded democratic possibilities, and rising real wages. Adamant that globalization is generating a "race to the top," not a "race to the bottom," Bhagwati claims the novelty of our new condition is a product not simply of technological changes that reduce time and distance, but also of public policy enthusiastically reducing barriers to trade and investment. "The story of globalization today," he wrote, "must be written in two inks: one colored by technical change and the other by state action."*[40] *That action would ideally include public policy to ease the transition costs of opening up hitherto-protected markets, but with great caution, lest even something as apparently innocuous as the harmonization of standards (food safety, labor, intellectual property, and so on) triggers "regulatory intrusionism"*[41] *that undermines the cost advantages enjoyed by developing economies.*
- *A more center-left take on the same theme of free trade inevitability tends to place the emphasis far more on the need to manage globalization, while recognizing the force of its progressive potential. "It is hopeless to attempt to stop globalization," a leading UK advocate of third-way politics said while acting as EU trade commissioner, "but it is equally wrong to think of globalization as a tidal wave where all we can do is let it wash over us, and leave it to individuals to sink or swim."*[42] *The world may be flat—Thomas Friedman is adamant that it is and that Ricardo was right—but with flatness comes new imperatives: to equip individuals with the skills necessary to compete in ever-more-exposed trading markets, and to equip economies with the infrastructure (and skill base) to do likewise. Center-left politicians and commentators generally share Bhagwati's faith in globalization's capacity to raise rather than lower real wages—Thomas Friedman, too, is a "race to the top" globalization advocate—but in his and similar writings lurks the fear that, without substantial policy change, economic decline will follow. "Education, education, education" was Tony Blair's solution to UK survival in the new globalized age. Likewise, Friedman: "JFK wanted to put a man on the moon. My vision is to put every American man and woman on a campus."*[43]
- *A globalized free-trade universe is something to be positively welcomed because its cumulative result is, and will continue to be, unprecedented levels of human progress. "In summary," Indur Goklany has written, "human well-being has improved and continues to improve for the vast majority of the world's population." Economic growth, technological change, and thickening trade flows mean that "gaps in human well-being between the rich countries and other income groups have, for the most part, shrunk over the last four decades," and where those gaps have widened "it is not because of too much globalization but too little."*

> *Rich countries are not richer because they took more from poor countries. Instead, "the poor are better off because they have benefited from the technologies developed by the rich, and their situation would have been further improved had they been better prepared to capture the benefits of globalization." The only culpability for global poverty that can be laid at the door of the developed world is the sin of protectionism. "If the rich can be faulted at all," Goklany concluded, "it is that by protecting favored economic sectors through subsidies and import barriers—activities that have not necessarily improved their own economic welfare—they have retarded the pace of globalization and made it harder for many developing countries to capture its benefits."*[44]

So overall we must say "no" to protectionism in any form: "no" to tariffs and subsidies, and "no" even to labor or environmental standards. The latter seek to homogenize the world in global trading systems in which "the major benefits of free trade derive from the differences among trading partners" and where the impositions of standards reflective of advanced industrial systems can only erode the capacity of developing economies to catch up. Free trade, so the argument does, "is fair when countries with different advantages are allowed to trade and capitalize on those differences."[45] *It becomes unfair precisely when the advantages of those differences are artificially suppressed. Matt Miller put it this way:*

> *The mother of all inconvenient truths is this. Global capitalism's ability to lift hundreds of millions of people out of poverty in China, India, and other developing countries comes partly at the expense of tens of millions of workers in wealthy nations. This awful, inexorable fact will soon pose an enormous moral and intellectual challenge for the American Left . . . the trade debate will bring special agony for progressives who see themselves as fighting liberals at home and global humanists abroad. We're at a hinge in history when it's no longer possible to pretend there's no tension between the two. Whose side are liberals on? The American people? Or people?*[46]

The case against free trade

The broad response has to be this: that what we desperately need to avoid here is not "psychic distress" of the kind anticipated by Matt Miller, but one-sided takes on complex processes of the kind common in the pro-globalization literature. The advocates of free trade perennially emphasize the upside of the exchange, glossing over complexities that suggest the presence of real costs whose avoidance needs to be managed. In the success story they tell, the active role of public policy is systematically downplayed, and the persistence of endemic contradictions is rarely addressed. That cannot be right. Moreover, the data linking free trade policy to economic growth is nowhere near as robust as advocates of free trade would claim; and because it is not, there is room for skepticism about many of the claims just surveyed—claims about the underlying economic theories and models, and claims about the data sets used in their defense.[47] We need to become familiar with all these complicating ramifications.

1. Given the current fragility of the American economy, U.S. vulnerability to untrammeled free trade is greater than is normally conceded

Those advocating a free trade solution to U.S. economic weakness paint a rosy picture of labor deployment—away from uncompetitive firms and industries into competitive and better paying ones. They treat the American trade deficit as a sign of foreign confidence in the role of the American consumer and in the strength of American financial institutions, and they see no structural problem in the outsourcing of manufacturing jobs to economies where labor is cheap. That optimism seems misplaced for at least the following reasons:

The adverse impact on wages and employment
For all the claims about redeployment to better paying jobs, we currently find ourselves in the United States with stagnant job and wage growth. Levels of employment in the private sector did not increase in the business cycle now coming to its end: growth in employment in expanding sectors was more than offset by job losses in declining ones,[48] and across the private sector as a whole, wage rates per hour now are no higher in real terms than they were in the 1970s.[49] Denying that, claiming that wages are actually rising, is so vital to the free trade case precisely because if they are not—and they are not—one of the great arguments (free trade linked to rising prosperity) becomes progressively more difficult to sustain. Consumption here in the United States has indeed gone up—pulling in cheaply made foreign imports as it does so—but it has been (and remains) consumption fueled less by a rise in real wages than by an increase in hours worked, by a rise in the number of family members working, and by an escalation in levels of personal debt. Credit card debt in the United States has quadrupled since 1989, and increased 41 percent since 2000 alone. It now totals more than $1 trillion and averages $9,827 for low- and middle-income households, one in three of which now rely on credit card debt to cover basic living expenses such as groceries, house payments, utilities, and insurance.[50]

The result is what we might term the *Wal-Mart* effect: low wages because of foreign competition sustaining a flow of cheap imports bought by workers too poorly paid to buy further up the value-chain. As was argued earlier, in *A Liberal Tool Kit*:

> It's not for nothing that Wal-Mart has become the United States' largest employer: for its cocktail of low wages, poor benefits, and cheap imported goods speaks to the central weakness of the modern U.S. economy. More and more American-based industries can no longer compete with the rising tide of particularly Chinese competition, and they can't because China's endless pool of displaced rural labor enables them to manufacture consumer goods at a fraction of the cost of producing them in U.S. factories paying U.S. wages. So those factories close or those wages fall, and people redeploy to the service sector where Chinese competition cannot reach. More and more American workers find themselves caught up in a globally generated "race to the bottom," obliged to turn to companies like Wal-Mart for the shoddy goods they need and the shoddy wages they alone still provide.[51]

Contrary to the claim that everyone benefits as consumers as imports bring prices down, it would be more accurate to say that free trade and the impoverishment of the average American family are currently going hand-in-hand, and are doing so because of the disproportionately adverse effect on the wages of those same consumers (the wages of those directly affected by competition from cheap imports, the wages of those closest to import-displaced workers in skills, and the wages of the rest of us as general levels of earnings experience the gravitational pull of their diminished pay). *It cannot be emphasized too strongly that the limited gains to American consumers brought by cheap imports are more than offset by the adverse impact of those imports on general wage levels.* Advocates of greater free trade too often overplay the benefits and understate the costs of letting in goods made in economies that pay lower wages than does the United States.[52] Josh Bivens has recently estimated those costs as an annual loss to a full-time median wage earner of $1,400 and to the typical two-income family of $2,500.[53] That was for 2006: for the longer time period (1973–2006), he thinks that "a reasonably cautious estimate is that global integration lowered the wages of American workers without a four-year college degree (the large majority of the U.S. workforce) by 4 percent. College-educated workers," by contrast, "saw 3 percent gains from trade, so inequality increased in this time, as well."[54] If those figures hold, then with Paul Krugman, "it's hard to avoid the conclusion that growing trade with third world countries reduces the real wages of many and perhaps most workers in this country."[55]

De-industrialization

The rosy picture of labor redeployment away from uncompetitive to competitive industries ignores the structural consequences of allowing into the United States manufactured goods made abroad behind tariff walls and/or significantly lower wages. As economies grow, the proportion of GDP and employment supported by the manufacturing sector does eventually fall—most mature economies can and do support large service sectors, without inflationary consequences. The ease of their ability to do so turns, however, on whether their deindustrialization is positive or negative in character.[56] In cases of *positive* deindustrialization, manufacturing employment shrinks as a proportion of the whole because the productivity of the firms in the manufacturing sector is so high that they can produce all the commodities required with fewer and fewer workers. In cases of *negative* deindustrialization, by contrast, manufacturing employment falls because local firms cannot compete on productivity and price with better-placed competitors abroad, and so are obliged to lay workers off. U.S. deindustrialization is increasingly of that second kind. Quite contrary to the free trade arguments that treat American deindustrialization as positive—explaining falling manufacturing employment here as a natural response to changing demand patterns and rising productivity—scholars at the Economic Policy Institute (EPI) attribute nearly 60 percent of U.S. manufacturing job losses since 1998 to increases in trade. The U.S. demand for manufactured goods has not dropped. What has dropped is the U.S. demand for manufactured goods made here in the United States. In 2003, domestic output met 76.3 percent of total domestic demand for manufactured goods. Between 1987 and 1997, it had met 90 percent.[57] This in an economy which now imports almost as much manufactured output as it produces.[58]

Again, a *Wal-Mart* dimension creeps in to explain that trend. To meet the low price requirements of major consuming outlets, American manufacturing firms are impelled to outsource their basic production to cheaper labor markets, of which currently the largest is China. In the process, American firms remain profitable, but American workers lose out. They lose employment, and they lose wage growth: the first through direct out-sourcing, the second through the fear of it in wage negotiations.[59] Big Box retailers like Wal-Mart essentially act as an export conduit for the Chinese economy, importing vast quantities of Chinese-made goods whose sale here triggers a shift in employment from one side of the Pacific to the other. Chinese wage rates are currently running 25–40 percent lower than those in the United States, and have remained largely stable since the mid-1990s, allowing the Chinese economy to accentuate a competitive advantage based primarily on currency manipulation, rising industrial productivity, and the suppression of labor rights.[60] Recent Chinese economic growth has been export-led growth, with Wal-Mart doing much of that exporting of Chinese products. The EPI's Robert E. Scott calculated the U.S. job loss/displacement directly resulting from trade with China between 2001 and 2007 at 2.3 million, with the American workers so displaced losing an average of $8,146 per worker/year.[61] The U.S. trade deficit with China was $84 billion in 2001. It was a staggering $266 billion in 2008. In August 2010, the monthly trade deficit with China was $28 billion.[62] The earlier impact of NAFTA on U.S. manufacturing jobs was similarly bleak, and equally driven by differences in wage levels each side of the border. Scott estimates the displacement of American workers from well-paid manufacturing jobs to less-well-paid service sector jobs resulting from the first decade of NAFTA at 660,000 and total job displacement at just over 1 million, with an associated reduction in the total wage bill of $7.6 billion in 2004 alone. Again, workers with only high school education were particularly hard hit.[63]

Trade imbalance

The U.S. corporate sector can sit astride the two sides of such trade flows, producing abroad and selling at home. But the economy as a whole cannot. Nor can either the federal government or the American worker. Trade imbalances have to be paid for. Running them year after year increases the dependence of the American consumer on the willingness of foreign workers to forego their immediate consumption by lending their surplus earnings back to the United States in the form of foreign direct investment. Rake's progresses always end badly, and ours will presumably be no exception. True, the U.S. foreign debt is now so large that the American economy is literally becoming too big to fail:[64] a collapsed dollar will hit the immediate consuming power of foreign creditors harder than it will hit the American consumer, though it will hit both. (A weak dollar stokes inflation here even as it eases the position of U.S. firms selling abroad.) But over time, funding a persistent U.S. trade deficit will become harder and harder to accomplish. As the deficit grows, American vulnerability to a run on the dollar steadily increases; and while the deficit persists, levels of U.S. policy autonomy necessarily diminish. It is very hard to pursue a vigorous campaign for human rights in China, for example, when the willingness or otherwise of the Chinese Government to buy U.S. Treasury bonds is so critical to current American standards of living; and it is difficult to take a strong pro-democracy stance in the Middle East with Saudi oil so vital an element in the U.S. energy supply, particularly when continued Saudi willingness to buy that oil in dollars is central to the balancing of our overall overseas accounts. As foreign capital flows in, ownership of key American industries flows out—with serious national security ramifications that grow over time. Having key American ports owned by companies based in countries sympathetic to Al Qaeda was too much even for the passionately free-trade Bush administration, and rightly so. The unregulated export of sensitive technologies does more than cost American jobs. It makes all of us that little bit less secure.[65] That cannot be a good thing.

2. The gains to the "south" brought by free trade are less than is claimed

As we have just seen, the case for lowering trade barriers between the advanced and developing world rests on a set of claims about the eradication of poverty, reduction of inequality, and avoidance of dependent development in the economies of the "south." The claims are excessive.

Poverty

The growth story in the conceptual "south" remains, at best, a patchy one, still framed by the uneven economic development left behind by Western colonialism, and still firmly embedded in the persistence of deep absolute poverty across vast swathes of the globe's surface. There are serious measurement difficulties here in relation to both poverty and income distribution which need to be acknowledged before generalizations are made;[66] but insofar as generalization is possible at all, it would appear that the recent marginal improvement in global poverty rates has been predominantly concentrated in just two countries: China and India. In 2007, the World Bank reported a welcome drop (2004–2006) of 260 million in the number of those living on less than a dollar a day, the standard measure of absolute global poverty; but the figure reported for that drop in China was larger than the global total: 300 million. *The number of those in abject poverty in 2006 actually grew in Africa and remained unchanged in Latin America.* If the World Bank figures can be believed, "Latin America and sub-Saharan Africa both have more people living on less than a dollar a day [now] than they did at the start of the 1980s"[67]—more, not fewer. Across great swathes of the global economy, growth and equity are not proving to be synonymous. So, advocates of free trade can claim, if they wish to, that eventually open markets will generate prosperity for all, but what they cannot do with any credibility is claim that the free trade initiatives of the 1990s have already created that generalized prosperity. They have not; on the contrary, the bulk of the conceptual south is still scarred by intense labor exploitation, desperate rural under-development and growing vulnerability to food shortages (vulnerability linked at least in part to the pressure on rural producers to replace domestic food crops with crops to be sold in global markets).[68] If free trade is going to be a success story for the world's poor, it has yet to become one.

Inequality

Nor can the advocates of free trade claim with any accuracy that open markets are a source of growing equality within and between countries. They are certainly not currently a vehicle for greater equality within advanced industrial economies, as we will see later; but nor have open markets generated greater equality within developing economies, or between those economies and the advanced industrial world. Again, the data is clear and readily available. The International Labor Organization (ILO) reported in 2008 that "since 1995 inequality between the highest and lowest wages has increased in more than two-thirds of the countries for which there is data,"[69] and that includes countries like Argentina, Thailand, and China. A parallel report by the New Economic

Foundation (NEF) "revealed that the share of benefits from global economic growth reaching the world's poorest people is actually shrinking . . . that growth was less effective at passing on benefits to the poorest in the 1990s than it was even in the 1980s—the so called 'lost decade for development.'" The NEF calculated that, "between 1990 and 2001, for every $100 of growth in the world's income per person, just $0.60 . . . contributed to reducing poverty for those living on less than a dollar a day."[70] The equivalent figure for the 1980s had been $2.20. None of this should come as a surprise. UNCTAD reported as long ago as 1997 that trade liberalization in Latin America widened wage gaps, hit unskilled wages the most, and created unemployment.

Moreover, in spite of deepening trade relationships, the gap between rich and poor countries created in the nineteenth century persists well into the new millennium. The data on that is also clear and readily available. The IMF in 2000, for example, when doing its millennium reflection, reported the world's income as actually *less* well distributed in 2000 than it had been in 1900, with virtually the same countries in the top and bottom quartiles of the per capita income tables at the start of the century as at its end.

Many other studies produce similar findings: showing that, as John Isbister put it, "the gap between the richness of the developed countries and the poverty of the third world is so huge that it is almost beyond our understanding." Almost beyond our understanding, but not quite—capable at least of being captured in bald numbers such as these: "In Switzerland in 2001, the average income per person was the equivalent of U.S. $36,970; in the United States . . . $34,870, and in Britain $24,230. In the poorest 49 countries, with almost half the world's population, the average income was $430—just more than one percent of the income of the richest countries."[71] Total output soared over the twentieth century, but its distribution by country and by class remained remarkably unaltered.[72] True, "the long term historical tendency for income inequality . . . flattened out in the last third of the century [but] the main reason [was simply] the rise of China, huge and (previously very) poor."[73]

Dependent development

Why? Because with the possible exception of very large economies such as China, the more normal pattern of economic growth in the conceptual south is still dependent growth, no matter how often advocates of free trade deny that dependency. It is dependent growth in that it is disproportionately controlled by multinational corporations headquartered in advanced industrial economies—predominantly still headquartered in the United States—multinational companies that then use third world factories and farms to produce components/commodities assembled or sold in northern markets, not southern ones. (The technology used, and the profits extracted, remain outside the south.) It is dependent growth in that the resulting commercial output is disproportionately designed to service the needs of export-markets in the north, and subject there to trading agreements that privilege the intellectual and commercial property rights of northern owning classes. It is dependent growth in that the price normally paid for access to those northern markets is the parallel opening of domestic markets to better-capitalized and better-subsidized northern competition, with predictably adverse impacts on local producers (small businesses, independent farmers, and day wage laborers alike)[74]. And it is dependent growth in that the opening of southern financial systems to global financial institutions inevitably leaves many developing economies vulnerable to sharp economic downturns whenever, as in 2008, northern banking failures and speculative excesses throw the global system into generalized recession.

The world is not organized on colonial lines any more—that much is true—but it is still organized on lines, and with centers of power first established in the colonial period. Political independence was hard enough to win from tenacious colonial rulers in the years after the Second World War. The winning of economic independence is proving more difficult still. Free trade on an economic map rendered unequal by more than a century of northern imperialism does not rub that map clean. It simply reproduces through the workings of the market inequalities that were previously politically created and imposed. Free trade in the nineteenth century was an economic creed preached by leading UK politicians and business owners to facilitate the establishment of British imperial rule and economic domination. Gunboat diplomacy opened some markets. Ideas opened the rest. For the last three decades at least, the tenets of neo-liberalism have been preached for similar reasons by a different generation of global hegemons, this time American rather than British in anchorage.[75] Free trade and imperial domination have spent the last two centuries as bedfellows. In the conceptual "south" throughout those years, and now, embracing the one inevitably leaves local economic actors vulnerable to the impact of the other.

3. Claims about globalization are scarred by class bias

So there is an immense amount of nonsense talked about the benefits of free trade, and about the necessities imposed upon us all by the unavoidable reality of globalization. It may suit global financial institutions to remove all vestiges of political control over the economic activity of foreign players, but it does not necessarily by that fact alone suit more domestically anchored economic interests. Globalization is as much an ideology and a class project as it is a trading reality.[76] The notion that globalization is something new needs serious debunking. The notion that, unregulated, it will generate a win-win race to the top needs serious questioning; and the notion that the free movement of capital automatically benefits everyone—whether they own capital or not—needs serious challenging: in the following ways.

Globalization and capitalism

As we noted in the previous chapter, capitalism did not at some point *become* global. It *began* global: global in the sense of world trade, and global, too, in a more basic spatial sense. Capitalism emerged initially only in certain places. Indeed, at first its capacity to develop depended on other places not being capitalist. Processes of unequal exchange between the capitalist and non-capitalist worlds were central to its emergence. Combined but uneven development was written into its global order from the outset. The capitalist world was always, to some degree, "flat." It was also always, from the beginning, driven by powerful inner tensions: tensions between capital and labor, over the rate and pace of work and the relative rewards accruing to each particular class, and tensions between capitalists themselves, and between different fractions of capital—tensions that drove each generation of capital holders perennially to search out new techniques, new markets, and new sources of labor. The dynamics of spatial expansion in capitalism are not new. Globalization is not a novel phenomenon. Marx described its core characteristics in *The Communist Manifesto* more than a century and a half ago. Indeed, if we are in a new phase of capitalist development, it is only because we seem at last to have reached the full flowering of the global reach of capitalism endemic to it from its inception.[77]

What we have to grasp are the specificities of this stage of capitalism development—two in particular: the rules currently governing interaction between particular national capitalisms (discussed here) and the balance of class forces those rules shape and preserve (discussed next). The current rules—the current institutional structures of global capitalism—are constructed ones, and recently constructed at that. The institutional architecture of global trade and development (the IMF, the World Bank, the GATT, now the WTO) were laid down in the 1940s under U.S. leadership, when the United States, as the world's leading economy, stood to gain massively from the opening of foreign markets. But the political requirements of the Cold War initially obliged Washington to tolerate in others, if not in itself, controls over capital flows and tariffs around domestic markets. The pressure was always there to bring those protective tariffs down. Free trade was and remains the preferred option of globally dominant economies, and by the 1980s that dominance did bring new free trade rules increasingly into play. But, paradoxically, by then, U.S. manufacturing dominance was slipping, challenged first by the re-emergence of strong industrial economies (particularly Germany and Japan) under the American umbrella, and then (as the Cold War ended) by the rapid industrialization of China (and to a lesser degree of India and Brazil). The United States now finds itself ideologically committed to the opening of markets in which the competitiveness of its firms is no longer assured, markets that are themselves becoming sites for U.S. outsourcing and the investment of American capital.[78] As global competition now hollows out U.S.-based manufacturing industry, U.S. corporations flourish; but increasingly, they flourish as global, not as American, players.

The altered balance between capital and labor

The freeing of trade flows and capital movements from government regulation does not in some magical sense put those flows beyond anyone's control. What it does, as we saw in the previous chapter, is leave control of them in the hands of the owners and senior managers of capital. CEO's decide where to invest, and what to build, and what to pay themselves in the process. They normally pay themselves handsomely. Those they employ, by contrast, find themselves facing an eroding social contract, and they do so because the size of the global work force—the number of people engaged in commodity production rather than subsistence farming—has quadrupled in a generation. Instead of the global economy possessing simply a "northern" working class strong enough to win decent wages and social benefits for itself and its dependents—social contracts that it took northern labor movements over a century to win in the face of the opposition to social reform by private business owners—we now have a northern working class under pressure because of the emergence of a "southern" working class still subject to Victorian-level wages and working conditions. Competition between firms based in the "north" and in the "south" is not raising southern wages and benefits so much as it is creating a new global norm of remuneration—one that is significantly lower than that hard won by northern workers in the first 50 years of the post-war period.[79] No wonder that even the IMF was obliged to report in 2007 that "labor globalization has *negatively* impacted the share of income going to labor in the advanced economies."[80]

In that sense, the world is not "flat," though it is "flattening."[81] It is not fully flat, in that there are significant differences in wages and social benefits between old and new working classes. The new working class of the south has the best technology that capital mobility can give it, but it does not enjoy the rights and payment packages of its European and North American equivalents. Indeed, "southern" workers attract foreign capital only to the degree that their wages and conditions are not "northern." "Northern" workers, by contrast, find themselves trapped in a race to the bottom—with their wages, their job security, and the social benefits that flow to them from publicly or privately funded welfare states everywhere under attack. Indeed, the conceptual distinction between "southern" and "northern" workers is increasingly *not* simply a spatial one. It remains true that average wage levels in China are lower than average wage levels in America: in that sense, one is "south" and one is "north"—but even within national labor forces, some workers find themselves part of global wage systems that make their wages "southern" even if physically they live in a rich northern country. Workers in textiles and furniture production in North Carolina, for example, currently have wages driven "south" by low levels of pay in textile and furniture-producing sectors in Asia, whereas workers with skills in short supply pull higher wages to themselves, even in China. The world is not flattened fully as northern and southern economies thicken the scale of their economic interactions. What happens instead is that wage inequality grows both *between* and *within* competing national systems.

Globalization as a class project

All of which means that what is good for General Motors is no longer necessarily good for America; indeed what once was good for General Motors is no longer good even for itself. Free trade is less a socially neutral panacea than a political project of benefit to just some players in the global marketplace. The movers of global capital benefit. Globally inert working classes do not. Globalization is not simply some technical thing, a consequence of transformations in the technology of communication. Globalization is a political and a social thing. It is a political thing—given its modern forms by the rules of international trade agreed in successive trade rounds; and it is a social thing—made possible in its present form only through the extensive proletarianization of labor. Capital is more mobile now not because of the internet—though that helps—but because of the removal of capital controls and the creation of new labor forces: capital is more geographically mobile now than in the past because of the existence of more workers on whom it can land. And because it is a political and social process, globalization is something that can be controlled. If its consequences are not to our liking, it is up to us to so reset the rules and working conditions, north and south, that those consequences change, and change for the better.

4. Right now, the consequences of unfettered free trade are deeply destabilizing

The contrast could not be sharper between the glowing image of an ever-more prosperous and interlocked world—the image regularly presented of the global economy in the free trade literature—and the reality of a global recession triggered by toxic assets initially created in just one housing market, that of the United States. Globalization has an underside—a really big one—that the advocates of unmanaged trade flows would do well to ponder.

Savings gluts or money gluts

The big debate in official policy circles these days is between those who explain our current global misfortunes in terms of excessive savings in key parts of the conceptual "south" and those who point the finger at excessive consumption in key parts of the conceptual "north."[82] On the "savings glut" side of the debate, our current economic difficulties are said to derive from an excess of savings over investment in China and Japan, and among oil-producing states in the Middle East—an excess which fuelled huge capital flows from the "south" to the "north," kept global interest rates low, and both facilitated and required a balancing bout of excess consumption in key developed economies. On this view of our present difficulties, the U.S. consumer is the victim and the savior, not the culprit, in the contemporary global economic story. On the "money glut" side of the debate, by contrast, the culprit role comes home. Lax monetary policy and inadequate financial regulation in the "north" is said to have fuelled a consumer boom without triggering an equivalent supply of locally produced goods, so pulling those goods from the developing economies at the cost of huge trade deficits in the "north" and the stockpiling of unwanted dollars in the "south." Either way, the steady deregulation of both capital and trade flows has left the global economy massively out of balance, able to function at all only by building a bigger and bigger deficit under the one currency currently accepted globally as "as good as gold."

No matter which side of that technical debate you come down on, one thing is clear: unfettered free trade will not produce prolonged and generalized economic prosperity unless it is accompanied by significant changes in public policy. We may need free trade—that is still in contention—but what is not in contention is that we also need government action. The current dispute among key policy makers and leading international economists is clearly not a libertarian one—no one is seriously arguing there that we need to get the state entirely out of the way. It is rather that the dispute replays at the international level the old battle between neoclassical and Keynesian economists of the kind surveyed in the previous chapter. Keynesians want the injection into the global economy of greater amounts of consumer demand, focused on the economies now in trade surplus. Neoclassical economists, by contrast, want a purging of, particularly, government welfare programs in economies with large trade deficits. But for our purposes here, the key point is not where they disagree. It is rather where, by implication, they are together: their shared recognition that a fully free trade global economy needs to be managed by actors other than the private companies engaged in that trade if the whole system is to avoid large-scale economic catastrophe. At the very least, the current state of the global economy demonstrates that free trade on its own is not enough, that global markets do not clear automatically, that, on the contrary, left to themselves, surplus economies continue to grow surpluses, and deficit ones to grow deficits, such that—without some form of coordinated public intervention—bringing the two into a more stable equilibrium can only be achieved by a world-wide economic crisis of truly gigantic proportions.

Persistent contradictions

This may come as a surprise to free market advocates brought up on the illusions of neoclassical economics, but it should not come as a surprise to anyone familiar with a Marxist understanding of the necessary contradictions of a capitalist economy. The perennial competition between capitalists for market advantage has always been, and remains, the key source of economic growth in economies dominated by privately owned companies, the key reason why economic activity spreads firstly locally, then nationally, and finally globally. That competition is both expansive and anarchic. No one controls it because no one firm, however large, can be big enough to close out all the rest, even though competition between firms over time does generate an ever smaller group of ever larger firms: what Marx termed "the centralization and concentration of capital." But even large firms are subject to the long-term tendency, within capitalism, for the rate of profit to fall, brought down by the difficulty of realizing the volume of sales necessary to sustain profit levels on an ever-growing body of fixed capital. The difficulty of realizing profits derives from capitalism's other great tension: that between the employers of labor and those they employ. If labor is scarce and well organized, firms find it difficult to increase the rate of labor exploitation: productivity, competitiveness, and ultimately profits stall, as in the great crisis of the 1970s. If labor is plentiful and weakly organized, as now, firms find it difficult to sell the totality of their output because general wage levels are low and blocked. It is in precisely those conditions that firms come under their greatest pressure to go global, in a desperate hunt for ever cheaper sources of labor and raw materials (to hold their prices down) and new sources of consumption (to hold their share of the market up).

In that sense, we are currently in a classic crisis of capital accumulation and profit realization of the kind last seen in the 1930s, but this time a crisis on a truly global scale that both lacks new markets to exploit and (let us hope) new global wars to wage. It is a crisis in which debt has come to be both the defining feature and the immediate source of crisis resolution: the debt of northern, particularly American and British consumers, which "solves" the immediate demand problem only at the cost of bringing forward wages not yet earned, but which are brought forward anyway in a gale of plastic credit cards; and the debt of whole economies, which are tolerated by their creditors only because a default would bring the whole global economic house crashing down around the ears of the privileged everywhere. Debt is central to this crisis in ways it was not in the 1930s. Financial institutions are everywhere the key players, and the fees they extract (and the exorbitant bonuses they pay themselves) are the only reliable income flows currently operating in the global system. Stabilizing that system will indeed require tighter bank regulation, the managing down of excessive "northern" demand, and the systematic expansion of consumption in "southern" labor forces that are currently seriously underpaid. But doing that will also require a diminution in the freedom of action of the social forces that created this impasse in the first place: the bankers, the CEOs, the purveyors of corporate capital who now dominate the corridors of power and the airwaves of even the "northern" democracies. A crisis rooted in the excessive power of capital will need to be resolved by strengthening the global power of labor, and doing that is literally impossible in a world whose governing institutions talk perennially the language of deregulated markets, limited state action, and unalloyed free trade.

The case for managed trade

1. The case of managed trade in the "South"

If that seems a little stark, remember this: it is one of paradoxes of the present debate on deregulated markets and deregulated trade that the economy whose growth record has outstripped all others in the last decade—namely China—practices neither. Johan Norberg may follow Hernando de Soto and claim growth in the Asian Tiger economies was a product of the establishment of clear property rights, but the thesis is quite simply wrong. As the fastest growing economy, China entirely lacks clear property rights, and indeed is currently struggling to put them into place. What China, South Korea, and Japan all have in common is that their takeoff to post-war economic growth was *state-led* rather than property-driven, was (and in China's case, still is) cushioned by both explicit and hidden walls of protection, and in the latter two cases was tolerated as such by the United States for reasons of Cold War politics. It was only when Japan and South Korea wound down their state-economic leadership, and in South Korea's case joined the WTO, that their growth stalled and their exposure to financial crises intensified. It is worth remembering that the adverse impact of the worst of those crises in the 1990s—the Asian financial crisis of 1997–1998—was actually greatest on economies which had already removed state controls on the import and export of capital (South Korea, Thailand, Indonesia, and Malaysia). The economies in the region that had not removed those controls—India, China, and

Taiwan—were the only ones able to tide out that storm without serious damage to their patterns of internal growth.[83]

Whatever else the Asian growth story tells us, it tells us that managed, not free, trade is one key to development. As regional scholars have regularly noted, "South Korea and Taiwan focused their economies on exports, but combined that outward orientation with high levels of tariffs and other forms of protection, state ownership, domestic-content requirements for industry, directed credit and limits to capital flows."[84] "China also followed a highly unorthodox two-track strategy, violating practically every rule in the guidebook."[85] Whatever these successful Asian economies practiced in their years of success, it was not free trade. The contrast with Latin America could not be more striking. "Since the mid-1980s, virtually all Latin American countries opened up their economies, privatized their public enterprises, allowed unrestricted foreign capital and deregulated their economies. Yet they have grown at a fraction of the pace of the heterodox reformers, while being buffeted more strongly by macroeconomic instability."[86] It was during earlier decades—the 1960s and 1970s—"when they were pursuing the 'wrong' policies of protectionism and state intervention, [that their] per capita income grew" most rapidly: decades that were, as Ajit Singh later put it, "*the* period of Industrial Revolution in the Third World."

The case for infant industry protection in developing economies remains a strong one, because too rapid an exposure to the full force of global competition too easily splits developing economies into disconnected sections: isolated export enclaves sunk inside traditional and unaltered production systems without any internal growth dynamic of their own. Developing a productive and competitive manufacturing base behind strong tariff walls is not easy—the ISI experiment demonstrated that[87]—but nor is abandoning the attempt to do so in favor of a free trade agreement—the Mexican experience of NAFTA demonstrates that. If free trade is the obvious answer to development issues, Vietnam should have lagged far behind Mexico once Mexico joined NAFTA. But it did not. Vietnam growth rates continue to outstrip Mexican growth rates, not least because since joining NAFTA small-scale farming in Mexico has taken a huge and irreversible hit: throwing at least 1.3 million peasant farmers off their land, and fueling the movement of illegal immigration northwards.[88] A decade of NAFTA has left the gap between rich and poor wider in Mexico, real wages and salaries at less than 1990 levels, and the economy as a whole increasingly dependent on global imports—hardly the success story canvassed for the free trade agreement in Mexico immediately prior to its signing. Even the cheap labor jobs that initially boomed on the border –in the *maquiladores*—are now slipping away in the face of cheap labor competition in Asia. Of the 700,000 new *maquiladora* jobs created in the first seven years of NAFTA, some 300,000 had been lost three years later.[89]

The trick for those seeking successful economic growth in the conceptual "south" is not to make trade policy meet theologically established standards of immediate openness. The trick is to forge a trade policy compatible with intelligently designed internal development programs: not free trade but realistic infant industry targets, an export strategy geared to the incremental lowering of protective walls as competitiveness increases, a state willing to discipline local firms which are temporarily receiving protection, and a state that is itself free of large-scale corruption. Neoclassical economics might argue otherwise: but two financial tsunamis in a decade (1997–1998 and 2008–2009) are already way too high a price to pay for that philosophy, and theoretical models are beginning to emerge clearly identifying "conditions under which protection might result in faster growth," protection understood "as a short-term strategy to prepare an economy to compete in the international market in the long term."[90]

2. The case for managed trade in the "North"

The case for managed trade for already fully developed capitalisms is less obvious but not less potent. History teaches us that their development was as intimately tied to managed trade in the past as their current impasse requires it to be in the immediate future.

We must never forget that no less an economy than that of the United States developed behind high tariff walls for more than a century. So, too, did the economies of most of Western Europe. American intellectuals may now be leading advocates of free trade, but in the years before the First World War, many were the great exponents of protectionism. We don't hear much about past U.S. protectionism these days, but "the historical fact is that the rich countries did not develop on the basis of the policies and institutions that they now recommend to, and often force upon, the developing countries." "Almost all of today's rich countries used tariff protection and subsidies to develop their industries"[91] from the last quarter of the nineteenth century to the first half of the twentieth. Without those tariff walls, local industrial development would have been blocked by powerful competition from the already globally dominant UK economy. As we have already noted, free trade is invariably the mantra of the already competitively strong. Other economies—including throughout the nineteenth century the majority of today's leading industrial systems—were engaged in economic catch-up. They needed (and indeed managed) to borrow UK technical know-how and UK capital funds; but they also needed (and instituted) protection for their own fledgling industrial endeavors. Once caught up, of course, their needs changed—easy access for their exports to growing global markets became as important to them as once it had been for the British—but prior to the modern period (really anything much before 1970), trade openness and growth did not correlate positively even for them, and, indeed, "protectionism was the rule rather than the exception." In this sense, even for the advanced industrial world "given its importance in current theory and policy, it is easy to overlook the fact that free trade is a historical aberration"[92] and needs to be treated as such.

The case remains strong for the institution of free trade between economies of equivalent levels of development. Where the case remains weak, however, is for free trade between economies that are developed and those still seeking to catch up. Catch-up and convergence can take two forms: a *positive* form—the pulling of under-developed economies up to the levels of productivity and output of their fully-developed equivalents—or a *negative* one, the pulling down of those fully-developed equivalents to the wage levels prevalent in newly industrializing economies. We have already noted how free trade can militate against catch-up and convergence in that first sense. What we need to see now is how it also intensifies the danger of catch-up and convergence in that second, and regressive, sense. We have already documented the evidence of such "northern" wage suppression linked to trade flows. It represents what Paul Krugman rightly called "a dark side to globalization . . . When we import labor-intensive manufactured goods from the Third World instead of making them here, the result is reduced demand for less-educated American workers, which leads in turn to lower wages for those workers. And no, cheap consumer goods at Wal-Mart aren't adequate compensation."[93]

Nor should sensible comfort to be taken from the view—widely canvased still—that only the jobs and wages of the low-skilled are currently at stake. The last vestiges of an imperial mindset enable some commentators to project a future of outsourced low-skilled jobs to former colonies, and the automatic retention of high-skilled jobs in the old metropolitan core. No such luck. Outsourcing is now a reality higher and higher up the white collar and managerial chain, as skilled workers in India and China offer globally mobile companies their developed skills at bargain-basement prices. "High wage professional jobs are [now] migrating to low-cost countries—still only a trickle at present," but nonetheless potentially heralding "a fundamental restructuring of rich world economies, akin to the globalization of manufacturing in the 1980s and the outsourcing of unskilled service jobs in the 1990s."[94] There is no reason why the existing global distribution of skills should remain frozen to the U.S. advantage, and much evidence that, on the contrary, skill patterns globally are now in flux. China, after all, produces "a third of a million new engineers a year, and is entering high-tech and service areas such as design, software, and digital technologies."[95]

Free trade under those conditions can have an immiserating rather than an income-enhancing effect on previously dominant economies; they can grow and become poorer at the same time. Recognizing that possibility, Dani Rodrik has recently called for a breathing space in the drive for lower tariff walls, arguing that:

> rich and poor nations need breathing space for different reasons. Rich countries need it so that they can revive the social compacts that underpinned the success of Bretton Woods. They need flexibility to interfere in trade when trade conflicts with deeply held values at home—as, for example, with child labor or health and safety concerns—or severely weakens the bargaining power of workers. Poor nations need room to engage in exchange rate and industrial policies that will diversify and restructure their economies, without which their ability to benefit from globalization is circumscribed.[96]

He is surely right. What we need, at the very minimum is a new three-pronged approach to the management of trade "north" to "south" We need:

- *The establishment of powerful labor standards designed to put a floor under remuneration and working conditions across the globe as a whole.* "The rationale for international labor standards is the same as for national standards: to prevent competition from reducing acceptable working conditions and to force employers to compete by improving productivity and quality."[97] The ILO has long advocated five core labor standards: freedom of association, right to collective bargain, abolition of forced and child labor, and freedom from discrimination.[98] Those five can only be a starting point, but even making access to U.S. markets contingent on simply their adoption would strengthen the rights of workers globally while contributing directly to an easing of the current U.S. trade deficit (which is higher with countries that fail to implement ILO-type conventions[99]). The evidence is clear that such standards do not undermine competitiveness.[100] Nor do they push the poorest of the poor out of employment altogether, as is so often claimed. On the contrary, if global trade rules are changed to reward countries that raise their labor standards, a new dynamic of rising wages can be built into the global trading system from the bottom up. The ILO's minimum labor standards simply require that international competition no longer be based on excessive labor exploitation. They set a floor. They still "permit countries to have low wages because of labor market conditions but do not permit countries to compete by artificially suppressing wages and working conditions."[101] And, like any good floor, over time they can be raised: a vital job for a strengthened Department of Labor.

- *The establishment of "fair trade" institutions overseeing trade between developing and developed economies.* It is entirely right and proper that the federal government should phase out the excessive subsidies currently provided to large U.S. agricultural producers while protecting, as do most economies, the basic incomes of small farmers battling the elements as well as competitors. It is right and proper that international action be sought against countries seeking to inflate their share of global trade by holding down the exchange rate of their currencies, as arguably is currently the case with China.[102] It is also entirely right and proper that special trading status be given to developing economies who meet labor and environmental standards, and that those economies should be allowed to use infant industry protective walls and public subsidies as, in the Cold War years, key allies were also allowed. Such "asymmetric protection," as Ha-Joon Chang calls it,[103] needs to be accompanied in the United States by the creation of a stronger social safety net for workers directly adversely affected by that asymmetry.[104] It also needs to be reinforced by developed "fair trade" campaigns by U.S.-based consumer groups, so building in incentives for companies to increase market share not by underpaying third world suppliers but by buying commodities from them at a fair and reasonable price.[105] In institutional terms, this leg of the new policy requires a strengthened Department of Commerce in Washington, and a clear timetable for the systematic phasing out of tariffs and subsidies as living standards north and south converge.

- *The immediate development of industrial policy designed to reverse U.S. de-industrialization in a progressive fashion—going back to industrial strength and strong middle class wages by going green.* As we will argue more fully in later chapters, it is time now to revisit arguments last widely canvassed in the 1980s on the need for center-left administrations in the United States to develop coherent and ambitious policies for industrial growth. Manufacturing still matters.[106] Finance still needs to be tamed. Consumption of goods as well as of services needs to involve, far more than it does now, commodities (and not simply services) made here in America. The United States needs again the high-wage high-productivity dynamic that sustained growth and affluence in the long post-war boom; and, as with that earlier dynamic, the fusion of high wages and rising productivity will not occur naturally. It will have to be called into existence by public policies that strengthen labor and support domestic manufacturing investment. The federal government has a long (if largely hidden) tradition of actively stimulating economic innovation, most recently using the Pentagon as a substitute industry ministry to galvanize American engineering firms for national defense. Now we need such a galvanization once more—not for defense against foreign enemies this time, but for defense against environmental degradation and climate change. In institutional terms, that requires a strengthened Environmental Protection Agency and the planned development of new energy-saving industries and industrial practices. The case for managed trade and the case for going green can and should be made together. The task of this chapter has been to establish the first of those cases. The task of the next chapter is to establish the other.

CHAPTER 4

Making the Case for a Green Economy

Making the case for a green economy is never easy in the United States. This is a big country with big roads, big appetites, and big heating and cooling systems. The current generation of Americans has become acclimatized to moving from place to place easily, cheaply, and in comfort: big cars, cheap air travel, readily available fast food and accommodation. The rest of the civilized world may have signed up to the Kyoto Protocol in 1999, but the United States—the largest per capita consumer of resources on the face of the earth, and the largest emitter of greenhouse gases—did not; and yet, as late as the 2004 presidential election, in the three televised debates between the leading candidates the question of environmental protection occurred only once.

But what a difference one presidential cycle and the threat of $4 per gallon gas then made. By 2007–2008, the questions of energy efficiency, energy security, and action to prevent global warming were at the center of political debate, and political luminaries were tripping over themselves in their newfound desire to prove their green credentials. By late 2008, George W. Bush had already made his unexpected U-turn on the question of climate change,[1] Arnold Schwarzenegger had signed groundbreaking environmental standards into Californian law,[2] and Al Gore had won an Oscar and shared a Nobel Prize for his work on the prevention of global warming. Each leading candidate in the 2008 presidential campaign had a fully developed "green" dimension to their domestic policy package. Barack Obama entered the presidency committed to a full set of carbon caps and targets, fuel efficiency measures, renewable electricity standards, and funding for a clean energy future.[3] His opponent, John McCain, was similarly innovative. In a sharp break with the previous administration, even the Republican flag-bearer in 2008 committed any McCain-led administration to the establishment of a mandatory limit on the emission of greenhouses gases.[4]

Political tides never turn alone, of course, and this one certainly did not. In 2004, the bulk of U.S. business leaders had been steadfastly opposed to the introduction of carbon controls. Yet by 2008, sensing the economic opportunities available in a green economy and the dangers inherent in green regulations imposed without a business input, major business leaders were in the vanguard of the call for change.[5] So, too, were more enlightened sections of the Christian Right, concerned with the desecration of God's chosen Earth, and security hawks concerned about terrorism threats and the U.S. dependence on foreign oil.[6] By then, a string of governors in states other than California had responded positively to calls for tighter environmental controls, and major pieces of bipartisan legislation were beginning to emerge from a Congress now in Democratic hands. Two pieces of proposed federal legislation were particularly significant in this regard: the December 2007 House energy bill that raised the minimum fuel efficiency standard for passenger vehicles (the first hike since 1975) and doubled the use of corn-based ethanol, and the later Senate *Climate Security Act* that created permits ("allowances") which global warming polluters would be required to purchase, creating funds (as much as $800 million over ten years, it was claimed) that could be directed to the development of clean-fuel technologies. The Lieberman-Warner CSA proposed a cap-and-trade system to be administered by the Environmental Protection Agency, and intended a declining cap on U.S. emissions of all types of greenhouse gas: down 4 percent by 2012 and by 71 percent by 2050.[7] Not to be left out, the Supreme Court, in *Massachusetts v. U.S. Environmental Protection Agency*, ruled in April 2007 that the EPA should revisit its unwillingness to define carbon dioxide as an air pollutant.

The Obama administration should, therefore, have had little difficulty in picking up and running with this tide of political enthusiasm for the greening of the U.S. economy—but in practice it did.[8] Campaigning was one thing, governing was quite another. Both domestically and abroad, the push for climate change legislation that the Obama administration inherited stalled. It stalled abroad late in 2009 when the U.N. conference convened in Copenhagen failed to produce a post–Kyoto climate change treaty. It stalled domestically early in 2010 when Republican senators threatened to filibuster a renewed version of the Lieberman-Warner carbon-emission targets for American industry. In December 2009, representatives from 193 nations gathered in Copenhagen amid high expectations and in the full glare of world publicity. But—in spite of Obama's complete reversal of the Bush administration's lack of enthusiasm for internationally negotiated targets on carbon emissions—the president actually swept in on the last day of the conference, trying (and failing) to trigger a general agreement—all that could be salvaged from two weeks of bitter wrangling was a non-binding three-page "accord" signed between the United States and four major developing nations (China, Brazil, India, and South Africa) to jointly monitor progress towards nationally specified emission reductions. With the global political initiative thus dissipated and Obama's own credibility as a green warrior seriously depleted, early optimism about a domestic bipartisan agreement on the same agenda then proved equally misplaced. The House did narrowly pass a cap-and-trade bill—the *Waxman-Markey Bill*—in 2009,[9] but the Senate declined to follow suit. In July 2010, the Republican capacity to bring business there to a complete halt persuaded Senate majority leader Harry Reid to abandon the Kerry-Lieberman bill, even though that bill had already retreated from a general cap-and-trade stance, proposing instead a weaker set of emission standards for specific sectors of the economy. In 2009–2010, fears of disadvantaging U.S. industries relative to their Chinese competitors, and the lobbying of coal and oil interests on the cost and price consequences of tougher regulation, blocked comprehensive energy reform at home just as effectively as tensions between developing and developed economies had blocked it in Copenhagen.[10]

This lack of progress in the Senate was all the more shocking because it occurred against the background of the worst environmental disaster in U.S. history (the BP oil spill in the Gulf of Mexico), and in spite of the broad consensus on global warming and its perils currently prevalent in scientific and political circles on both sides of the Atlantic. That consensus turns on a string of linked propositions: that the Earth is warming at an unusually rapid rate; that rising temperatures threaten to disrupt weather patterns, sea levels and economic activity; that the rise in temperature was a direct product of recent human economic activity; that policy to reverse global warming is both necessary and available; and that such policy could be a key source of long-term economic growth. It is a broad consensus deeply rooted in the relevant scientific communities, but it has never been a complete one. On the contrary, and not just in the United States—though primarily here—the consensus on the need to go green remains under challenge. In the United States it remains under challenge from political and scientific forces that are predominantly anchored on the American Right—forces which subscribe, to a lesser or greater degree, to the widely cited view of Republican Senator James Inhofe (chair of the Senate Environment Committee 2004–2006), that global warming is the "*greatest hoax ever perpetrated on the American people.*"[11] The convincing case for a green economy is readily available; but it is a case that here in the United States has constantly to be defended and remade. If you think arguing for regulated markets is an uphill struggle, try this one instead. Particularly with so many new "climate-change deniers" elected to Congress in the 2010 midterm elections, you are likely to find that arguing for a green economy makes arguing for market regulation seem like a stroll in the park!

Why: because of this passionately held conservative case against going green.

The conservative case

1. Global warming as a manufactured issue

There are many conservative commentators and scientists who share James Inhofe's view of global warming as something entirely without empirical foundation. Like him, they see the current uproar about global warming as a great hoax perpetrated on the American people by liberals bent on the erosion of civil liberties, the regulation of U.S. business, and the dismantling of U.S. federalism. As usual, Rush Limbaugh is among the more colorful of those conservatives, criticizing liberals for "wag[ing] war on phantom threats like CO_2 *while ignoring the real battle to the death [with Islamofascism] that has already begun,'*[12] *and dismissing "the global warming hoax as nothing more than a religion." In January 2008 he told his radio listeners:*

> *if you look at global warming, it has all the elements of every major religion on the planet. It has the creation of the divine; it has original sin; it has the Garden of Eden; it has penance; it has everything. The most important element that it has is faith, because the people who believe in it can't prove it. So, it is nothing more than a religion for people who have not a whole lot of foundation in their lives.*[13]

Limbaugh is not alone in making such claims, or in dismissing the Al Gores of this world as "environmental wackos." Representative Paul Broun of Georgia told the House of Representatives in June 2009 (apparently to a round of applause) that climate change is nothing "but a hoax perpetrated out of the scientific community."[14] *Thomas Sewell, too, has written that "a new cult of pagan nature worship has sprung up, in which the slightest inconvenience to any toad or bug is enough to call a halt to even the most urgent human needs."*[15] *Likewise, Fred Singer has written of what he calls "the true agenda of the Green Movement. It really isn't about 'global warming' or even about protecting Nature. It's about shutting down the world's leading economies and imposing on the world's population—both rich and poor—a lifestyle they would not freely accept."*[16]

On climate change, the hoax claims have a certain sequence and logic.

- *They invariably begin by asserting that the hysteria about global warming is based on bad and politicized science. It is based on bad science: too heavily reliant on necessarily limited computer modeling, on errors in the collection and use of data, and on the violation of standard forecasting principles[17]–on what Richard Kintzen once called "junk science."[18] It is also based on politicized science. The widely cited IPCC report (of which more later) is invariably dismissed this way: as "a political document, not a scientific report,"[19] one overlaid by bureaucratic interventions.[20] The widely respected IPCC is dismissed in similar fashion: as "an activist enterprise from the very beginning," its agenda being nothing more or less than "to justify control of the emission of greenhouse gases."[21] "The problem with the IPCC process," Steven Hayward writes, "is that the scientists and experts participating in each iteration have become increasing biased towards climate alarmism. It is getting harder to separate the ideologically motivated . . . from the honestly worried scientists."[22] Particularly, it would appear, a scientist working at the University of East Anglia in the United Kingdom—the leakage of 3,000 of whose e-mails in 2009 triggered a veritable "Climategate" of claims of fabricated and suppressed data.[23]*

- *The parallel claim is, then, one of closure: the closing off of debate through a liberal media conspiracy and the denigration and witch-hunting of dissenting scientists. We are told of a liberal conspiracy to block out alternative views on global warming: a systematic denial to skeptics of access to programming by all three major television networks, and an over-reliance there on politicians and rock stars rather than scientists as global warming is discussed.[24] We are also told of something akin to a witch-hunt, within both the media and the scientific community, against naysayers on global warming. "Scientists who dissent from the alarmism," MIT professor Richard Lintzen has written, "have seen their grant funds disappear, their work derided, and themselves labeled as industry stooges, scientific hacks or worse."[25]*
- *Then add to those arguments claims about the dangers of scientific consensus and of the interlocking dynamic of exaggeration and funding. That there is a scientific consensus is regularly denied.[26] That such a consensus would be desirable, were it to exist, is also questioned. Skepticism, not consensus, in what proper science requires: not fashion-followers but a Galileo or an Einstein. Richard Lintzen reminds us that the "consensus science of eugenics was equally 'settled' 100 years ago."[27] Funding logics, too, he tells us, also distort. Scientists make meaningless or ambiguous statements, advocates or media personalities translate statements into alarmist declarations, and politicians respond to the alarm by feeding scientists more money, so starting the cycle again! The result is what he called "the sad tale of the iron triangle (of alarmism) and the iron rice bowl (of science),"[28] or what researchers at the Tyndall Centre in the UK have termed "the social construction of a quasi reality"; the scientists emphasize doubt and contention, but the public hear only certainty and consensus.[29]*
- *There is even one strand of the hoax argument that treats the case for global warming as not simply manufactured but also false: false because, in truth, the*

Earth may well be cooling rather than becoming warmer. Phil Chapman has written that "all those urging action to curb global warming need to take off the blinkers and give some thought to what we should do if we are facing global cooling instead." Phil Chapman is a former MIT staff physicist and Mission Scientist on Apollo 14.[30]

2. Global warming as an exaggerated issue

Not everyone uneasy with the global warming thesis necessarily wants to go that far. More moderate voices within the skeptical camp simply say that global warming may well be occurring, but the scale of it—and the dangers it is said to represent—are being wildly exaggerated. Maybe we have global warming, maybe not: but what we certainly do not have is any doomsday-like problem of global temperature change. In Bjorn Lomborg's words, "we need to cool it"[31]*—the debate, that is, rather than the world.*

Again, there is a certain logic to the pattern of skepticism here.

- *For some of the more moderate skeptics, global warming is something that happens periodically, and should give no cause for concern. Indeed, global warming may well be beneficial.*[32] *"History shows," Dennis Avery has argued, "that a warmer world is better for human health on average." It raises agricultural productivity, stabilizes weather patterns and facilitates population growth. "From the perspective of human health," as he put it, "people have far more to fear from the next full Ice Age than the modest warming" now before us.*[33] *"While cutting* CO_2 *will save some people from dying of heat, it will simultaneously cause more people to die from cold."*[34] *In June 2007, Avery, then NASA's chief administrator, said to much fury that he was "not sure that it is fair to say that it is a problem we must wrestle with. To assume that it is a problem is to assume that the state of the earth's climate today is the optimal climate."*[35]
- *For other skeptics, the scale of global warming is just not big enough to warrant the fuss, nor the causal linkage with carbon dioxide strong enough to warrant the policy debate. As Richard Kintzen has written, "let's start where there is agreement." Global temperatures have risen about one degree Celsius since 1900. Levels of carbon dioxide in the atmosphere are 30 percent higher now than then (they were 0.03 percent of the atmosphere, they're now 0.04 percent); and more* CO_2 *should add to global warming. "These claims are true," but they "neither constitute support for alarm nor establish man's responsibility for the small amount of warming that has occurred."*[36] *After all, greenhouse gas concentrations increased steadily through the twentieth century, but the global average surface temperature did not. It actually fell from 1940 to 1975.*[37]
- *For yet other skeptics, the information we have on temperature change is so problematic and tentative that using it to say anything definitive about climate change*

is fraught with difficulty. We can't even be sure that we have accurate data on surface temperatures over time,[38] *and we certainly can't test the relationship between* CO_2 *and global temperature in any direct and scientific manner. We can't pump greenhouse gases into some parts of the atmosphere and leave other parts unpolluted; and the computer climate models we use instead, for all their current sophistication, can't even backcast, let alone forecast, with any degree of accuracy. They can't even "match up greenhouse emissions with the climate record for the last 30 years."*[39] *The IPCC has come in for particular criticism in this regard. "The forecasts in the Report were not the outcome of scientific procedures," Green and Armstrong complain. "In effect, they were the opinions of scientists transformed by mathematics and obscured by complex writing . . . Claims that the Earth will get warmer have no more credence than saying it will get colder."*[40]

- *For many of those unconvinced by the Al Gores of this world, the unnecessary concern about global warming is rooted in a profound misunderstanding of normal weather patterns. The institutionally skeptical NCPA put it this way in a briefing in May 2005: "only in the last 20 years have scientists begun to understand that the earth has a moderate, persistent 1,500-year climate cycle that creates warmer and cooler periods of time."*[41] *We may be simply at a warming part of that general cycle, not at a point of crisis at all. Certainly some scientists think so. At it, and at its end. "I expect to live," William Gray has written, "to see the start of a global cooling pattern and the discrediting of most of the anthropogenic warming arguments. The world has more serious problems to worry about."*[42]
- *For yet others, even if global warming is occurring and will go on occurring, there is simply no way of being certain that human activity is its prime or even its major cause. Natural forces are at work here, too; for some, even divine ones. William Gray has suggested we focus instead on natural changes associated with the slowdown of the oceans' deep water.*[43] *Danish researchers have recently attached importance to variations in cosmic ray intensity.*[44] *Fred Singer has added "continental drift and mountain-building, changes in the Earth's orbit, volcanic eruptions and solar variability."*[45] *The list of "drivers" here is potentially endless. And for the record, volcanoes were once Rush Limbaugh's favorite, too. "Mount Pinatubo in the Philippines," he wrote in 1993, "spewed forth more than a thousand times the amount of ozone-depleting chemicals in one eruption than all the fluorocarbons manufactured by wicked, diabolical, and insensitive corporations in history."*[46] *How, Al Gore, are we supposed to discipline volcanoes?*

3. Global warming as a hyped issue

Of late, critics of the global warming thesis have been particularly incensed by the claims made by Al Gore in his book and film An Inconvenient Truth, and by the hype that has surrounded the former vice president's participation in the campaign to green global politics. Al Gore has been feted by the liberal media and the global establishment, and censored in equal volume by those believing that his film is "science fiction" and he himself "bad for the planet."[47]

- *Partly, the irritation is simply with the hype. Scientists with long years of work in the field despair of the speed and range of coverage of the presentation of a complex issue by a scientific amateur, and they share a common frustration at Gore's capacity to mobilize opinion globally (the eight coordinated Live Earth concerts he triggered in July 2007 were genuinely global—Tokyo, Johannesburg, Shanghai, Hamburg, London, New York, and Rio de Janeiro).*
- *There is also a degree of muckraking—criticism of Gore for his own personal energy use and for his well-placed corporate friends. Critics see in his apocalyptic vision an unhealthy flow of dollars to companies that support him, to companies in which he has investments, and to government programs that he favors and they don't.*[48]
- *But the main irritation is with what skeptics find to be a series of simplifications and inaccuracies in the content of An Inconvenient Truth. Challenged in court in the UK in October 2007, the presiding judge reported 11 errors of fact or presentation in the video version of the Gore argument. These included the claim that the sea will rise up to 20 feet because of the melting of either West Antarctica or Greenland in the near future, and the claim of a direct coincidence between the rise of carbon dioxide in the atmosphere and the rise in temperature over the last 650,000 years. The judge found the first an exaggeration (the process would take thousands of years) and the second overstated ("Although there is general scientific agreement that there is a connection, the two graphs do not establish what Mr. Gore asserts," the judge said). He was similarly uncomfortable with claims directly linking global warming to Hurricane Katrina, recent polar bear drownings, the diminishing ice-cap on Mount Kilimanjaro, and the bleaching of coral reefs worldwide.*[49]
- *Critics prefer instead to point to data that does not fit the Gore case. Expanding glaciers in Norway, New Zealand, and the United States, for one; NASA temperature data for another—data that has 1934 as the hottest year in the last 127, and the 1930s, not the 1990s, as the century's hottest decade.*[50] *They certainly think Al Gore is correct to point to a recent explosion of hot air. They just think that it is Al Gore the alarmist, and Al Gore the global traveler, who has created it.*[51]

4. Global warming as an excuse for bad policy

Given the degree of uncertainty about the scale and consequences of any change in global temperatures, skeptics have consistently argued that a new body of public policy should not be developed; and that if the United States does face the potential of an energy shortfall, there are plenty of domestic sources of energy to which we can easily turn. For skeptics, bad policy comes in the form of cap-and-trade schemes of the Kyoto type, and it comes in the form of tight EPA regulations and standards. Good policy comes in the form of renewed drilling for oil, the development of clean coal technologies, and the expansion of reliance on nuclear power. The bad policy first:

- *No more Kyoto. Kyoto-type cap-and-trade schemes stand condemned, and not just by conservatives, as both ineffective and destructive of better alternatives. They stand condemned as ineffective—Kyoto, in particular—because their targets are rarely met, because key polluters other than the United States (China, for example) are excluded from the required standards, and because their climate effects are miniscule and delayed, while their economic costs are huge and immediate.[52] The conservative website 'Human Events' called the cap-and-trade legislation proposed by Democrats in 2009 "a massive energy tax that will dramatically raise the cost of just about everything you produce or consume."[53] Cap-and-trade schemes also deflect attention from more effective methods of reducing greenhouse gas emissions, particularly the development of new fuel-efficient technologies and their distribution worldwide.*
- *No tighter EPA standards. Advocates of tighter environmental standards systematically downplay the costs of their implementation, and skeptics should not. The 2007 House energy bill was said by researchers at the Heritage Foundation to be likely to raise gas prices from an average of $3.06 (the price as the bill was passed) to $5.02 a decade later.[54] Any consumer tax on fossil-fuel use, or special levy on oil company profits, is bound to do something similar; and any other kind of environmental legislation is bound to generate the kind of "industrial-strength EPA red tape that routinely imposes hundreds of thousands, if not millions, of dollars in compliance costs."[55] "Heritage estimates a nearly $7 trillion cumulative decline in GDP by 2029 from such regulations, and up to 3 million lost manufacturing jobs."[56] EPA ozone standards are stringent enough— "more than sufficient to protect public health"[57]—and do not need to be raised.*
- *Honesty about the downside of alternative green fuel technologies. Taxing fossil fuels just generates "a slush fund for solar energy, windmills, biodiesel, ethanol and other green gadgetry boondoggles"[58] that simply does not work. The scale of wind farms required to significantly affect energy generation would be an ecological disaster of an entirely new order,[59] and we have already seen that encouraging farmers to grow corn for ethanol has an immediate and disastrous effect on the general price of food.[60] And if public policy—of the kind proposed by the Obama administration—creates new jobs in "approved" fuel industries, it will do so only by destroying jobs in industries no longer approved. Currently, one million people work in the coal, oil, gas, nuclear, and automobile industries. Are they all to go?[61] As Ben Lieberman has it: "a green stimulus is [simply] a contradiction in terms."[62]*

5. Market solutions to global warming

Anyway, why cross the river to fill the pail when solutions to energy shortages and possible environmental side effects are so readily to hand? "Drill, baby, drill" was the mantra of the Republican base throughout the McCain presidential campaign, and rightly so: for market-based solutions are immediately available. These include:

- *Drilling for oil within the U.S. itself: offshore and in the Arctic National Wildlife Refuge. Both were part of the McCain–Palin energy plan, and both have their advocates: offshore drilling, because of its capacity to ease long-term dependency on foreign sources of oil; and drilling in the ANWR, because of its potential size. "The Arctic National Wildlife Refuge and the off-limits parts of the outer Continental Shelf are estimated to contain 28 billion barrels of petroleum . . . enough to fuel all the vehicles for 7.4 million households for 50 years."*[63] *Why not go for it?*
- *Making full use of existing and new coal reserves. This, too, was a major plank in the McCain–Palin energy plan. Had they been elected, they were committed to investing critical resources into the development of clean coal technology, so generating jobs in traditional coal-producing states: including Colorado, Ohio, Pennsylvania, and Virginia.*
- *Expanding our reliance on nuclear power. The Heritage Foundation's Jack Spencer is particularly keen on this, and he is not alone. With the existing nuclear industry in the United States already producing 20 percent of the nation's electricity and 73 percent of its* CO_2*-free electricity, he at least sees an important role for nuclear power in any program to reduce levels of carbon dioxide emissions, and wants the United States to commit to open commercial nuclear markets.*[64]
- *Use economic growth, not government regulation, to get to a better climate. Ultimately, whether weather conditions kill people turns not simply on the conditions but on how well prepared people are to deal with them. Generalized economic growth is the guarantor of their ability to deal with them better. An over-regulated economy slows that growth.*[65] *"Because the warmest world, which is also the richest, is superior to the other worlds through the foreseeable future, it is unnecessary to launch an urgent program to reduce climate change at this time. If there is any urgency at all, it should be to increase the level of economic development and . . . technological prowess, particularly in developing countries."*[66]

Skeptics of global warming regularly remind us that the United States already possesses an impressive record on environmental conservation. It does not need to apologize to the rest of the world for its environmental record, particularly when it is the rest of the world who are now increasingly the great polluters. China certainly is, and China is a communist, not a capitalist, country. It is in that direction that liberals want to move the United States, and that is exactly the wrong direction in which to go. What is needed in the field of energy conservation and environmental protection is less government regulation, not more: less government and more market.[67] *We don't need a green crusade, or a green economy. We just need to rely on that American ingenuity and enterprise that has stood us in such good stead these last two centuries. Private enterprise, not government regulation, is the key to both sustained economic growth and a better climate. That, at least, is the claim.*

A liberal response

1. Climate change is no hoax

Nor it is a joke, nor a communist plot to destroy private enterprise, nor a liberal initiative to destroy individual liberty and bring down American federalism, nor the work of Satan. All these claims are simply ludicrous. Climate change is a reality. It would appear to be also a growing reality; and because we are talking of climates, it is a growing reality which necessarily transcends national borders, let alone internal state ones. European conservatives seem to realize that: global warming is not purely a "left-wing" issue in an EU context, and is certainly not widely dismissed there as a figment of some overheated liberal imagination. Climate change is necessarily an area in which certainty is difficult and projections tentative; but over time, the stock of scientific knowledge on trends has grown and become more reliable, so that there are certain reasonably hard facts that we can definitely know.[68] We know, for example:

- That although greenhouse gases (predominantly, but not exclusively, CO_2) constitute only a very small part of the Earth's atmosphere they are critical to making the Earth habitable. Even modest changes in CO_2 levels can be expected to have long-term consequences for average global temperatures, and, hence, for the conditions (or indeed possibility) of human life on Earth; and "climate-change science is clear. The concentration of atmospheric carbon dioxide . . . stands at 389 parts per million . . . higher than it has been for at least 650,000 years."[69]
- We also know that human activities—especially deforestation and the burning of fossil fuels—have recently generated an increase in those greenhouse gases. Human activity is not the only, or indeed even the main, source, of carbon dioxide, even now; but it would appear to be the main source of the recent increase in CO_2 levels. These are up 35 percent since the start of the industrial revolution, with 80 percent of that increase occurring since 1950. Interestingly, the emission of manmade greenhouse gases was forecast by the International Energy Agency as likely to *fall* by 3 percent in 2009, because of the financial crisis[70]—economic activity and greenhouse gases moving hand-in-hand in bad times as in good.

- Global temperatures have risen and fallen many times through the history of the world, and have increased less than one degree Celsius since 1900. Almost half of that increase occurred before 1940, and so before CO_2 began to rise; but with the rise of greenhouse gas emissions, two recent developments give great cause for concern. One is that the rate of increase of temperature would appear to be quickening: the 11 hottest years on record have all occurred in the last 13. 1998–2007 was the warmest decade on record. The other is that alongside those rising temperatures have come clear signs of climate-induced environmental change: diminished snow accumulations, rising river and sea levels, extensive wildfires, and greater heat-induced illnesses and death.

The issue before us is whether we are approaching some human-induced climate tipping point and that, if we are, whether there is anything we can do to prevent it. "There are three specific events that . . . are especially worrisome and potentially imminent . . . widespread coral bleaching that could damage the world's fisheries within three decades; dramatic sea level rise by the end of the century that would take tens of thousands of years to reverse; and, within 200 years, a shutdown of the ocean current that moderates temperatures in northern Europe."[71] Unless those changes are totally fanciful, we do seem to face a pattern of climate change with which carefully calibrated policies ought progressively to deal.

2. "Seven ayes, one no—the no's have it" is no way to make public policy

As we contemplate how, we need to remember that the debate on green issues has attracted two camps, not one: one that favors addressing climate change with new public policies, and one that does not. Those opposed to public policy on climate change like to present themselves as isolated and underfunded individuals, battling against the tide—if you'll forgive the inappropriate imagery here—but, in reality, they are neither isolated nor underfunded, though they are certainly battling. On the contrary, what we now face—on the green agenda, as on others—is a set of academics and think tanks who have built their reputation on challenging the emerging orthodoxy, and who have been rewarded and funded for doing so. It is their material that was cited extensively earlier in this chapter. But though vocal, the skeptics in this debate are nonetheless a minority[72] in a wider scientific and policy-making universe in which there is now a compelling level of agreement.[73] That agreement is not the product of the findings of one report but of many. It is the product not of just an occasional report but of a steady stream of them. It is a set of shared understandings anchored in a huge mass of research findings that, individually and collectively, suggest that the climate *is* warming, that it is warming at a significant rate, and that it is warming as a result of human action. It is a set of understandings that was and remains embedded in a wider group of arguments warning of generalized resource depletion because of unregulated human economic behavior.

Even before the publication of the controversial fourth IPCC report, the scientific case had already been made—by scientist after scientist after scientist—for taking the threat of global warming seriously and for recognizing the dangers of generalized global resource depletion. Given the numbers of scientists involved, and their status within their professions and the policy-making world, it seems ludicrous to dismiss them all as either fools or knaves, which is all the options their critics appear to allow to us if we are to set their findings aside. Those findings are invariably dramatic and occasionally apocryphal. Take for example:

- The *Stern Report*, prepared for the UK government by a former chief economist at the World Bank and issued in October 2006. It estimated that although effective policies to curb carbon emissions would incur a one-off 1 percent reduction in global GDP, without such policies in place it seemed wise to anticipate anything between a 5 percent and a 20 percent reduction in global GDP by 2050 because of climate-induced economic disruption. The report warned of floods from rising sea levels possibly displacing 100 million people, melting glaciers causing water shortages for one person in six, and droughts that could create tens or even millions of "climate refugees." "The benefits of strong early action considerably outweigh the costs," was Sir Nicholas Stern's own initial summation of the findings he had gathered.[74] "Looking back" later, his view was even starker: namely that his own report "under-estimated the risks and under-estimated the damage from inaction."[75]
- Prior to that, in 2005, a report backed by 1,360 scientists from 95 countries had warned that as much as two-thirds of the world's resources are currently being depleted by human activity. That activity "is putting such a strain on the natural functions of the Earth," the report concluded, "that the ability of the planet's ecosystems to sustain future development can no longer be taken for granted." How could it be otherwise when because of human demand for food, fuel, and raw materials, more new land has been claimed for agricultural use in the last 60 years than in the previous 200 years? Water withdrawals from lakes and rivers have doubled in the last four decades. Since 1980, 35 percent of mangroves have been lost, and 40 percent of coral reefs destroyed or degraded . . . The study concluded with what it called a "stark warning" that basic ecosystems are

being irretrievably damaged,[76] a warning echoed in the later World Wildlife Fund (WWF) report, *The Living Planet.* The WWF calculated that we are currently using 30 percent more resources each year than the Earth is capable of replenishing. Without restraint, their report concluded, at this rate we will need *two* planets by 2030!

- Likewise, the UK's chief scientist warned the UK government in May 2006 that, without action now, the globe faced the possibility of a 3C degree rise in average temperatures, with devastating consequences for crop production and coastal flooding: this in response to the EU decision to commit to policies designed to set a 2C degree cap on global temperatures. The warning by Professor King was based on a report from the UK's Hadley Centre, *Avoiding Dangerous Climate Change.* The Hadley scenarios were based on estimates of carbon dioxide levels of 550 parts per million in the atmosphere. The EU's were on 450 ppm of CO_2. If Hadley is right, half the world's nature reserves and a coastal wetlands face imminent destruction.
- Similarly stark findings are to be found in other official reports launched in London and New York. These include one from the chief adviser to the UK Department of Agriculture, Fisheries, and the Environment warning of a 4C degree temperature rise (August 2008); another from the UK's government's own climate committee (*Building a Low Carbon Economy,* December 2008); plus the dramatic findings of Kofi Annan's Global Humanitarian Forum (2009)—namely that global warming is already killing 300,000 people a year and affecting 300 million people's daily lives—numbers that can only grow if climate change remains unchecked.[77] The adverse effects of climate change on grain yields, according to the *2010 U.N. Human Development Report*, might on a worst-case scenario reduce per capita cereal consumption by a fifth by 2050, leaving 25 million additional children malnourished, especially in South Asia. "Climate change," the report said, "may be the single factor that makes the future very different, impeding the continuing progress in human development that history would lead us to expect."[78]
- But by far the most potent of the reports warning of impending irretrievable damage has come from the Intergovernmental Panel on Climate Change, particularly from its fourth report issued February/April 2007. Drafted by 174 lead authors and 222 contributing authors, and drawing on the work of more than 2,500 of the world's leading climate scientists, its findings were extremely stark: that, if CO_2 levels continue to rise as predicted, global temperatures would be three degrees Celsius higher by century's end—with serious food and water shortages for millions of people, lower crop yields, the spread of tropical diseases, the loss of at least one-third of animal species, extensive flooding, greater risk of

wildfires, the loss of one-third of coastal wetlands, increasing storms and hurricanes, and the mass migration of people away from the worst affected regions. It is this report whose accuracy and bias has been most called into question—but though questioned, not faulted. The Climate Research Unit at the University of East Anglia was fully exonerated after a lengthy inquiry by the House of Commons Science and Technology Committee;[79] and the IPCC report itself was exonerated of all but a handful of minor errors—including an error on forecasts of the loss of Himalayan glaciers by 2035. A thorough Dutch review of its findings concluded that they were "well founded."[80]

- Finally, to bring the data back home: in May 2007, the National Academy of Sciences reported that from 2000–2004, global industry emitted approximately 7.9 billion tons of carbon dioxide, an amount *greater* than that assumed in even the worst of the IPCC's scenarios.[81] In May 2008, U.S. scientists reported higher levels of CO2 in the world's atmosphere than at any time in the last 650,000 years;[82] and in July 2010, the U.S. National Oceanic and Atmospheric Administration—in the first major new research since the Climategate scandal—reported global warming as "undeniable," with clear signs in its data of a "human footprint" in that warming. It took 11 indicators of climate, found each one pointing "to a world that was warming owing to the influence of greenhouse gases."[83]

With data of these quality, sources and profusion, it can't all be liberal hype and a commie plot, can it?

3. Making a clean green break with the immediate past

Skeptics of global warming often counter their critics by pointing to the impressive track record of the United States on environmental issues—making the case that it is no longer we who need to reform, even, on occasion, pointing to George W. Bush's leadership, late in his presidency, on issues of climate change. While what they say is true, what they fail to include in their accounting is that the United States remains the world's greatest polluter, that George Bush was a late and reluctant recruit to the green cause, and that we remain blighted by a uniquely retarded opposition to even moderate attempts at policy change.

In response to any emerging skepticism about the need to do more, we need to say:

- *There is nothing foreign or imported about environmental protection.* On the contrary, it is as American as apple pie—even Republican apple pie. It was Theodore Roosevelt, after all, who created the national parks; and the United States has certainly cleaned up its act in relation to environmental degradation, and done so under both Republican and Democratic administrations. The *Clean Air Acts* of 1970 and 1990 were particular landmarks, as was the creation of the Environmental Protection Agency in 1970.[84] The data is there: in spite of rising population, rising affluence and increased road traffic, the United States has witnessed significant improvements over time in the quality of air, water, food standards, personal hygiene, even carbon emissions—all because of sensible public policy. The United States is now bringing its emissions levels down faster than newly industrializing nations like China and India—and that is all to the good.[85]

- *George W. Bush did indeed have some kind of green epiphany late in his presidency.* He used his 2007 State of the Union Address to acknowledge the U.S. "addiction to oil" and to set a target of a 20 percent reduction in oil consumption by 2010. He also reversed course on the need for international targets for global warming. Long an opponent of the Kyoto accord, he argued in June 2007 that the world should agree to new greenhouse gas targets in a post-Kyoto age, and a year later he was willing to "seriously consider" the G8 commitment to a 50 percent reduction in global emissions by 2050, so long as China and India were included in the agreement. But the Bush adoption of a green agenda was late and limited, and we should never forget that, either side of his epiphany, his administration remained a consistent deregulator of business practice and a destroyer of rules limiting environmental damage by corporate America. To the very end, the Bush administration's policy on environmental protection and climate change was rendered ineffective by the questioning of the science underpinning the case for regulation, by the excessive role of business lobbyists in the design of those regulations, by an entrenched preference for ineffective voluntary agreements over binding statutory ones, and by a willingness to scale back existing environmental standards and budgets. George W. Bush may have been many things, but a green warrior was never one of them.
- Nor should we forget that, in spite of a long record on environmental protection and the more recent openness of first the Bush and now the Obama administration to serious diplomacy in pursuit of emission targets, *the United States remains the largest single polluting nation on earth* and has yet to sign up to any major climate agreement for the post-Kyoto world. We are no longer the world's largest consumer of energy—that title has recently slipped into Chinese hands—but with just 4 percent of the world's population, we still consume 25 percent of the world's total

> output of oil and put down a per-capita ecological footprint that is four times the world average and twice that of the European Union.[86] We also generate 20.6 percent of all greenhouse gases, more than any country other than China, and more than the EU taken as a whole;[87] and we do this through lifestyle, not population size. Our per-capita emission of CO2—at 19.8 metric tons—is double that of other leading industrial economies, including the UK, Germany, and Japan.[88] It takes an excessive number of old-fashioned coal-burning power plants and state-of-the-art large automobiles to get figures like that. When the World Economic Forum produced its 2008 Environmental Performance Index, ranking 149 countries on 25 indicators tracked across six established policy categories,[89] it placed the United States 39th in that list—down 11 places on its 2006 ranking, and well behind the majority of industrialized countries, particularly those in Western Europe from Scandinavia to Spain.[90]

However, this pattern of excessive resource use and limited federal regulation is not entirely unexpected, given the uniquely ill-informed character of the environmental debate still prevalent in conservative circles here in the United States. It would be laughable, were it not so tragic, to hear the widely respected IPCC Report dismissed as the work of hired political hands, given that those opposing global warming are themselves so often heavily subsidized by oil, gas, and auto interests. We have it on record that American climate scientists have come under political pressure to tone down their warnings of impending problem,[91] that business lobbyists have doctored government reports on climate change,[92] and that energy industry funds have been used to actively recruit scientists willing to argue the skeptics' case.[93] We also know that a senator like James Inhofe, the scourge of the green lobby, receives significant campaign funds from oil and gas interests. Here in the United States, we are still locked into a political dialogue on environmental issues that is at least a generation behind that prevalent elsewhere in the advanced industrial world. We are still debating whether global warming is occurring, when political debate elsewhere is focused almost exclusively on how to slow it down.

4. For once, genuinely taking a lesson from Europe

Which is why, for once, being open to European ideas and practices is of enormous importance right now. The IPCC Report made it abundantly clear that three-quarters of all greenhouse gases now being emitted were generated either in the United States or in the EU, with each party equally guilty.

Governments in the EU countries know that. They know it is an EU-wide problem; and they have already moved to address its resolution.

- There is widespread recognition across Europe of the need to address climate and resource issues. We have already documented a string of reports and policy proposals emanating from countries in Western Europe, and we could have documented more. Take the UK, for example: as late as 2005, the then New Labor government set itself a target of reducing 1990 CO_2 emission levels by 20 percent by 2010—a tougher target indeed than the 12.5 percent by 2012 initially agreed at Kyoto. Too tough in the event—the UK will probably undershoot by as much as one-third—but an 80 percent reduction by 2050 is still the target for which UK policy continues to strive: policy that stretches from taxation on high-emission cars through building codes for new energy-efficient buildings to the increasing use of renewable energy sources (wind, solar, bio-fuels, even nuclear) and the building of eco-towns.[94] The UK currently possesses a cabinet-level Department for Energy and Climate Change, and a target for renewable energy use—15 percent of all energy to come from renewable sources by 2020. Such climate change targets were accepted in the UK not simply by its former center-left government but also by its current center-right one.[95] This is the key difference between the United States and the UK on climate change. In the UK, there is clear majority support among the electorate for policies (including taxation) that address the issue of climate change. Here, there is not. There is still too much *misinformation* floating around in the United States, misinformation that needs to be quickly and decisively challenged for the nonsense that it is.

- The collective response within the European Union has also been to establish targets for the reduction of greenhouse gas emissions over time, and the adoption of policies in pursuit of those targets. The current target is a 20 percent reduction in 1990 levels of CO_2 emissions by 2020, with the promise to increase that to 30 percent if other countries follow suit. It is a target more criticized in Europe from the Left (as too modest) than from the Right (as unnecessary); indeed the center-right German government led by Angela Merkel was the major architect and advocate of that target when it was first formulated in 2007. Among the policies adopted in its pursuit are legally binding commitments to have 10 percent of vehicle fuel be comprised of bio-fuels by 2020, the creation of 12 clean coal power plants by 2015 (to show the potential of carbon capture and sequestration), the creation of an Emissions Trading Scheme in 2005 ("the only large-scale attempt so far to set a carbon price"),[96] and new legislation on more energy-efficient consumer products, particularly cars. The European Commission in 2007 proposed Europe-wide rules requiring an 18 percent cut in CO_2 emission by European car-makers by 2012. It had initially wanted a 25 percent cut, and eventually settled for 2015 as its deadline. The Merkel government also pressed in 2007 for an EU commitment to another 20 percent target by 2020—this one for the percentage of European fuel use coming from renewable energy sources[97]—and the Sarkozy government in France introduced in 2009 a €17 carbon tax on every tonne of carbon dioxide emission. Whatever else the European center-right may or may not be, it is definitely *not* as out-of-touch on climate change issues as its American counterpart. The EU remains committed from its March 2007 summit to its so-called 20/20/20 goals: a 20 percent cut in emissions and 20 percent of primary energy to be delivered by renewable fuel sources by 2020. There is an important reference point for us in those particular targets. If the EU can adopt them, why not the United States also?

5. So what can we do? We can make the general case . . .

The first thing we can do is recognize that the public regulation of greenhouse gas emissions is vital. Left unregulated, markets will not produce a green outcome, no matter how often conservative forces in the United States insist that they will.

Indeed, there is a particular irony here on which it is worthwhile momentarily to dwell. The irony is this: that the very idea normally used to defend private ownership against collectivism and public regulation—*the tragedy of the commons*—plays entirely the other way when environmental policy is in the frame. In the classic formulation of the tragedy, a commonly held piece of land is systematically overgrazed by the individuals who share it, because no one individual has a personal short-term interest in the commons' long-term conservation. The normal solution is private ownership of land, the parceling up of the commons into private plots that each individual farmer has an interest in conserving long-term.[98] But, the climate cannot be parceled off, and privately owned in bits. It is an unavoidably shared entity. It is the ultimate public good. So the logic of individual competition threatens it directly. No individual corporation has an interest in restraining its own use of this free good. On the contrary, each corporation has a powerful incentive to exploit existing climate conditions fully before they degenerate, precisely because its overuse will guarantee that degeneration. *The market, left to itself, guarantees global warming.* For that warming to cease, collective restraint is required, and that restraint will have to be a created one—the product of the restructuring of private corporate interests by systematic and sustained public intervention.[99] Private corporate interests will inevitably resist such public regulation, claiming it will weaken competitiveness, but in making that claim they will be entirely wrong.[100]

That potential resistance serves to remind us, however, that our problem here, as guardians of a better climate, is not the moral superiority of unregulated markets. It is the incredible difficulty of imposing a moral order on a fully functioning, privately run economic system. Indeed, a body of literature already exists arguing that environmental degradation (including global warming) is so endemic to capitalism that nothing short of a socialist transformation of the capitalist order will save the planet. Private ownership, and the logic of market competition, is presented in this literature as a "second contradiction of capitalism"—a contradiction so entrenched that it cannot be managed away.[101] This is the new Malthusianism; not global degradation through population growth per se, but degradation resulting from the commodification of the natural environment and from the inexorable pressure on finite natural resources created by the unrestrained consumption of increasingly affluent populations—their insatiable appetite for more and more manmade goods.[102] Costas Panayotakis has termed this "working more, selling more, consuming more" as "capitalism's third contradiction."[103] It is the very productivity and avarice of capitalism that is said, in this literature, to be driving the global economy towards the precipice, such that only a brake on growth, a lowering of affluent living standards, and a retreat from private ownership can (literally) stop the rot.

If that is too unpalatable a message for many progressives, then the time is short for us to prove otherwise: to demonstrate by policy and action that a green capitalism is both possible and within our grasp, that we do not need (and, indeed, cannot afford) to wait for a fundamental transformation of property structures for which, however desirable, no major constituency now exists. In the absence of global socialist movements, if the planet is to be saved, then it can and must be saved by public policy that restructures private capitalist interests—by initiatives of at least the following kind: (a) the establishment of progressively higher standards, and tougher penalties, on the energy-efficiency and environmental protection of existing technologies and products; (b) the negotiation of an effective post-Kyoto global agreement on the lowering of greenhouse gas emissions as economies industrialize and grow; and (c) the development of new carbon-free sources of power and transportation in both advanced economies and developing ones. All that, of course, is easier to type than to do—because individually, each of those policy transformations will be system-changing, and because collectively that will initiate a total and essential resetting of the relationship between capitalism and nature.[104] Green politics, whatever else it is, is not a politics for the fainthearted—it is a politics that requires a tough-minded and totally focused progressive commitment on a daily basis over a prolonged period of time—a politics requiring not simply strong nerves but also stamina.

6. . . . and we can make the specific steps

Transforming the U.S. economy in a green direction will be neither easy nor quick. It will be a tough struggle, and one that will be resisted every inch of the way. Fortunately, however, there are already a whole set of "shovel-ready" proposals out there, available for use by a progressive administration. Green politics in the United States does not have to begin from an entirely clean slate.

Among those "shovel-ready" proposals are a string of proposals that combine energy conservation with much-needed job creation and the re-invigoration of the U.S. manufacturing base. These include:

- The *NRDC*'s "Plan to Secure America's Energy Future" by capping carbon emissions, saving 2.5 million barrels of oil a day by 2015, expanding investment in energy efficiency, increasing the role played by renewable energy supplies, and reducing pollutants from power plants.[105]
- The *Hamilton Project*'s three-prong strategy for climate change and energy security: pricing carbon and oil correctly to reduce their use; increased public investment in basic research and long-term energy technologies; and reasserting U.S. global leadership on climate-change targets.[106]
- There is also the *Centre for American Progress*'s ten-year, $100 billion "green recovery" program focused on six energy efficiency and renewable energy strategies: retrofitting buildings to improve energy efficiency; expanding mass transit and freight rail; constructing "smart" electrical grid transmission systems; wind power; solar power; and next generation bio-fuels.[107]
- Plus the *Apollo Alliance*'s program to rebuild America clean and green, with 25 percent of U.S. power coming from renewable sources by 2025, energy efficiency of buildings up by 30 percent, U.S. industry retooled to build renewable energy systems and high-efficiency, alternative-fuel vehicles, and American workers retrained for green-collar jobs.[108]
- The *Economic Policy Institute*'s call for a renewable energy industry based on government support for basic science, R&D, and technology commercialization; and for the job-training necessary to avoid supply-side bottlenecks and labor skills gaps.[109]
- There is also now Thomas Friedman's widely read program—his *Plan A* (there being no "Plan B")—his "win-win" solution to America's energy crisis: his strategy to "help ease global warming, biodiversity loss, energy poverty, petro-dictatorship and energy supply shortages—and make

> America stronger at the same time." Clean power and energy efficient technologies which, even if they are followed as a response to a global warming crisis that turns out to have been hyped, will still leave us with "cleaner air and water, more efficient products, more workers educated in the next global industry, higher energy prices but lower bills, greater productivity, healthier people, and an export industry in clean power products that people across the world will want to buy." Oh yes, and in addition, greater world respect and fewer wars![110] How could we resist that?

So there is no shortage in the United States of ways forward to a green economy, and we do at last now possess, for the moment at least, an administration in Washington, DC, committed in principle to the pursuit of at least some of them. The Obama administration entered office promising to win Congressional support for a cap-and-trade program to reduce emissions (80 percent by 2050). It entered office promising to invest in secure domestic energy supplies and to diversify energy sources (it proposed 10 percent from renewable sources of energy by 2012, and 25 percent by 2025). It entered office promising to invest in a smart grid, and to weatherize 1 million homes annually.[111] And it entered office promising to improve fuel efficiency in cars, trucks, and SUVs (it spoke of 1 million hybrid cars by 2015). Barack Obama entered office, that is, with, at long last, an embryonic green agenda—and with his own "green team"—a powerful group of administrators committed to new and radical energy policies.[112]

But as we have seen, Congressional support for a cap-and-trade initiative has so far proved elusive—the big prize continues to slip away—and we are left instead only with the reality of small gains.

- Those have partly come, thus far at least, through the administration's willingness to use the Environmental Protection Agency to pursue a number of its more modest green goals. These include rapid moves to reverse many of the Bush administration's more intransigent rulings (including the Bush EPA refusal to comply with the Supreme Court ruling obliging the EPA to examine the effects of greenhouse gases from vehicles, and to regulate them if necessary). The EPA under Lisa Jackson did comply, and in December 2009 ruled that carbon dioxide and five other greenhouse gases were indeed a danger to public health and welfare, so requiring regulation. New rules then followed—applicable to large facilities emitting more than 25,000 tons of $C0_2$ a year—some 70 percent of total U.S. carbon dioxide emissions. From July 2011, under powers already legislated in the *Clean Air Act*, major emitters of greenhouse gases—coal-powered power plants, particularly—will need permits to operate if they release more than 100,000 tons of such gases annually, or if they increase those emissions by as much as 75,000 tons. The EPA also let it be known (July 2010) that it would be particularly responsive, when drafting its environmental regulations and when issuing its permits, to the health concerns of low-income and minority populations.

- Very early in his administration, President Obama directed the EPA to do something else that the Bush-led EPA had declined to do: reconsider granting California and other states waivers to set their own higher standards of car emissions of greenhouse gases. He also instructed the Transportation Department to draw up new interim mileage standards to ensure that from 2012, new vehicles reach the 35-mile a gallon level set by Congress for 2020. Those standards, when they came, required new cars and light trucks to average 35.5 miles to the gallon by 2016—moving to that standard in a set of 5 percent annual improvements in fuel efficiency—standards which, though still low in international terms, were welcomed at the time by bodies like the Natural Resources Defense Council as likely to leave new cars some 30 percent more fuel-efficient by 2016 than they were in 2008.[113]
- In addition, the Obama administration used its stimulus package and its first budget to give a huge boost to clean-energy products and fuel-efficient technologies. $59 billion of the $787 billion ARRA, and $150 billion (over ten years) of the $3.35 trillion budget proposal for fiscal year 2010 were so earmarked. Both included tax credits to stimulate private sector research and development in new clean-energy technologies, and funds to directly sustain clean-energy research in the Energy Department's national laboratories. "By a stroke of his pen," as the appropriately surnamed Joshua Green put it in *The Atlantic*, "President Obama made a federal agency the world's largest venture capitalist" and "essentially saved the renewable-energy industry in the United States."[114]

7. Avoiding weaknesses, picking strengths

Not everything in the green policy agenda is problem free, however, and so we do need to be very aware of various downsides to proposals as we chose between them. There are real problems of scale and cost to be considered in many of these plans, and proper weight to be given to the length and character of the transition they envision from an energy-wasteful economy to an energy-efficient one. So we need to be careful, and aware.

- Wind and solar power are not likely, with existing or looming technologies, ever to provide more than a modicum of relief from the existing energy crunch. There is a limit to how many wind turbines can sit astride a mountain without constituting a new form of environmental degradation, or how many solar panels can be gathered in one place without becoming a new form of urban blight. Wind and solar power may be free, but neither is uniformly distributed through time and space; and neither can be captured without machinery that has itself a potentially damaging environmental presence.[115]

- Nuclear power—advocated by some—has long been recognized by most green activists as part of the energy problem rather than a solution to it. Issues of nuclear waste disposal and potential military spin-offs rightly remove it from the progressive agenda for many, this writer included.[116]

- The extensive cultivation of bio-fuels had its own adverse impact on food prices in the first half of 2008—anywhere between 3 percent and 75 percent, depending on which report you read—and there is clearly no gain in clearing forests (with their immense capacity naturally to absorb CO_2) merely to grow more crops for emission-reducing purposes. ("Profoundly stupid" was how that tradeoff was described by the UK's new chief scientific adviser.)[117] Bio-fuel advocates now talk of the need for "next generation bio-fuels" that can give us clean energy without undercutting vital food production systems. Gone are the days when corn-based ethanol could be offered as a quick and easy fix.

- Cap-and-trade solutions also rightly have their critics. Some of the criticisms are political and contingent—what is the point of having a global agreement when major polluters like China and India do not participate, and when those who do systematically fail to meet their targets—do we really need an energy equivalent to the impotent League of Nations? But other criticisms cut deeper still: that there is no commensurate saving of greenhouse gas emissions to match the effort and costs involved in the creation of such a trading system, and that carbon markets are vulnerable to extensive fraud, being in essence "invitations to engage in pork-barrel corporate subsidy politics on a massive scale."[118] Moving rights to pollute around, so the argument goes, is no solution to the systematic erosion of that right in general—particularly when, for many, a strong carbon tax could achieve the same ends without the equivalent downsides.[119]

It is certainly better to concentrate on raising the energy standards of existing products, funding research and development on new energy-efficient technologies, and exploiting the long-term potential of hydrogen fuels and biomass energy.[120] We know what the great polluters are: coal-fired power plants that do not capture and sequester their emissions; and cars and trucks that belch out carbon dioxide as they go. Insulated buildings, hybrid and alternative fuel vehicles, clean coal technology, and a culture of efficient energy use—these are clearly vital elements in any coherent strategy to slow the rate of global warming. They are also vital elements in any growth strategy geared to long-term competitiveness and the generation of high-paying secure employment.[121] You don't have to be green to see the potential for employment in industries creating wind turbines, or for job security in industries that are energy efficient. You don't have to be green to see that if those jobs are not based here in America, they will be based abroad. But if you are green, then there is one thing of which you can be absolutely certain. Better a green technology with drawbacks than an economy that continues to pollute as modern ones do.

Ultimately, we need to recognize this. There is a very real sense in which the onus of proof is no longer on us—the advocates of a green technology. The onus is rather on our critics—who have to explain to us why the Cheney principle worked for many of them in Iraq but does not work for them on climate change.[122] The Cheney principle—the one that said that if there was just a 1 percent chance that Saddam Hussein had weapons of mass destruction, invading Iraq to avoid the possibility of their use made perfect sense. Well, if 1 percent chances justify war, they certainly justify defense—defense of an environment now under serious threat from the polluting activities of modern industry.

CHAPTER 5

Making the Case for a Reform of the American Model

History is replete with nations that thought themselves too powerful to fail, nations whose capacity to dominate neighboring areas and economies seemed for a time a necessarily permanent feature of the global landscape. Invariably, the self-confidence of those nations peaked at the very moment of their impending demise, as though collective self-delusion was itself a product of dominance and a key to decline. We saw that with Rome in the fourth century of the modern era, with Spain in the seventeenth, and with the United Kingdom in the twentieth. In each case, pride came before the fall. There is a lot of pride in contemporary America.[1]

So is history to repeat itself, or will the United States prove on this, as on so much else, to be exceptional? There is a case to be made for and against the notion of American resilience. We need to examine them both.

The case for American superiority

The case for American superiority is of long standing and of wide sweep. The very reasons that people fled old Europe for the new world quickly crystallized out, in their descendants, into a central belief in the uniqueness of their new home; and as the Washington political elite reset itself in the twentieth century as a major global player, that generalized faith in the special quality of the United States as a society then colored American understandings of the role that its government, its military forces and its private companies found themselves able to play on the world stage. The general case for American global superiority goes something like this.

1. American exceptionalism

The United States of America is said to be a unique place, and one long celebrated as such in a rich and varied literature. That literature stretches back to at least John Winthrop's seventeenth-century description of the English colonies as "a city upon a hill." It certainly includes Alexis de Toqueville's nineteenth-century enthusiasm for the new Republic, and Ronald Reagan's much more recent farewell address as president, in which he likened the nation to a "shining city"; all three of them, in fact, articulating a shared thesis of "American exceptionalism" that has been given its fullest and most recent expression in the extensive writings of the late Seymour Martin Lipset.

Lipset's claims for American exceptionalism were many sided and complex, but they were almost entirely arguments that emphasized difference rather than superiority. Indeed, he saw this exceptionalism as a "double-edged sword,"[2] *as something that gave the United States profound economic strength but also left in its wake significant social problems (including higher than average rates of poverty, incarceration, and divorce). These social problems, he argued, were the price we have to pay for living in the only nation founded on a commitment to a particular value system—founded on what G. K. Chesterton had earlier called "a creed," the one "set forth with dogmatic and even theological lucidity in the Declaration of Independence."*[3] *That creed, Lipset said, "can be described in five words: liberty, egalitarianism, individualism, populism, and laisser-faire."*[4] *Free of aristocratic political conservatism because of the flight of Tories into Canada after the Revolutionary War, and brave enough to establish a democratic franchise long before Western Europe managed anything of the kind, the United States, according to Lipset, created a unique society. It was one in which self-fulfillment and expressive individualism were paramount values, one in which a healthy skepticism about governments and politics prevailed (and still prevails), and one in which national pride and belief in the superiority of America as a social system remains general through the population as a whole.*

The United States of America is unique, so the argument goes, because "America" is an idea and a code of living as well as a place, and because it is understood as such by the bulk of its citizenry. As the "first new nation"[5] *one that is meritocratic in its social structure and uniquely philanthropic in its treatment of the poor, the United States has escaped the extensive public welfare provision and socialist (or social democratic) ideas and institutions that so burden Western Europe.*[6] *Not for America the need for the heavy hand of the redistributive state: on the contrary, a uniquely American "commitment to equality of opportunity implies that achievement should reflect ability, justifies higher differentials in rewards and rejects taxing the successful to upgrade the less advantaged."*[7] *Indeed, and because rather than in spite of the separation of church and state, the United States has managed to avoid much of the secularization—the retreat from religion—that has been such a feature of modernization elsewhere: so that, uniquely, most Americans now remain "utopian moralists who press hard to institutionalize virtue, to destroy evil people, and eliminate wicked institutions and practices."*[8]

2. Economic superiority

Yet even Lipset could not fully escape the national pride he saw as so critical to American exceptionalism: when recording the outstanding twentieth-century performance of the U.S. economy, even in his writings claims about difference often slid into claims about superiority. In this he was not alone. On the contrary, a quite separate literature now exists—one that is regularly updated—asserting the superiority of the American way of organizing economic life and defending it against its critics: asserting the superiority of what Olaf Gersemann has recently labeled "Cowboy Capitalism."[9] *The very absence in the United States of strong trade unions and large publicly funded welfare bureaucracies, we are told, has left the U.S. economy less burdened than those in Western Europe by heavy government regulation and excessive corporate taxation. Because it has, the U.S. record is so much stronger than that of its leading competitors across the full economic board: better on wealth generation, better on innovation, better on job creation, better on avoiding unemployment, and better on generalized affluence. The U.S. economy has been since the 1940s, and remains now, a uniquely successful one, with its uniqueness rooted in the superiority of the unregulated market competition that is defining of the American economic model.*[10]

The claims for economic superiority here are extensive. The United States economy is presented as a uniquely dynamic one, capable of creating wave after wave of new industries, new technologies, and new job opportunities. Many of the more conservative commentators making those claims are not happy about current waves of immigration, for example, but they often point to them anyway as indicative of the superiority of the U.S. model. Americans do not emigrate. Instead, people emigrate to join them, and they do so because American living standards and social freedoms are so much greater than those available elsewhere. That superiority applies even in relation to the economies of the European Union, prone as they are to a debilitating "euro-sclerosis"—a structured resistance to economic change rooted in their generous labor laws and safety net provisions.[11] *The message to European Christian and Social Democrats, Gersemann has written, "is simple: while U.S.-style capitalism may or may not have delivered results to be proud of, its performance as measured by economic and social indicators has clearly been superior to that of its continental European counterparts" such that "the price Americans are paying for the benefits of their cowboy capitalism is surprisingly small, and it is likely that, if Europeans decided to Americanize their economic systems, they would gain much more than they would lose."*[12] *As Martin Wolf once put it: "[T]he U.S. is unique. It is the 'capitalist' country: the engine of the future."*[13]

3. The home of the brave and the land of the free

The "political" strand of the "exceptionalism and superiority" case has both an internal and an external face. Internally, it is an argument about the unique American capacity for individual freedom—freedom from state oppression as in Old Europe, and freedom to rise socially in ways that Old Europe could never replicate. The roots of that freedom are said to lie, as with Lipset's arguments, in a unique set of values that are deeply rooted in the U.S. population as a whole. Americans uniquely combine a reverence for their Constitution with a deep suspicion of the governmental institutions created by that Constitution. They believe in the rule of law, and the Bill of Rights, and look to courts rather than governments for the protection of their liberties. They look to ability rather than birth as the source of an individual's social standing—the United States has long carried little or none of Old Europe's concern with class position and social background. On the contrary, for a society that was once "politically isolationist and racially intolerant," the United States has proved over time to be "an astonishingly open"[14]*—one with a particular genius for the incorporation of immigrants. Where else but the United States would "huddled masses yearning to break free" have found so welcoming and accommodating a home?*

The very antipathy that many Americans hold towards extensive state regulation of civil society has long left a space in which private philanthropy has flourished. State welfare provision for the poor may be parsimonious by the standards of contemporary Western Europe, but private generosity is not. Americans are uniquely free to choose whether or not to give; and they do give. America has many serious social problems, of course—problems it largely shares with all industrial societies: "a large underclass, the continuing isolation of many blacks, reduced economic mobility, a deeply polarized electorate, substance abuse among the young, many families in crisis, and a popular culture that is at once immensely creative and often debased."[15] *But to the degree that those problems are more acute in the United States than in other advanced industrial economies, they have to be understood, so the argument goes, "as the large and unfortunate costs of freedom," American style: and "freedom is America's watchword."*[16]

4. A beacon for the world

The external face of the "exceptionalism and superiority" argument offers the United States as a model society for others—a beacon of freedom in the world—and insists upon the uniquely benign and altruistic role of American power abroad. "I do not believe America is the problem in the world," Rush Limbaugh told the readers of The Wall Street Journal in April 2010, "I believe America is the solution to the world's problems."[17] *The case has recently been most eloquently and extensively put by Thomas Madden, in whose writings U.S. power abroad is presented as an "empire of trust" rather than as one of conquest (like the Soviet's) or of commerce (like the British). As against the British, for example, the drivers of American global expansion are said to be qualitatively different and morally superior: "Britain actively sought to build an empire, while the United States has actively sought to avoid one."*[18] *Thus, Madden's United States was and remains a reluctant global power—isolationism being in his view "woven into the DNA of the American character"*[19]*—one drawn into foreign alliances, much like the young Roman Republic, only in response to external threats; and once so drawn, obliged to play a progressively bigger role only to honor the trust placed in U.S. support by its allies. "The overriding dynamic behind Roman and American expansionism," he tells us, "was not to build an empire of the vanquished but a community of allies."*[20] *Madden even develops a diagrammatic encapsulation*[21] *of the way in which the American "desire to be left alone"*[22] *has been systematically thwarted by the twin force of attacks on allies and appeals from friends. It is this twin force, we are told, which has cumulatively obliged a reluctant hegemon to develop, not a colonial empire—heaven forbid—but rather a global network of military and economic obligations. The widespread peace created by that military and economic generosity then generated the space within which those same allies could both run down their own armies and even engage in a degree of ungrateful anti-Americanism. Western Europeans are particularly to be condemned for this, their attitude to the U.S. being not unlike the antipathy to Roman rule once demonstrated by the Greeks. But that is to be expected and discounted. It is certainly not to be used, as American-born critics of American imperialism are prone to use it, as evidence of the malevolence and fragility of American power abroad. On the contrary, according to Madden at least, though currently "we may not be able to see the end of America's road" in world affairs, "its direction seems clear enough. And, for both America and the world, it is a good road to follow."*[23]

If the Madden position is an extreme one in the defense of America's global role, it is not the only one. There are many similar if slightly less gung-ho defenses available in both the academic literature and the political commentary.[24] *Indeed, President Obama made one himself, when accepting the Nobel Peace prize in Oslo in December 2009.*

> *The world must remember that it was not simply international institutions—not just treaties and declarations—that brought stability to a post-World War II world. Whatever mistakes we have made, the plain fact is this: The United States of America has helped underwrite global security for more than six decades with the blood of our citizens and the strength of our arms. The service and sacrifice of our men and women in uniform has promoted peace and prosperity from Germany to Korea, and enabled democracy to take hold in places like the Balkans. We have borne this burden not because we seek to impose our will. We have done so out of enlightened self-interest—because we seek a better future for our*

> *children and grandchildren, and we believe that their lives will be better if others' children and grandchildren can live in freedom and prosperity.*

5. Corrosive forces

The underside of the case for American exceptionalism and superiority is one concerned with the potential instability of that superiority—one listing things that could easily undermine the strength of the U.S. economy and its capacity to do good in the world. Internally, the threats normally signaled out are those deriving from the institutions and disloyalty of the American Left: such things as strong trade unions, extensive welfare taxation, or over-regulatory federal governments. Externally the threat used to be communism. Now it is Islamic fundamentalism. The neoliberal political scientist Mancur Olson once explained "the rise and decline of nations," including America, by the depth of sectional interests operating within them, particularly trade unions and powerful welfare interests.[25] *More recently, Rush Limbaugh has given voice to a long-established view of those who criticize America's strength and uniqueness in the world. He is worth quoting on this at length:*

> *They have no concept of the thing I refer to as American exceptionalism, and a lot of these people are found in the Democratic Party. In fact, the whole concept of American exceptionalism embarrasses them. The whole concept of American exceptionalism is a problem, it makes them feel guilty . . . They look around the world and they see the poor, the wretched, whatever, and they blame this country for it. "Why, if we weren't so prosperous and we weren't stealing all the resources of the world, why, these people wouldn't be as poor. So it's only right that people from anywhere be allowed to come here and claim and take back what is theirs in the first place because the wretched, evil white European American founders stole it from them!" And that's what's driving this immigration business. It's not about immigration. It's the latest chance for the left to wreck and ruin this country.*[26]

The case for rethinking the American model

The general case for a resetting of the American model is one that challenges the Limbaugh position at its core. It is a case made by those who, quite contrary to his claim, wish America well and care deeply for the security and prosperity of its people. They simply see that security and prosperity threatened by the recurrent mythologies of the American Right of the kind that Rush Limbaugh regularly reproduces. The case for rethinking the American model is one that challenges both the claims for exceptionalism and those for superiority, seeing in a wide set of contemporary trends troubling signs of impending U.S. global decline and social implosion. If such forebodings are valid, then reform, not celebration, becomes the appropriate order of the day.[27]

1. Revisiting the claims about U.S. "exceptionalism"

First, this: that there is an alarming degree of self-delusion in the arguments about American exceptionalism, and also some danger in them.[28] Leaving aside the tendency of all nations to think of themselves as different and superior—there are many "exceptionalisms" out there in both the popular and the academic literature—the claims about American exceptionalism have at least three particular weaknesses. They cherry pick from the rich array of American values and practices in ways that downplay the less ennobling side of the American story (downplaying what Geoffrey Hodgson correctly calls "the dark side of American exceptionalism").[29] They write out of the historical narrative key elements and moments of American political and social development (downplaying the driving force of social class), and they entirely reverse the proper direction of causality between cultural systems and social forces.

Cherry picking your way to glory

It is entirely legitimate to point to the greater role of individualism and anti-statism in modern U.S. popular culture when contrasted with dominant belief systems in Western Europe. But it is not legitimate to present "liberty, egalitarianism, individualism, populism, and *laissez-faire*" as exhaustive of dominant American values, now or in the past. The American story is made up of much more than that. The United States was, and to a large degree remains, a society scarred by more than excessive individualism. It was and is also scarred by ethnic tensions, and certainly by unalloyed racism.[30] It would be more accurate to talk, as Paul Smith has done, about the "hot" and "cold" elements in American popular culture:

> The hot: the dynamic and progressive aspects of a society dedicated to growth and productivity, marked by mobility, invention, innovation, and optimism—in short, a super-charged modernity. The cold: rigid social forms and archaic beliefs, fundamentalism of all kinds, racism and xenophobia, anti-intellectualism, cultural atavism, and ignorance—in short, the primitive.[31]

Certainly, the "gift of the franchise" was a joke in the South until the mid-1960s—no gift there, certainly not for African-Americans[32]—and was a missing element in the American story even for white women until the 1920s. The United States was actually the last, not the first, major democracy to establish a fully universal franchise. It did not complete that journey until the 1960s; and like all its equivalents, its dominant culture and practices to this day retain large elements of the racism and patriarchy that until recently went unchallenged everywhere.

It is also quite wrong to slide from an argument about anti-statism (*laissez-faire*) to any claim that the federal government is uniquely *un*involved in U.S. private enterprise. As we first noted in Chapter 2, American governments have always played, and still now play, a critical role in the profitability of key sectors of the economy.[33] To take but three: federal authorities are major supporters of U.S. agriculture. They are the main funder of the military-industrial complex, and the main purchaser of medical services from the health industry. The Cato Institute's Stephen Slivinski put the total bill for direct and indirect federal subsidies to U.S. corporations in 2006 at $92 billion; and that was before the huge bailout of financial institutions triggered by the meltdown that began in September 2008. Boeing, Xerox, IBM, Motorola, Dow Chemical, General Electric[34]—the list of major companies currently subsidized is potentially endless. So while it may be good political rhetoric in the run up to elections to portray the United States as "cowboy capitalism," it would be equally valid—if, no doubt, less electorally successful—to characterize many of America's leading economic cowboys as "crony capitalists" whose success is periodically dependent on state largesse.

Writing labor out of the U.S. story

Moreover, talking of seamless and persistent individualistic values that stretch in a direct and unbroken line to the Founding Fathers not only over-simplifies the debates of the 1770s and 1780s, it also completely writes out of the American nineteenth- and twentieth-century story any mention of the role of organized labor. Collectivist ideas were strong in late-nineteenth-century America. Industrial militancy was then a regular feature of U.S. industrial life. Indeed, there were more strikes (and more bitter strikes) in the United States in the run up to the First World War, and again in the 1930s, than anywhere else in the emerging industrial world. Only Russia matched the United States for the number of times state troopers broke strikes between 1900 and 1914, in what Graham Adams has properly called "The Age of Industrial Violence."[35] And not just industrial militancy: rural radicalism, too, swept the Midwest and the rural South in the first half of the 1890s—Jim Crow was at least in part a concentrated attempt to avoid an electoral alliance between disgruntled farmers, white and black.

The United States in the age of the robber barons was periodically home to mass radical parties: of artisans (the Knights of Labor), of farmers (the Populists), and even of unskilled workers (the Industrial Workers of the World (IWW)). May Day as a working-class holiday, the eight hour day as a working-class goal, the public ownership of the banking and railways systems as a weapon of working-class strength—all these entered the lexicon of the twentieth-century global Left from their beginnings in nineteenth-century *American* labor history. They all happened first here! Indeed, the Socialist Party of America received a similar percentage of the popular vote in the presidential election of 1912 to that received by the British Labor Party in the UK's two elections of 1910; and while Europe went fascist in the 1930s, the United States went center-left, producing in the New Deal moves towards a modern welfare state that the rest of the advanced industrial world would only consolidate, under U.S. military leadership, more than a decade later. When that New Deal then faltered in the 1940s, strong industrial trade unionism replaced it, raising wages and benefits for that section of the working class employed in mainstream U.S. manufacturing industry. Trade union strength was a critical trigger to the long post-war boom in American living standards that began in 1948—trade union strength and solidarity, not individualism or *laissez-faire*. We are not told our history in that way anymore, but it remains our history even so.[36]

Writing class out of history

This hidden history then reminds us that Lipset's cultural stories actually *reverse* the causal relationships at work between dominant belief systems and social forces in modern America. The contemporary American Left is not weak because of American values. Socialism did not fail here because of the prior existence of a uniquely anti-collectivist mindset. The American mindset and Lipset's quintessentially American value system remain as they do today because the Left here was roundly defeated, first in the 1920s and again in the 1960s, by conservative political forces more powerful than its own. As we have just noted, late-nineteenth- and early twentieth-century America witnessed bitter struggles between social classes, and a fierce backlash against black emancipation. In the great clashes between capital and labor in the United States that peaked in 1920, socialist elements within the American labor movement lost out, allowing socialism to be entirely written out of the American story. Indeed, many of the leading socialist campaigners of that First World War generation were literally shipped out of the United States in Palmer raids in 1920 overseen by the young J. Edgar Hoover. For all the glory of the New Deal, Hoover's long and consistently focused career epitomizes the continuity of state and employer hostility to working class industrial and political movements in twentieth-century America.[37] If we are looking for real American exceptionalism, we might do well to concentrate our attention here. What has been really exceptional about U.S. twentieth-century history—looked at as a whole—has been the strength of capital, and the weakness of labor, in so many of its decades.

For, in our generation as in any other, the political values and historical stories that people carry around in their heads have to be put there. Those values and stories do not fall from the sky, or slip into mind simply from drawing on the water supply. Values reflect political power, particularly the power of whole social classes and dominant ethnic groups. Values and stories do not bring that power into existence, but they do help to keep it there. If the Great Depression radicalized American labor and gave us the New Deal, Cold War McCarthyism then closed that chapter down, leaving modern American conservatism far to the right of its Western European equivalent. Conservative hostility to public welfare provision is greater here than among German Christian Democrats, and hostility to the state direction of industry is greater among American conservatives than among French Gaullists—not because American values are unique, but because the forces of the American center-left have for so long been ineffectual. Conservatives everywhere have to be trained to be civilized—trained by progressive forces that are too strong electorally to be ignored. The contemporary tragedy of our politics is that U.S. progressives have lacked that electoral potency throughout the lifetime of most living Americans. It is a potency whose restoration is desperately needed.

2. Challenging the assertion of U.S. economic superiority

The American economy is undoubtedly still the most significant economy in the global system, and U.S. technology and prosperity did play the leading role in the post-war reconstruction of both the Western European and the East Asian economies. That is not in dispute. What is in dispute is whether the U.S. economy is *still* the world's strongest, and whether the future is in that sense still American. The claim that it is rests on two insecure foundations: an under-estimation of American economic fragility, and an over-statement of particularly Western European economic sclerosis. Economic power is shifting East right now. It is a shift that we would do well both to recognize and to counter.

American danger signs

Maintaining the superiority of the "American model" is significantly more difficult now than it was before the financial meltdown of 2008—2009. Clearly, sectors of the U.S. economy once thought of as invincible and worthy of emulation—its leading investment houses and hedge funds certainly, its uniquely buoyant housing market possibly—now look decidedly tarnished, and rightly so. The balance of finance and industry in the economy has shifted dramatically in the last three decades, to the detriment of the long-term stability and superiority of the American economy as a whole. A manufacturing sector that was indeed once a world leader is a world leader no more.

- The U.S. *balance of trade* has been negative with the rest of the world economy since 1975, and has become significantly more negative of late, to stand by 2008 at a worrying 4.9 percent of GDP. The June and July 2010 trade statistics showed the U.S. economy running a goods and service deficit in June of $49.8 billion and in July of $42.8 billion, with a significant increase in both months in the volume and value of imports of crude oil, automotive vehicles and parts, pharmaceutical preparations, computer accessories, and other household goods. Things made in the United States and exported out into the global economy prior to 1975 are now increasingly made elsewhere in the global economy and exported back to us.

- The *productivity* lead which U.S. labor enjoyed over its major rivals in the first half of the post-war period has now narrowed or evaporated, depending on which economy you use as comparator and which measure of productivity you favor—it is just still there if you measure productivity per worker, but not if you measure productivity per hour. In 2007, if U.S. GDP per hour worked was 100, it was 136 in Norway, 110 in Belgium, 108 in Austria and 103 in France.[38] The post–2008 recession may well have narrowed those gaps—but not because of any greater increase in investment per worker in the U.S. economy—but rather because of a generalized intensification of the work process here, in a domestic economy in which a recovery in business output and profits has not yet triggered either significant job growth or rising wages.[39]
- The *job creation* record of the U.S. economy, so strong in the 1990s, is now no longer internationally superior. "The economic expansion from 2001 to the end of 2007 added jobs more slowly than any other expansion since World War II . . . 0.9 percent a year, about one-third of the 2.5 percent posted by the average postwar expansion."[40] The U.S. economy then *lost* 7 million jobs in 18 months in the immediate wake of the 2008 financial meltdown. (The U.S volume of job loss at the peak of the crisis—December 2008 to May 2009—was almost twice that of Europe and three times that of the Asia Pacific economies surveyed by the ILO.[41]). Indeed, the number of *private sector jobs* available in the contemporary United States is at best stuck, or more likely now diminishing. As was first noted in the chapter on managed trade, private sector job growth over the full business cycle that ended with the 2008 financial meltdown was virtually zero: with job gains in leading service sectors being more than compensated by job losses in core American manufacturing industries.
- *Unemployment*, so long the thing that the U.S. avoided more successfully than its Western European equivalents, is now higher in the U.S. than in broad sweeps of continental Europe. American unemployment in the wake of the financial meltdown peaked in October 2009 at 10.2 percent, when the joint under-employment and unemployment rate stood at 17.5 percent. (Unemployment among African-American men that month touched 34.5 percent, and among young Americans as a whole

hovered around 18 percent!) There are no European and Japanese equivalents to figures as appalling as these. As late as the Fall of 2010, the official unemployment rate in the United States remained stuck at 9.6 percent. The equivalent figure for Japan was 5.2 percent. For the UK, it was 7.8 percent and for Germany 8.2 percent. Official figures in all cases failed to capture high levels of under-employment and (in the U.S. case, high levels of hidden unemployment among undocumented immigrants, and the softening impact on jobless levels of a uniquely large jail population); but the official figures were still sufficiently robust to demonstrate a U.S. under-performance here in comparative terms of at least one or two percentage points.

- *International League Tables,* once dominated by the United States, now have new national leaders. The 2009 IMF listing of countries by nominal GDP per head, for example, put the United States in ninth place, behind countries such as Norway, Denmark, Switzerland, and even Ireland. The World Economic Forum's annual review of competitiveness, from the body that sponsors the annual gathering at Davos, ranked the United States fourth overall, behind Switzerland, Sweden, and Singapore, and gave the U.S. very low rankings on such things as macroeconomic environment (87th), strength of corporate reporting requirements (55th), cost to business of terrorism and crime (84th), and government budget balance, government debt, and national savings rates (all in the 130s).[42] perhaps most striking of all, on the Department of Labor's own figures, U.S. hourly wage rates in manufacturing industries in 2007—at $30.56—*trailed* those in both Norway and Germany by more than $20.[43] Long gone are the days when U.S. blue-collar workers were the best paid by far in the entire global system.
- Where the United States does lead these days are on economic indicators that nobody really wants. The U.S., for example, has "the dubious honor of being the only *no-vacation nation,* i.e., no legally required paid time off and of course some weeks fewer actual days off per year than our European counterparts enjoy."[44] In 2006, average annual hours worked in the United States numbered 1,804. In Germany, they were 1,436.[45] U.S. performance on maternity and paternity leave is equally unimpressive, and again an outlier. The United States is the only industrial economy that does not provide at least some vestigial paid maternity leave as of right.[46] This is not entirely surprising perhaps, given the weakness of American trade unions relative to their Western European equivalents; and it is surely significant in this regard that in 2010 the ultra-orthodox *Freedom House* was unable to list the United States as one of the 41 countries in which it could score workers' rights as "free." The United States was relegated in the Freedom House survey to the

> subordinate category of "mostly free," putting it—in the Americas—in the same group as the Dominican Republic and Costa Rica, and *behind* the Bahamas, Barbados, Belize, Canada, Chile, and Uruguay.[47]

Some of this under-performance may be temporary, but the narrowing of the gap between the United States and the best of the rest most definitely is not. The claims for the superiority of "cowboy capitalism" on productivity, innovation, job creation, and employment levels are excessive, and we have to recognize that. We have to recognize, too, the immense importance to long-term economic growth of adequate amounts of top quality *social capital*—labor skills, transport systems, functioning inner cities—and wonder if, by failing to chart U.S. performance on those, advocates of unregulated market capitalism fail to see weaknesses in the U.S. model, weaknesses linked to the difficulties that government agencies have here in correcting the imbalance between private affluence and public squalor that J. K. Galbraith first pointed to more than a generation ago.

European strengths[48]

Gaps are narrowed between economic leaders and their pack of followers both by leadership under-performance and by economic catch-up; and there is no doubt that both Japan and Western Europe did eventually catch up with U.S. levels of economic performance in the last decades of the twentieth century. They did so initially by adopting American-generated Fordist-type production systems, and more recently by generalizing through their economies new information technologies that were originally American in conception and design. That catch-up is largely complete, and has been achieved within social structures of accumulation (settlements between capital, labor, and the state), which are qualitatively different from that prevalent in the United States itself. It is one of the great ironies of the post-war global economy that the United States used its military and diplomatic power abroad to call into being at each edge of the Cold War stand-off (Germany in Europe, Japan in Asia) economies that were not simply replications of itself. Instead, the United States oversaw the creation of successful capitalist economies in which state direction (Japan) and extensive welfare provision (West Germany) played a major role in ways that they did not do here. In Japan and Germany, U.S. levels of social inequality were avoided. No social time bomb now ticks away in either of these leading economies, as arguably it does in the American inner city. Instead, economic growth in what are now the two most successful non-American capitalist economies was combined with (a) a stronger education and training system than we find here in the United States, (b) a stronger welfare safety net (even in Japan), and (c) the establishment of more long-term and committed relationships than in the United States between major industrial producers and the financial institutions on whose credit flows they depend.

Japan may indeed have overdone the latter—a lack of faith in over-leveraged Japanese financial institutions has blocked economic growth there since the early 1990s, redirecting Japanese investment funds into Wall Street throughout their "lost decade." It is a wasted decade that many commentators fear may now be in America's future, too. But Germany certainly did not settle into crony capitalism, and because it did not, performance there (and in the core EU economies linked into the German growth machine) now regularly matches or outperforms the U.S. on productivity, product innovation, and job creation, while providing levels of universal welfare provision for which America still strives.[49] Remarkably, rates of individual social mobility are now higher in many Western European welfare states than they are in the United States itself, as the social inequalities that have built up in "the land of the free" drain that freedom of much of its economic content for the more than one-third of U.S. families now living within one tranche of the poverty level.[50] And it is in Western Europe, after all, and not in the United States, that all citizens enjoy either entirely free or very inexpensive access to quality health care, but where health care spending as a percentage of GDP remains significantly *lower* than it is here in America. Even the much-derided UK—whose expenditure on health care is well under the Western European average—spends on providing health care to *all* its citizens that percentage of GDP which in the United States provides health care only to those aged 65 and over.

The coming of China

If that is not evidence enough of a slippage in U.S. economic competitiveness, then add to the mix the remarkable recent rise of China as a manufacturing power. China has now joined Germany and Japan as one of the global system's leading "surplus" economies—economies whose internal growth is fueled by the successful export of manufactured goods to other economies, including to major "debtor" ones like the United States and the UK. As we noted earlier, the Chinese trade surplus with the United States soared in the first decade of the new century—from $83 billion in 2000 to $268 billion in 2008 and $226 billion in 2009—as China passed Japan to become the second largest national economy in the global system and passed Germany to become the world's largest exporter of manufactured goods. China, not the United States, is now the largest consumer of automobiles and the largest consumer of energy. Its annual growth rate remains around 10 percent; and it is primarily Chinese funds that, flowing back into the U.S. financial system, sustain both public borrowing and private consumption in contemporary America. Economic power is visibly sliding east and sliding south. Since 2007, "the BRIC economies (Brazil, Russia, India, and China) have accounted for 45 percent of all global growth, compared with 24 percent between 2000 and 2006, or 16 percent in the 1990s."[51] They will likely account for a third of total global GDP by 2030, matching by then the output levels of both the United States and Western Europe. The United States began the post-war period as the capitalist system's major exporter and supplier of investment funds, as well as its major military protector. The military role remains and the dollar is still for the moment the global system's major reserve currency; but U.S. export domination has entirely vanished and it is American debt, not American largesse, which now helps to sustain global economic growth. A rakes progress of this sort is hardly the basis for a secure and prosperous future in a multi-polar world, which is why it needs to be recognized for what it is—unreformed, a recipe for future decline—and addressed as such.

3. Warning signs of long-term economic decline

At the risk of playing the Jeremiah, the current weaknesses of the U.S. economy are probably best understood as emblematic of deeper and longer-term problems that we would all do well to address. Hegemonic economic powers have slipped before. We have the shining example of the United Kingdom in front of us, and there are some alarming parallels with that decline in elements of the current U.S. economic configuration: three in particular.

Education and training

For more than a century, the United States was a world leader in mass education, sending children to school in unprecedented numbers on the premise that a functioning democracy required an informed citizenry. Long before other societies followed suit, the United States also developed an extensive system of college education—universities and community colleges, both. Even now, the quality of its best universities stands global comparison, and the proportion of high school students currently graduating with a high school diploma is at an all time high. But not much else in contemporary American education and training gives cause for congratulation. The rise in the proportion of Americans with a four-year college degree appears to have leveled off, so that suddenly "younger cohorts are now no better educated than the soon-to-retire baby boomers." Indeed, on one measure they may even be less well educated. "In 2006, Americans aged 55–59 collectively possessed *more* masters degrees, professional degrees and doctorates than Americans aged 30–34."[52] Moreover, American high school students consistently underperform in international test comparisons, relative to the best of the rest elsewhere. The United

States is never last—scoring better on math and science than many European countries, including Italy and Norway—but never matching performance scores from high school students in Singapore, Taiwan, South Korea, Hong Kong, and Japan.[53] Paradoxically, underperformance seems to grow the longer American students are in school;[54] what is even more alarming is that the international slippage seems to be intensifying over time.[55]

There would appear to be problems at both the high skill and low skill ends of the American education and training system. At the high end, the United States currently lacks a sufficient supply of indigenously generated high flyers in the key math, science, and engineering skills vital to industrial innovation. It is a gap the United States is currently attempting to fill by immigration. At the bottom end, education performance is highly and adversely affected by dimensions of class, gender, and ethnicity. Currently, 20 percent of African-American boys fail to graduate from high school. Some 30 percent of Latino children are equally unsuccessful. Overall, the dropout rate from American high schools for men aged 16–24 is currently running at more than 18 percent.[56] Post-school, U.S. industry increasingly lacks the incentive structure to regularly train and retrain its key personnel, particularly at the level of intermediate skills. Despite the existence of an extensive system of community colleges, apprenticeships are rare in the United States and in-company training remains patchy and non-standardized. Skill poaching, rather than skill growing, is the inevitable logic of a labor market in which employers are free to hire and fire, and employees are free to job hunt with impunity.

In the world of industrial training there are high skill trajectories and low skill ones.[57] The United States, like the United Kingdom, runs the risk of being trapped in a low-skills training equilibrium, at a time when levels of skill required in successful industrial economies are systematically on the rise. Overall, the United States is no longer the most highly educated society on earth—indeed it is slipping back all the time, as other economies and societies catch up. If David Mason is to be believed, "the educational system, once considered the world's best, now ranks near the bottom among developed nations, and a sizeable proportion of U.S. citizens is now functionally illiterate."[58] Certainly, the American labor force in general remains, by the best global standards, increasingly under-educated and under-trained; and many commentators have quite rightly pointed to the dangers which this loss of educational leadership poses to the long-term viability of the U.S. economy. Thomas Freedman has recently been among the most vocal, though by no means the only voice, in this particular chorus of doom. Arianna Huffington has become another.[59] As the conclusion of the latest report from the National Academy of Sciences put it, "In spite of the efforts of both those in government and the private sector, the outlook for America to compete for quality jobs has further deteriorated over the past five years."[60]

> Here is a little dose of reality about where we actually rank today . . . sixth in global innovation-based competitiveness, but 40th in rate of change over the last decade; 11th among industrialized nations in the fraction of 25- to 34-year-olds who have graduated from high school; 16th in college completion rate; 22nd in broadband Internet access; 24th in life expectancy at birth; 27th among developed nations in the proportion of college students receiving degrees in science or engineering; 48th in quality of K–12 math and science education; and 29th in the number of mobile phones per 100 people.[61]

Research and development

Perhaps slippage in world leadership on general educational performance would matter less if the U.S. record on research and development, product innovation, and market share remained stellar, as well: but again it does not. The warning signs are here, too, of catch-up by competitors, slippage by U.S.-based companies, and of innovation portfolios distorted by the heavy dependence of U.S. engineering firms on military contracts. The last of these we will discuss in the next section, on the costs of empire. What we need here is clarity on the weakening position of the United States as the world's generator of new ideas, new products, and new modes of producing them, and some sense of whether the United States is currently generating the volume and quality of skilled engineers and scientists that successful innovation in the immediate future will surely require. On this dimension of our collective future at least, the data is mixed but troubling, as the 2008 CRS Report to Congress on the state of the nation's scientific and engineering skill base made clear:

> The number of workers in science and engineering occupations grew significantly—7.7 times larger in 2000 than in 1950 . . . The STEM growth rate in the 1990s was a little more than three times that of the overall labor force. More recent data . . . shows a decline in STEM professionals as a percentage of the employed labor force beginning in 2000. On the other hand, BLS reports that science and engineering occupations are projected to grow by 21.4 percent from 2004 to 2014, compared to a growth of 13 percent in all occupations during the same period. It is anticipated that 65 percent of the growth in science and engineering occupations will be in computer-related occupations.[62]

This is presumably why both the Bush and Obama White Houses have put their support behind calls for more science and engineering teaching, and more federal funding for pure science. Well they might, because currently the United States ranks only sixth in the number of bachelor degrees awarded in engineering.[63] China now graduates almost four times as many engineers as we do, raising the distinct possibility that "the next generation of scientists in other countries may not speak English."[64] That would indeed be a sea change of considerable importance.

Already, the leadership role of American engineering is slipping away, as the percentage of GDP generated by manufacturing—currently down to 13.9 percent—now sits below that of every advanced industrial economy except France. As we noted earlier, China has recently (2009) replaced the United States as the world's largest manufacturing economy, and though much of that Chinese output was concentrated in low-tech production of the kind that is invariably globally mobile, much of it was not. By 2009, the United States was the world leader in only five product areas—computer hardware, software, biotechnology, aerospace, and entertainment—and many U.S.-based and owned technology companies had relocated some or all of their production capacity abroad. "In 2000, 40 percent of the world's telecom equipment was produced in America. [By 2006] that share [was] 21 percent and falling."[65] By 2002, indeed, U.S. trade in advanced technology products had gone into sustained deficit—exports earning less than imports cost by $16.6 billion; by 2006 that deficit was $381 billion[66]—with wider consequences of the kind noted by Richard Elkus:

> In large part because of early losses in consumer electronics, the United States is suffering from a competitive disadvantage in the automotive industry and losing ground in semiconductor fabrication . . . the United States is rapidly and unwittingly losing its competitive position in the world of information and image processing . . . areas in image processing such as displays, recorders, cameras, and cell phones, which in one form or another affect the entire U.S. communication industry, are being usurped by Asia. Software, which is enabled by these electronic platforms, will ultimately be at risk as well . . . the fundamental fact is that information technology and its resulting products are prerequisites for America's competitive industrial base. Lacking those prerequisites, the United States will be forced to depend on its competition for much of the strategic infrastructure essential for advancement . . . under those circumstances, the ability of America to control its economic and political future will certainly be diminished as U.S. economic power quietly passes to those who produce and own the resources America needs most.[67]

Outsourcing has already partially denuded the U.S. industrial landscape of industries as vital to daily life as textiles and furniture, and America has yet to find sufficiently strong equivalents to break the cycle of persistent trade deficits that have been with us since 1975. The large-scale factory-based semi-automated production systems of the first half of the post-war period—the period when Detroit was at its peak and the U.S. car industry was without serious internal or foreign competition—have long gone: replaced in dominance by Japanese style *just-in-time* production systems in many industries and by Italian-style *small batch* production in others. Michael Porter, among others, has pointed to serious long-term weaknesses in the U.S. industrial portfolio: too much de-industrialization, too slow a rate of productivity growth, too heavy a dependence on fickle foreign-based sources of investment funds, even too limited a volume of internal demand as U.S. wage rates stagnate. Weaknesses like that help to explain the recent slippage in the position of the United States in the Global Competitiveness Index published by the World Economic Forum: first in 2008–2009 and second in 2009–2010, but down to fourth in 2010–2011 behind Switzerland, Sweden, and Singapore.[68]

Impatient capital

One of the other weaknesses of the "Anglo-Saxon model" of capitalism often cited by its critics is the *impatience* of its capital–providers and the associated *short-termism* of even its industrial management.[69] Raising capital publicly on stock markets rather than privately through banks, U.S. industry traditionally had greater access to investment funds, particularly when economic difficulties elsewhere were (as in the 1990s) bringing huge flows of foreign investment directly into Wall Street. But the price to be paid for that greater access was greater vulnerability to loss of investor confidence, hostile takeovers, and managerial shakeouts, all of which predisposed American industrial and financial managers to judge their success by the level of their next quarterly dividend payout. The case made, even in the decades of U.S. economic superiority, was that this disadvantaged long-term investment programs and cost American companies market share, when competing with companies whose close relationship with a supporting banking system enabled their managers to take the longer view. The United States was once the heartland of what Lenin long ago called *Imperialism*—the economy where banks and large corporations rose and fell together. In the age of the robber barons, American companies grew large rapidly because American financial institutions bankrolled them; but their very success turned them into global players, American banks into global conduits, and the American state into the global policeman. American companies now face a globally active U.S. financial system, one where banks and other financial institutions increasingly make their money on a global, not a national, playing field. And as capital goes offshore—as the history of both the UK and Japan demonstrates—a gap necessarily opens up between "capital" and "industry." American capital may prosper and its financiers flourish: but at the cost of seriously de-industrializing the home economy on which they now no longer so heavily rely.[70]

The result is a society and economy whose living standards have recently come to depend disproportionately on the willingness of *overseas* investors and savers to sustain the American way of life. Dependence on foreign largesse is neither a sign of strength nor, indeed, a guarantee of stability. Rather, as David Mason correctly has it, "increasingly, foreigners have been subsidizing the American binge, but that certainly cannot continue, just as large-scale deficit spending cannot continue forever." [71]A U.S. financial system that was once a guarantor of American industrial supremacy has now turned itself into a/the major source of U.S. (and indeed global) financial insecurity. American financial institutions are riding high, but the U.S. economy as a whole is riding low. The politics of the casino have taken over from the politics of the factory. An economy dominant when U.S. factories were strong has now come under challenge from factories strong elsewhere because U.S. finance and consumption helps makes them profitable at the expense of their U.S. equivalents. We are increasingly locking ourselves into a self-sustaining downward spiral from which escape is vital: that spiral in which capital export by U.S.-based financial institutions sustains foreign competitors whose capture of market share comes at the expense of U.S. manufacturing firms who are then left even weaker than before in the competition for the next round of capital injection. John Gray put it this way:

> In a number of respects the U.S. now resembles an emerging country more than the advanced economy it was some decades ago. Its industrial base is largely gone, sold off or off-shored, and its public infrastructure is in visible disrepair. Because of the severity of the real estate collapse, parts of its housing stock are being abandoned and once-thriving neighborhoods are now slums . . . The bail-out of the banks . . . is a prime example of the crony capitalism against which the U.S. ceaselessly railed in emerging markets.[72]

If that seems overdrawn, note this: the decision taken at the global economic summit in Pittsburgh in September 2009 to take responsibility for the collective management of the global economy away from the G-7 and give it to the larger G-20. Time was (in 1944, for example) when the world came to America to design international economic architecture that would enshrine American global leadership. Not any more: now the world came to America to enshrine the shift of world economic power from the North to the South, and even quietly to discuss ways of reducing global dependence on the dollar as the international medium of exchange. U.S. global economic power has not gone away: but it is now power exercised in a multi-polar world, a pluralism brought more quickly into existence than might otherwise have been the case by the rapid development of the U.S. trade deficit with China and by the devastating global impact of a financial meltdown caused by under-regulated financial institutions based on Wall Street. Well might Jeffrey Sachs write in *The Financial Times* that "the G-20s true significance is not the passing of the baton from the G-7/G-8 but from the G-1."[73]

4. The consequences of imperial over-reach

The notion that the post-war United States has been a reluctant and ultimately benign imperial power would be laughable, were it not so dangerous. The notion is *laughable*: U.S. expansion was deliberate. It was planned. It was extensive and it was often covert. And the notion is *dangerous*, (a) because it closes off any capacity fully to understand the resulting anti-Americanism; (b) because it treats neo-con excesses as exactly that—deviations from a more benign norm—when in truth they are nothing of the kind; and (c) because it understates the enormous costs of empire which we regularly and currently bear. As Andrew Bacevich put it so well, when responding to the Obama description of the U.S.'s global role quoted earlier: "[I]t is such a sanitized view of our history in the past five or six decades that it shouldn't pass the laugh test. Yet . . . it's an excellent example of the way political leaders perpetuate the credo: Obama putting his stamp of approval on an image of our role in the world that everybody, at least since Franklin Roosevelt, has embraced."[74] It is a credo from which we need sharply to break.

A deliberate empire

The United States may not colonize directly in the manner of nineteenth-century European powers, but, like them, its government regularly intervenes to reshape other people's political furniture. The United States is an imperial power. It has a long record of supporting military dictatorships, even of initiating them: as in Iran in 1953. Guatemala (1954), Brazil (1964), Indonesia (1965), Chile (1973) . . . the list is long, as is the U.S. record in supporting anti-democratic forces if American regional interests are thought to be at stake. The Contras in Nicaragua were simply one in a long line of anti-democratic forces supported covertly by CIA operatives funded without public Congressional approval. The United States has long practiced what Chalmers Johnson rightly called "stealth imperialism." The U.S. may not seize territory, but it does build military bases. In fact, it builds and maintains lots of them: at least 865 of them in 2008, distributed globally in more than 40 countries, at an estimated cost to the American taxpayer of $102 billion a year.[75] As world players, U.S. political leaders invariably laud human rights and claim no territorial ambitions, but in practice they often sustain dictatorships whenever regional interests are at stake, and tolerate human rights abuses in their allies which they decry in their opponents. The rhetoric of American freedom is fine, but in the sphere of foreign affairs it is so often hollow—as indeed so much of it was as the invasion of Iraq loomed. The Bush administration decried weapons of mass destruction and the spread of lethal arms; but the United States remained the world's largest exporter of the very non-nuclear military hardware against whose dispersal it claimed to be fighting. Shades of 1984.

A military-industrial complex

The United States exports arms because this country has a very extensive engineering industry geared to arms production—arms the United States needs for its own global role and arms its political leaders sell or give to overseas allies who reinforce that role.[76] Whole local and regional economies within the United States rely on little else: there is even a literature presenting the United States now as in essence a garrison economy, dependent for job creation on the proliferation of arms to be sold abroad and prisons to be maintained at home.[77] Certainly, the United States has an extensive military, a Pentagon prepared to orchestrate arms production and sales, and a secret state apparatus (16 national security agencies at least), all geared to national defense and the pursuit of U.S. overseas objectives. A kind of *military Keynesianism* operates at the very heart of U.S. public policy—heavy procurement programs and extensive overseas aids packages that have to be paid for, normally regardless of the state of the rest of the public finances. That military expenditure has at times strengthened the civilian economy that runs alongside it—NASA's innovative moves in the 1960s, for example, generated computer technology that spun off into greater labor productivity across the economy as a whole.[78] But, more normally, as now, the growth of a large military industrial complex distorts and weakens civilian economic competitiveness: absorbing the energies of America's best scientists and engineers, softening the competitiveness of the engineering sector as a whole by the scale of the soft military contracts on which engineering firms can draw, and absorbing tax dollars that could have been spent developing the economy's wider social infrastructure.

The costs of empire

Diminishing international competitiveness is not the only cost of empire, however, though it is a major one. There are other serious costs to empire, too. At their most visible, these are costs borne by the military themselves, sadly best measured by the number of body bags returning to these shores and by the number of military families devastated by loss or debilitating injury. The less visible costs of empire are equally potent and of more general impact. Imperial regimes find their political leaderships preoccupied with global matters, lacking adequate concentration and focus on the weakening of the domestic economy on which those leaderships ultimately depend. Too often indeed, in the U.S. case, the strengthening of competitive economies, the export of American capital and know-how, and the inflation of the exchange rate of the dollar all became central elements of post-war foreign policy, even though each of them over time inevitably weakened the competitive position of the overall American economy. Even the simple cost of all the foreign bases—that $102 billion a year figure mentioned earlier[79]—eats away at the capacity of U.S. governments to sustain welfare spending at home and a strong currency abroad, and, of course, the economic cost of major regional wars (from Korea and Vietnam to Iraq and Afghanistan) has proved particularly destructive of U.S. financial strength and American domestic consumption. Introducing his *"The War is Making You Poor" Act* in 2010, Representative Alan Grayson claimed that the $159 billion earmarked for "emergency wars" by the Obama administration—if not spent—would leave every American earning up to $35,000 a year free of income tax.[80] We might question the math, but not the point: wars cost money as well as lives—and the United States is currently fighting more of them than any other country on earth.[81]

There are also cultural costs inevitably linked to the creation of empires: particularly the generation of a popular culture within the imperial center that treats foreign peoples as inherently inferior, as legitimately open to manipulation by imperial proconsuls, and as inexplicably ungrateful for the advantages of imperial (in this case, American) leadership. Domestic parochialism, racism, xenophobia, and general cultural insensitivity are all endemic to the imperial mission, as the long history of British colonialism so visibly demonstrates. Endemic, too—abroad—is resistance to the presence of foreign troops, local outrage at the inevitable collateral damage of military interventions, and deepening anti-Americanism. In the U.S. case, that domestic cultural insensitivity is of very long standing, and predates the move from continental expansion to global dominance. The United States, after all, has long referred to itself as *America* as though neither Canada nor South America actually existed. But exist they do, and they—like other recipients of unwanted American interference in their politics—are often extremely resentful of American power.[82] *Blowback* is the ultimate price imperial powers always pay for the exercise of their global reach, and 9/11 must stand as the starkest and most dramatic example in our lifetime of that inherent feature of imperial dominance. Blowback does not excuse the brutality of that day but it does help to explain its occurrence.

The danger of "bread and circuses"

Chalmers Johnson recently counted the number of large and medium-sized overseas U.S. military bases in 2005, and found there to be 38—a number "almost exactly equal [to] Britain's thirty-six naval bases and army garrisons at its imperial zenith in 1898" or to the 37 major bases used to police the Roman empire at its zenith in 117 .D;[83] we all know what happened to those empires. Of course, the numbers may be coincidental and the comparison specious, but they are suggestive of the possibilities of looming imperial decline. The National Intelligence Council's global trends report—prepared as normal for an incoming administration—made news late in 2008 by reversing its 2004 projection. In 2004, the NIC had told the returning Bush administration to expect "continued U.S. dominance" as late as 2025. Four years later, it told the incoming Obama administration something entirely different: that by 2025 "the United

States will remain the single most powerful country but will be less dominant," that by then "shrinking economic and military capabilities may force the United States into a difficult set of tradeoffs between domestic versus foreign policy priorities."[84] Earlier imperial powers had reached such a moment: the Roman Empire in the fourth century, the British in the twentieth, and in each case, the slowness of their governing classes to recognize the realities of decline only brought the decline on still faster. We have the benefit of hindsight to guide us—the ability to learn from their errors—but we can do so only if we first recognize the basic similarities of our conditions.[85]

But self-awareness is rarely a dominant reality in moments of imperial decline. It certainly was not in Rome, where the fragility of the imperial order was hidden from the general Roman citizenry by the state-orchestrated outlandish provision of bread and circuses; and it might not be again in contemporary America, sealed as so many of us are from the reality of a weakening economy and a diminishing culture by the equally outlandish if privately orchestrated provision of *American Idol* and the National Football League. Policy-making now on matters of the gravest public importance has to operate against the backcloth of a huge entertainment industry whose presence in the daily lives of each and every one of us is made ever more intrusive by the development of increasingly sophisticated means of mass and personal communication. We have the technology to be well informed as never before, but it is a technology heavily clogged with material that blocks that information flow. It is possible in contemporary America to live in a completely noisy world full of rock stars, sports idols, and ranting shock jocks—a world from which even the broad outlines of a calm and rational discussion of key choices in national policy can be entirely excluded—and many of us understandably do chose to live in such a noisy silence.[86] At the very time when the Republic needs as informed and engaged a citizenry as it can generate, a potent mixture of political and religious conservatism, mind-numbing reality television, and ubiquitous American sporting moments is combining to close down the democratic political space for more and more Americans. "Turn off the television," was President Obama's advice in 2009 to parents wanting to see their children flourish at school. "Turn off the sports channel," might well be the equivalent mantra in 2010 and beyond to citizens keen to see their economy and society flourish globally again.

5. The looming time-bomb

If all that has been written earlier in this chapter is true, then—as David Mason has written—"the United States is headed for hard times and major adjustments."[87] Our imperial endeavors alone, if Chalmers Johnson is right, "will, sooner or later, condemn the United States to a devastating trio of consequences: imperial overstretch, perpetual war, and insolvency."[88] And even if that fear is overblown—and probably it is not—there is certainly trouble looming at home, trouble for which we all need to be prepared, and trouble that we would do well to avert by systematic and extensive social reform before it occurs.[89] For if the challenges abroad are linked to empire, at home they are linked to poverty.

Per capita income in the United States remains high. We are still a rich society. We are currently one of the ten or 12 richest in comparative terms, though the United States is no longer in per capita terms the richest—that title has recently moved to Europe (to Luxembourg, Liechtenstein, Monaco, or Norway, depending on who is doing the counting). But the title we do hold is the *inequality* one. The United States remains unique among developed societies in combining its huge riches with significant pockets of the desperately poor. The United States currently "has both the highest level of inequality and the highest level of poverty (including child poverty) of its peers. In other words, much less of the vast income of the United States is reaching the lower end of the income distribution"[90] than is normal in other advanced industrial economies, including even in the UK. Poverty levels in the United States in 2009 returned to those last seen in 1994. Some 14.3 percent of all Americans—one American in seven—lived that year on incomes below the official poverty level.[91] That was 4 million more Americans in poverty than had been there 12 months before, a poverty that remained ethnically uneven. One white American in ten knew poverty in 2009, one African-American in four, a quarter of Hispanic America, and one Asian-American in eight. It was the American poor, and the near-poor—some 51 million in total –who also went through part or all of 2009 without any form of health care coverage. Health care coverage may now be poised to change—if the *Affordable Care Act* survives its challenge in the courts and the Congress—but the poverty that made those health care changes necessary is not going away any time soon. Nor are we likely easily to lose the urban ghettos in which so much of that poverty is currently so heavily concentrated.

If that were not enough to give us cause for alarm, we must remember that the American middle class is not currently in great shape, either. The years between 2000 and 2009 were a "lost decade for family income" in the United States, the "worst for American families in at least half a century" as "the inflation adjusted income of the median household . . . *fell* 4.8 percent"[92] in just nine years. In December 2009, one in five Americans was either "unemployed, underemployed or just plain out of work. One in nine families [couldn't] make the minimum payment on their credit cards. One in eight mortgages [was] in default or foreclosure. One in eight Americans [was] on food stamps. More than 120,000 families [were] filing for bankruptcy each month [and] the economic crisis [had] wiped more than $5 trillion from pensions and savings." Little wonder, then, that Elizabeth Warren could contemplate an "America without a middle class,"[93] a society polarized between the super-rich and the poor; or that Arianna Huffington should chose to describe the contemporary United States as *Third World America*. "I deliberately chose a title that is very jarring," she said, "because I really believe that we are on this trajectory, where the middle class is crumbling."[94] She has a point, for as she spoke, "one out of every six Americans [were] in government anti-poverty programs. More than 50 million [were] on Medicaid. Forty million receive[d] food stamps, and 10 million receive[d] unemployment benefit."[95] That is hardly a stellar economic performance.

Then there is, as there always is in the United States, the hidden hand of racism. The level of black unemployment is double that of white. One young African-American male in nine is currently in jail. African-Americans are concentrated in urban areas from which white flight has sucked tax revenues, jobs, and decent public infrastructure; and if you are black and male, you have a four times better chance of being executed by the state for crimes that, if you were white, would leave your life intact. Black or white, Latino or Asian, Americans now work in an economy whose long hours, low pay, and an inadequate health care system leave them disproportionately vulnerable to bankruptcy if sick, poverty if unemployed, and stressed if at work.[96] The American dream is in reality an illusion for more and more Americans, replaced for so many by what Jeremy Rifkin called "the American daydream . . . substitutes—legal gambling, celebrity television and the like—grounded in fantasy and delusion."[97] There are now two very different Americas—one in the suburbs and one in the cities. Those two Americas met briefly in riots in the hot summers of the late 1960s. With inequality now more severe than in the 1960s, how long will it be before they meet in similar conditions again?

Fortunately, we don't need to wait for urban rioting to realize that America is rapidly coming to the end of a particular road.[98] As we noted in Chapter 2, twice now in the post-war period the United States has seen sustained prosperity. Between 1948 and 1973, it was a prosperity based on a strong manufacturing performance and on high levels of domestic consumer demand rooted in rising industrial wages. Between 1991 and 2008, by contrast, enhanced consumption was based on stagnant wages and rising income inequality, an extension of the hours worked by the typical family, a stock market bubble for the wealthy and, for the rest of us, by the maxing out of our credit cards. In the first of those periods of growth, people spent the wages they had already earned. In the second, they spent income they hoped they would earn in the future. For 30 years, conservatives have been preaching at us the virtues of unregulated markets, the dangers of trade unionism, and the self-fulfilling nature of anti-poverty programs. But by surrendering the war on poverty, they allowed poverty to flourish and debt to grow. The unregulated markets for which they campaigned culminated not in sustained growth but in a global recession that brought involuntary unemployment to at least 50 million people world wide. Senior bankers are already back to paying themselves bonuses, as though they bore no responsibility for the parlous economy in which the rest of us struggle to survive, and as though the crisis which they generated has now passed. But it has not passed, and they (and their conservative acolytes) have to be particularly foolish, or particularly selfish, to tell us again that we should solve the problems of the second growth period in which they alone flourished by replicating them in a third.

The task before us now is not to build another brief period of credit-based consumption. Sand is not a strong foundation on which to build a house. Our task now is to find a way back to the conditions of prosperity characteristic of the first period of post-war economic growth. Simply going back to the 1950s settlement is neither possible nor desirable. We face a new international division of labor, and we also face a domestic society that is no longer as tolerant as was that in the 1950s of racism and patriarchy. Our task, rather, is to find a way forward that, amid these new global and domestic conditions, can reproduce the manufacturing strength and rising wages of the "golden age" of American capitalism. We will not do that successfully without a root-and-branch transformation of the imperial and financial America that has brought us to our contemporary impasse. The time for tinkering is over. As former President Bush put it so elegantly in the middle of the financial crisis, "this sucker could go down."[99] Yes, it could, and sadly it might yet, which is why the time for fundamental reform is well and truly upon us. The capacity and direction of reform in the United States is, unavoidably, the overarching question of the age.

CHAPTER 6

The Politics of Winning

The intensity and partisan bitterness of day-to-day politics in the contemporary United States mask one underlying area of general agreement on which we would all do well to dwell. Indeed, contemporary politics is as bitterly divided as it is only because of this one thing on which so many politically active Americans agree. What they agree on is this: that the future of this country will be a bleak one if the political system fails to deliver a fundamental change of direction. What they disagree about, of course, is the new direction that is required.

This fundamental disagreement on direction makes the perennial pursuit of bipartisanship ultimately hopeless, because though our political leaders may agree on the details of certain policies—on which bipartisanship then becomes a possibility—there can be no agreement across the aisle on the overall line of march. In fact, even bipartisanship on the detail of agreed policies can be hard to reach because of the underlying relationship between those details and the longer-term trend, and because any agreement on detail might strengthen electoral support for the other party—the one taking the country off in what its opponents feel strongly to be completely the wrong direction. The Republican minorities in the Senate, for example, delayed aid to small businesses in the Fall of 2010, not because they opposed aid to small business *per se*—of course not—but because they opposed increasing the federal deficit without compensating cuts elsewhere, and because for short-term electoral reasons they were determined to deny the Obama administration the legitimacy of success on even this modest issue.

Politics in the contemporary United States is currently bitter and partisan because different American futures are believed to be at stake. The way to win the progressive argument is not to deny that fact. It is to make a more powerful case than the conservative one for the future we think worth winning.

The scale of the task before us

To win that argument, it is first necessary to clarify the depth of the problem before us. If the material in the early chapters is accurate, the main problems we face are deep and wide. They are embedded in core economic and social institutions and processes, such that their resolution requires a major resetting of both. That resetting is difficult partly because of its scale, and partly because of the defensive interests that can and will be mobilized against any serious program of reform. The United States has big problems that require strong political leadership, and yet currently possesses a political system so dysfunctional as to make that leadership almost impossible. At the end of this chapter, we will need to consider how best to break the political logjam that is currently Washington, DC. But first we need a clear sense of the interests faced and the institutions in need of change; and, in the case of the U.S. economy, that requires that we take a very close look at the structural underpinnings of the financial crisis whose legacies remain so dominant around us.

1. Mighty finance

We are all aware, I am sure, that the Dodd–Frank financial reform legislation is less than perfect, and that in the fight over the detail of the new regulatory codes, lobby activity financed by major banks and other Wall Street institutions will play a critical role. So we can anticipate that any shortfalls in the potency of those new rules will partly be caused by the arrogance, influence, and selfishness of key figures on Wall Street, who will no doubt vigorously defend their turf and their privileges, with little regard for a wider public interest. They will buy influence and they will buy politicians as they always have, so that reforming America's leading financial institutions will remain an uphill task even after all the damage that their earlier recklessness caused. But if lobby activity was all that was at play here, a straightforward if politically difficult solution would be immediately to hand: we would simply need new and more restrictive rules on lobbying activity and political finance of the kind commonplace in other industrial democracies—rules that would take the money out of politics. That is a worthy goal anyway, but to focus on it alone would be to miss the deeper point: that the power of money in American politics is itself a reflection of the structural position of financial institutions in the U.S. economy and political system. Pulling the Masters of the Universe to heel requires first that we cut them down to size.

We must chart our way forward recognizing that although the immediate origins of this particular credit crisis lie in the specificities of the U.S. housing market and in the particular lack of transparency associated with securitization, the vulnerability of the global system to crises of this kind does not. The vulnerability is systemic and potentially irremovable. Depending on which particular body of radical scholarship you follow, the dominant role of uncontrollable finance can be variously explained as a response to overproduction and under-consumption in the age of monopoly capitalism,[1] to the dwindling profitability of investments in manufacturing plant or equipment over time,[2] or to unavoidable contradictions in the maintenance of American global dominance;[3] but whatever its origins, excessive "financialization" has to be understood as structural rather than accidental, and as such, as extraordinarily difficult to reverse. Hegemonic capitalist economies inevitably become the global banker. The dwindling profitability endemic to mature capitalisms necessarily stimulates speculative activity. On the most orthodox of Marxist readings of the financial crisis, public policy of any kind is at best a temporary palliative and more likely an irrelevance. "Stuff happens," as the Bush people used to say: it has happened before and, so long as capitalism remains, it will happen again.

Certainly the United States, like the UK, suffers from what Martin Wolf called the "strategic nightmare: it has a strong comparative advantage in the world's most irresponsible industry."[4] The great curse of our present condition is that over time, the United States—like the UK—has come to be overly dependent on the international competitive strength of its financial institutions. The figures on financial dominance in this economy are striking and politically important. In 2002, the financial sector generated 41 percent of all corporate profits in the American economy—41 percent, when from 1973 to 1985 the percentage had never exceeded 16 percent—and average pay in the sector, pretty close to industry-wide norms as late as 1982, was by 2007 running at 181 percent of the average for all U.S. industries. In parallel, by 2008, U.S. private indebtedness was running at 295 percent of GDP. In 1976, that figure had been 112 percent.[5] The story told by the data is clear. The U.S. is finance heavy—its financial institutions play a bigger role in the domestic economy than in any leading industrial economy other than the UK—leaving the rest of us disproportionately vulnerable to finance's rise and fall. Addressing that weight, and not just the lobbying generated to protect it, needs, therefore, to be a central element in any program of progressive reform worthy of the name.

In the world of political economy, however, things can only be heavy if other things are light; and finance is heavy in the U.S. economy because of two linked and parallel "lightnesses" elsewhere in the economic order: with the strengthening of which progressive policy needs also to be concerned.

2. The lightness of labor

Capital in general is heavy economically and politically in the United States because organized labor is not. The stagnant real wages experienced by the majority of working Americans since the end of the Vietnam War, and the rising inequalities in income and wealth associated with that stagnation, speak to that labor weakness. A successful employers' offensive against labor unions and worker rights effectively put financial institutions, and not manufacturing products and wages, at the heart of the second great post-war wave of U.S. economic growth now so firmly behind us. As we saw earlier, unlike the first wave of post-war U.S. economic growth (1948–1973) that had been built on rising wages for unionized workers and on their purchase of U.S.-made manufactured goods, this second wave (1992–2008) rested on borrowing and debt. The incomes of the wealthy minority, deposited in U.S. financial institutions for safe keeping and growth, were leveraged by those institutions to create credit for ordinary U.S. consumers—consumers who borrowed heavily to maintain living standards that could no longer be enhanced simply by working longer hours and by sending all adult members of the family out to paid work (though both those things also occurred). As Leo Panitch and Martijn Konings correctly put it:

> constrained in what they could get from their labor after the defeats suffered by the trade union movement in the 1970s and 1980s, U.S. workers were drawn into the logic of asset inflation in the age of neoliberal finance not only through the institutional investment of their pensions, but also via their one major asset: the family home . . . The era of neo-liberalism did not bring about an absolute deterioration of living standards for most American working families: high levels of consumption were sustained by the accumulation of household debt and the intensification of labor—more family members working longer hours, under harsher conditions, subject to the discipline of having to meet debt payments.[6]

In the years of Clinton and Bush II, U.S. consumers had a last long fling—as consumers of last resort for domestically based service providers and increasingly also for foreign-based manufacturing firms—but the fling was in reality a rake's progress. It was a fling sustained only at the cost of the exorbitant interest rates and excessive bank fees that fed into the great bonuses enjoyed by the Wall Street elite. Over more than two decades, American workers borrowed incomes they had not yet earned, and paid bankers big fees for the privilege. However we go forward in both economy and society in the next decades, we cannot and must not go forward on that basis again.

3. Deindustrialization and the weakness of industrial capital

Finance institutions enjoyed those bonuses as manufacturing firms did not because of a second source of "heaviness" for finance in the U.S. economic model. With the deregulation of capital flows in the 1980s, and the entry into the global labor force of vast new numbers of workers for hire as the Cold War divide fell (in Russia) or weakened (in China), the U.S. economy as a whole experienced, as we saw in more detail in earlier chapters, "negative deindustrialization." The economy experienced deindustrialization—manufacturing industry shrank as a proportion of GDP and as a source of domestic employment—and the deindustrialization was negative, in that much of that shrinkage was the consequence of an increasing inability to compete effectively in both overseas and domestic markets with foreign firms equipped with the latest technology and a seemingly unending supply of both skilled and unskilled labor paid significantly less than their U.S. counterparts. The result was the rapid emergence over the Clinton and Bush II years of entrenched global imbalances: imbalances between economies in which saving exceeded consumption and exports exceeded imports, and economies in which exactly the reverse was the case. Financial institutions acted as the critical intermediary of those global imbalances—the privileged few taking again huge fees and bonuses in the process—but the feast at which they presided was one during which the U.S. economy slipped from its immediate post-war pre-eminence as the world's leading lender to its current position as its leading borrower.

This slippage was not simply accidental. It was the consequence of policy—the result of the prolonged pursuit by recent presidents of both parties of a particular economic strategy. Clyde Prestowitz's review of the pattern of industrial subsidies in post-war America led him to this judgment on the nature of that strategy:

> It is to over-consume, and to promote weapons production, financial services, construction, medical research and services, agriculture, and oil and gas consumption and production. Further, it is both to offshore production and provision of all tradable manufacturing and services as well as, increasingly, high-technology R&D, and to expand the domestic retail, food service, and technical medical services industries. At the macro level, the strategy is to run up massive debt and borrow as much and as long as possible.[7]

Notice that last dimension of recent economic strategy—debt. The structural basis of our present economic impasse is debt at two key levels: *personal debt,* particularly mortgage and credit card debt; and *international debt*, an American inability to pay its way in the world. The immediate crisis has added a third kind of debt, *public debt*, as governments everywhere have spent lavishly to keep employment levels up and banks in business; and right-wing critics do have a point. Financing that third debt will be problematic, the longer it persists: though if it works, the resulting private sector growth should provide the tax revenues eventually to bring it down. But ending fiscal largesse, whether easy to finance or not, will not of itself help to solve either of the other structural underpinnings of the 2008 financial meltdown. There is a personal and an international debt issue in U.S. economic and social policy that remains unresolved, and is the great ticking time bomb of the age.[8]

What that scale tells us

The scale of our current problems tells us certain things. It tells us that the next period of U.S. economic growth will have to be based on an entirely different set of internal and global conditions. It tells us that the creation of those new conditions is not entirely within our control; and it tells us that the conditions that are within our control will need to be fundamentally transformed.

1. No going back

What is particularly clear is that business as usual will not solve economic and social problems of the scale now before us. There is no possibility, or desirability, of constructing another brief period of recovery on the same basis as the last one. It is not possible—the unending faith in the availability of credit, and the associated willingness to stack up higher and higher levels of personal debt, has been entirely shaken by the speed and severity of the recession. American consumers will not go that route again—nor should they. If history is any guide, it is that generalized prosperity can only be rooted in rising productivity and a fair distribution of the resulting growth in goods and services. Without significant political intervention to put the U.S. economy back on to that more stable track, the danger of a Japanese-style lost decade looms before us. Lack of confidence (in banks by companies and companies by banks—and by both in relation to consumer demand) will keep credit distribution low and investment down. The resulting stagnation in demand will become self-reinforcing: with companies not hiring, unemployment not falling, demand kept low by the fear of job loss, houses foreclosed for the want of salary. If a new basis of recovery is not *constructed*, the shadow of the old one will hang over all of us for a generation. The economy might slowly limp back to strength and Wall Street flourish again, but generalized living standards will not rise with them. As Robert Reich put it, "the question, then, is how to move from a vicious cycle to a virtuous one—how to restore the widespread prosperity needed for growth, and how to get the growth necessary for widespread prosperity." His answer seems particularly sound: "a fundamentally new economy is required—the next stage of capitalism." "There are essentially two paths from here," he said, and "only one of them will get us to where we want to be."[9]

2. External constraints

From an immediate policy point of view, the necessary construction of a new basis for generalized recovery will be hamstrung by two, not just one, feature of the old order now in disarray around us. It will be hamstrung internally by special interests and by Republican ideological idiocy—their constant chorus of *leave it to the market*, as though the market was not the thing that brought us to the impasse in the first place. It will be hamstrung externally by the global imbalances that grew up within it between economies that successfully exported and those that survived by debt-financed imports. "The globalization of the Clinton–Bush era not only lacked safeguards for labor but rested on two mutually reinforcing flawed models of growth: debt-financed consumption in the United States and other Anglo-Saxon economies, and over-saving and under-consumption in the production-oriented export economies of Asia."[10] For that reason, any return to rapid global economic growth will require new sources of demand to replace American consumers without credit or confidence. It will require an internal turn of focus by leading exporting economies—a move that will be difficult enough to do for a German economy at the prosperous heart of the European Union, and one that will be immensely more difficult for developing economies whose comparative advantage in the old order lay in their large flows of cheap labor. They made competitively priced goods but could not sell them to the workers who produced them: at least they could not sell enough. That now needs to change. The rise of a powerful Indian, Brazilian, and, crucially, Chinese middle class is not something that Washington can order, though it is something that Washington requires—and quickly.[11] Export economies facing stagnant American markets need it, too—it is in the interests of governing circles in America's key competitors, as well as here at home—but whether politically it can be achieved remains an open question. The need is economic, but the blockage could be political. How the Chinese Communist

Party creates a prosperous internal market without losing its monopoly of political power is the great unanswered question facing progressive politicians everywhere in the wake of the 2008 financial tsunami.

3. Internal reform

It is not, however, the only question. The other one—the one over which Americans have almost total control, no matter what the Chinese do—is how to effect a profound internal realignment of domestic policy and global stance. Regardless of the Chinese and their condition, our condition is far from ideal. We are overstretched abroad, no longer able fully to pay our way in the world. We are de-industrialized at home, too dependent for our economic growth on a financial sector hard to regulate and a service sector low on labor productivity. Our general living standards depend too heavily on the deployment of personal and governmental debt; and too many of us live in, or on the edge of, debilitating poverty. Putting all that to rights will require more than simply "leaving it to the market," as Republicans would have us do. No matter what they claim, unregulated markets lock economies onto an existing growth path. They do not enable an economy to move from one growth path to another, as we need now to do. Moving from a low to a high growth path will require a profound change in the totality of U.S. public policy: and, unfortunately (given how hard that will be), nothing short of such a move will ultimately suffice. As Joseph Stiglitz put it, the resetting of the U.S. economy "will take resources, and it will take public spending. Resources will have to move from some sectors that are too large (like finance and real estate) and some sectors that are too weak (manufacturing) to others that have better prospects for sustainable growth."[12] What progressive forces must, therefore, now put on the U.S. political agenda is the issue of complete *rupture*—the design of a road map to a totally new economic and social settlement reflective of the novel internal and global conditions of a new century.

At the very least, a permanently successful regeneration of prosperity at home will require three fundamental changes. It will require a different global role for the United States (effectively, an incremental retreat from empire), an extensive reindustrialization of America's industrial core, and a complete reversal of the drift towards social inequality and ethnic separation characteristic of the post–Reagan years. Each of those changes will be enormously difficult to deliver politically, but each is essential and time is no longer on our side. Courage, not caution, therefore, needs to be the watchword of the hour, because, as Thomas Friedman rightly put it: "We simply do not have another presidency to waste. There are no more fat years to eat through. If Obama fails, we all fail."[13]

Getting from here to there

Getting into our contemporary mess took effort enough. Getting out of it is going to take even more. But there is a way. It is perhaps best illustrated by visualizing the ripples caused when a pebble is dropped in a pond. Whenever that pebble is dropped, the ripples race out from the point at which the pebble entered the water to finish their journey away in the distance at the pond's edge. So it must also be with progressive public policy. There are policy changes that must and can be made here and now, policies whose effects will be visible and immediate—policies close to the pebble, as it were. There are other policy changes that can and must be made, policies whose effects will be long-term and less easy to discern—much like the ripples vanishing at the edge of the pond. Both sets of policies need to be in play this side of the next presidential election—*the pebble needs to be dropped*. As Arianna Huffington correctly put it, "[I]t's not too late to change course. The financialization of our economy didn't just happen. Decisions were made that made it possible—and decisions can be unmade."[14] The best place to start? Why not with immediate policies on houses and jobs, to make them more secure, followed by longer-term policies, to guarantee that that security will last.

- *Housing*. Immediately we need action on home foreclosures.[15] The brief foreclosure moratorium triggered in October 2010 by improper banking procedures should have been extended, even made permanent. Banks holding mortgages in arrears need to be given extra instructions rather than extra resources—they have already been given more than enough publicly subsidized resources[16]—to enable homeowners exposed to negative equity and involuntary unemployment to stay in their houses. Keeping householders in their homes both protects them and their families, and breaks the vicious cycle now so prevalent—the dumping of foreclosed homes on the housing market triggering falling house prices, negative equity, and the creation of yet more foreclosed homes! Renting, not eviction, should be the order of the day, and the financing of that reform should be clearly placed in HUD and/or the Department of Labor—not in the Treasury—to signal the administration's belief that access to affordable housing is a civic right, not an accidental casualty of market position.[17] As this volume goes to press, the administration is not buying this argument, but even its HUD Secretary is on record as saying that "the more quickly we provide help to families—whether it's to stay in their home, to ensure that they buy new homes, or to help them to transition to affordable rental housing—the sooner our neighborhoods will stabilize and the sooner our economy will recover."[18] He is quite right on that.

- *Banking.* If public direction of the banking sector is still possible—it certainly was immediately after September 2008, but that political moment was definitely lost—then the banks should be directed to lend long-term to small businesses in return for job creation, using for that purpose money not paid out in excessive bank bonuses. Since the banks paying the bonuses and the ones doing the lending to small business tend to be different—the first large and Wall Street-based, the second small and regionally anchored—the next round of financial regulation needs to strengthen the latter at the expense of the former. We need to get bank money back in the hands of those close to Main Street, and dependent for their own success on that of the rest of the real economy. Quantitative easing by the Federal Reserve may be politically easier to effect than a new round of financial reform—and over the long period could well increase the flows of credit to Main Street again—but a prolonged period of interest rate reduction always runs the risk of generating another speculative bubble, especially when consumer confidence is low and viable private sector investment projects are hard to come by; for those reasons, this is no adequate substitute for a real jobs program orchestrated by the federal government.

- *Stimulus.* Which is why we also immediately need a further stimulus package, and the use of public funds to directly employ significant numbers of those Americans now without work. Infrastructure programs, publicly funded, do what private banks seem incapable of doing in the midst of severe recession. They create work. They strengthen long-term economic competitiveness, and they move the focus of public money from the funding of failure (job loss) to that of success (infrastructure development). Conservative fear-mongering about the dangers of expanding the federal deficit should be exposed for what it is—class-biased fear-mongering. A successful jobs program will actually bring the federal deficit down, by generating the growth and tax revenues that are always the other half of the federal spending equation. In fact, direct job creation is one of the most effective ways to reduce the deficit—job creation by direct employment for infrastructure development, *and* job creation by the funding of state spending on education, training, and law and order—both of which stimulate demand and tax flows faster than any other form of public expenditure. A jobs crisis as deep and tenacious as this one requires direct action by public authorities; and, no matter what the critics say, the design of the necessary programs is hardly rocket science. Indeed, there are plenty of excellent "shovel-ready" programs already to hand, not least the Economic Policy Institute's *American*

Jobs Plan advocating job creation through a strengthening of the safety net, fiscal relief to state and local governments, increased investment in social infrastructure, new public sector jobs, and a new job creation tax credit to encourage private sector employment growth.[19]

- *Poverty.* The attack on poverty needs both a public and a private face, and, as such, will take much longer to effect.[20] Publicly, it will require sustained commitments to progressive taxation, to affirmative action, to the extension of effective education and training programs, and to the making of child care support accessible to both lone parents and low-paid, two-income working families. Privately, it will require renewed commitment to personal educational development, to the prioritizing of child care over adult indulgence, and to the rediscovery of the powerful work ethic on which this country's economic growth was initially anchored. There is a clear role for public policy in the establishment, enforcement, and incremental raising of minimum tolerable standards of life, and there is definitely a role for progressive movements in challenging and inverting the normal priorities of public discourse—the ones that privilege business interests over social consequences, the ones that legitimate huge CEO salaries in an economy scarred by poverty wages.[21] Again, there are major blueprints available on the shelf, ready and able to be implemented in the pursuit of this goal. Among the most developed of those right now is the Center for American Progress' 2007 *From Poverty to Prosperity: A National Strategy to Cut Poverty in Half*, a strategy that included the sorts of proposals commonplace in anti-poverty programs elsewhere in the industrial democracies: raising and indexing the minimum wage, expanding Earned Income Tax Credits, strengthening trade unions, guaranteeing child care for low-income families, providing housing vouchers, reforming the means-tested benefit system, and strengthening the links for disadvantaged teenagers between school and work.[22] Poverty eradication is always and everywhere very difficult unless income distribution is squeezed, unless welfare traps are sprung, and unless low-paid workers are incrementally paid more; even then, cycles of deprivation between generations inevitably widen the distribution of necessary skills and capacities between social classes over time, so that it is the children who suffer most of all. But there is nothing unique about American poverty that makes it any more intractable than poverty elsewhere in the advanced industrialized world. As we have seen in Scandinavia, poverty can be reduced by public policy if the political will to pursue that policy is there. Given the scale of poverty in contemporary America, it is time to assert that political will again.

- *Wages.* The reconstitution of a debt-free base for general U.S. affluence requires a rise in general U.S. wage levels, and that, in its turn, requires a strengthening of the one institution committed to that goal above all others: the American trade union. As Robert Reich wrote, the central challenge before us now "is not to rebalance the global economy so that Americans save more and borrow less from the rest of the world. It is to rebalance the American economy so that its benefits are shared more widely in America, as they were decades ago."[23] That rebalancing requires a rolling back of the forces that have weakened organized labor in America for nearly half a century: listed by Dorian Warren as "(1) the exceptional anti-unionism of American employers; (2) the post–1960s breakdown of the post-war social contract; (3) the historically weak administrative capacity of the federal government; and (4) the regulatory capture of the state by big business."[24] The rebalancing also requires an actively pro-worker Department of Labor willing to enforce existing labor laws and safety codes. The Department of Labor under the Obama administration's Hilda Solis has proved light years better in this regard than its Republican predecessor; but liberty is eternal vigilance—and the employers' offensive is already on again,[25] with much talk in the media of overpaid federal employees and excessively generous public sector pensions—so enforcement here needs the support of new policy and law. The AFL-CIO and its affiliates remain an important source for suggestions on how best to raise general wage levels without a loss of competitiveness and employment. These include the passing of a strong *Employee Free Choice Act*, the use of government contracts to oblige private sector employers to meet high labor standards, better pay for publicly employed workers, the widespread use of living wage laws, and forms of corporate taxation that reward investment and job creation in U.S.-based factories and offices.[26]

- *Trade.* With poverty in the United States so tied to the issue of stagnant and low wages, neither an anti-poverty program nor programs to raise middle class wages can fully succeed without the development of a supportive trade policy. Policymakers will need to break decisively from assumptions now dominant in governing circles: the assumption that free trade is automatically the same thing as fair trade; and the assumption that the outsourcing of low wage jobs by American-based companies will somehow be automatically balanced by the retention here of related jobs higher up the skill and value-added chain. Neither assumption is currently valid. The global economy is awash with mercantilism,[27] and we need to pursue a little of it ourselves.[28] U.S. trade policy needs to be redesigned to draw a broad tranche of well-paying jobs back into this economy. Free trade will not bring those jobs back. American middle class prosperity will not return without policy consciously designed to replace the current race to the bottom in wages and working conditions with a global race to the top. If the last decade has taught us anything, it is that high American wages and unregulated trade with low wage competitors do not go together; so while the weight of American demand is still a significant factor in particularly China's capacity to maintain its levels of domestic employment, progressive voices here must actively support internal Chinese calls for human rights reforms, and more generally advocate trade agreements privileging the improvement of wages and working conditions abroad. The governing principle in a progressive trade policy should be that trade between economies of roughly equivalent wages should remain unregulated, while trade between economies with different average wages should be managed, and managed in ways that narrow the wage gap over time by raising the base rather than by deflating the top.

- *Industry.* Reversing market logics set in train by negative deindustrialization requires the design and implementation of an active industrial policy different in focus than the one currently implicit in federal spending decisions.[29] This is definitely the hardest of all the tasks now before us in contemporary America. A service-based economy will not generate the labor productivity vital to rising long-term living standards, nor create the volume of export earnings necessary to offset the flow of manufactured goods back into the United States. Manufacturing still matters.[30] The debates of the 1980s on the need for industrial policy remain relevant—an opportunity lost then needs now to be regained. Regaining industrial strength will require the deliberate orchestration of new green technologies at the center of a coherent energy policy geared to greater self-sufficiency. It will require major expenditure on industrial training and skill regeneration. It will require publicly funded infrastructure development—both inherited and new infrastructure—not least through the creation of a national infrastructure bank,[31] and it will require a national competitiveness strategy of the kind advocated by Richard Elkus,[32] Jeffrey Sachs[33] and Clyde Prestowitz,[34] among others. As we first noted in Chapter 3, the United States has a long track record of successful government–industry partnership in the development of modern weaponry. The federal government has long used the Pentagon as its equivalent of Japan's Ministry of International Trade and Industry (MITI). That same capacity now needs to be forged in the area of civil production—a genuine partnership of government, industry, and labor in the strategic planning of a better balanced economic structure—one committed to the creation of an economy in which more things consumed in the United States are actually made here, by Americans paid decent wages and protected by strong and supportive labor laws.[35] A high-wage high-productivity manufacturing-centered economy works in Germany, an economy whose key institutions were put in place immediately after World War II under American leadership. What one generation of American leaders could do there, another generation of American leaders needs now to do here—reset key economic institutions to guarantee long-term high-productivity economic growth.

- *Empire.* One thing the Germans did not have, of course, after 1945, was an extensive set of military commitments overseas. The countries that lost the Second World War eventually won the economic peace—left free of foreign military entanglements and so able to focus their economic strategy on the winning of foreign markets. The economies that bore the cost of "defending" those markets from the threat of communism—the United Kingdom and the United States, in particular—both ultimately saw the economic dominance that had propelled them to military victory slowly erode. The UK has scaled back its military capacity and reach. It was not politically easy to do, even there. It took a string of sterling crises in the 1960s to pull UK troops back from east of Suez, in the process beginning a long period of de-colonialization and re-orientation towards the European Union that is still not complete. To ease the economic pressures now upon us, the United States needs to make an equivalent reorientation, pulling back from the extensive global network of bases and alliances constructed by the State Department and the Pentagon since 1941. The transition was slow and difficult in the UK. It will be even slower and more difficult here, but the truth remains the same. Solving imperial overreach requires military withdrawal and a resetting of U.S. foreign policy. Chalmers Johnson, among others, was full of suggestions for the route that such a resetting should take: including reducing the size of the army, the scale of arms exports, the use of civilian contractors, the number and size of bases, and the funding of ROTC and the School of the Americas.[36] And he was not alone: Arianna Huffington recently reported that the money earmarked for ballistic defense in 2011—$12.6 billion—could, if earmarked for other things, hire 190,873 extra police officers.[37] The cost of sending a single American soldier to Afghanistan is currently equivalent to the cost of providing free health care for 588 children or of employing an additional 17 teachers.[38] As we saw in Chapter 5, wars have serious opportunity costs, as well as more direct costs to the people actually waging them. Tough economic times require tough policy choices—one way of not wasting this crisis would be to begin a public dialogue on the appropriate role of America in the world.

The politics of winning

It would be naive to the point of idiocy to expect the Obama administration to come out fighting hard on the full range of these issues, particularly after the kind of midterm setback that the Democrats have just experienced. Obama the candidate and Obama the president seemed dangerously radical—and still do—to members of the paranoid right, but to the saner ones among us he and his administration remain firmly in the center of American politics. Yet centrist though he may be, both the severity of the economic crisis still upon us, and the electoral logics at play in a world full of conservative politicians and conservative media outlets, mean that Obama and his team would be wise to start down this list if the Obama presidency is both to last and to have a lasting impact. Our job as progressives is to push the administration as far down the list as we can persuade them to go, both for their benefit and for ours.

Campaigning for the 2012 presidential election began the day after the midterms, and why not. The gridlock in Washington that existed before November 2010 is now more entrenched than ever, and that gridlock plays straight into the conservative argument that Washington doesn't work, that politicians can't be trusted, and that business deregulation and low taxation will restore U.S. prosperity faster than fiscal stimuli and quantitative easing.[39] A political system designed to effect major change only on the basis of broad consensus can be—and is being—crippled by well-placed elites determined to block the emergence of any such consensus. Washington, DC, was always in that sense a rigged town[40]—requiring an incredibly high level of crisis in the wider society before it could/would respond with progressive legislative change—but what is remarkable in this crisis is how much more rigged Washington, DC, has so rapidly become.[41] In the wake of the Supreme Court ruling on *Citizens United*, unprecedented amounts of private money immediately flowed without any transparency[42] into conservative campaigns determined to reverse the reforms of the health care and financial systems squeezed through in Obama's first two years in office. Concentrated conservative money is winning the battle for influence right now, getting its candidates elected and sustaining the campaigning of the Republican base. A president elected on a popular mobilization financed by small money is being blocked at every turn by money that is neither small nor popular.

The question is, how will and how should Obama respond?

The danger (disturbingly visible in the president's first press conference after the midterm elections[43]) is that his administration will respond with more of the same—striking deals with an empowered Republican congressional caucus to win small legislative concessions and to defend existing reforms against campaigns of a thousand cuts. We saw that strategy—the strategy of a

Rahm Emanuel and a Larry Summers—drain the spirits out of the Democratic Party base when control of Congress was formally in Democratic hands. As a continuing strategy, it is bound to be even more draining of spirits if repeated in the more gridlocked context now before us. What the president needs to do instead is to lead the counter-offensive to Republican conservatism, using the one media tool he alone commands—the bully-pulpit of the White House. An ideologically offensive president would do at least the following:

- He would put to rest the bizarre notion that private enterprise in the U.S. economy flourishes because of its distance from government, and does so because it is by its nature more efficient and effective than government can ever be. Both ends of that proposition are entirely false. If the financial tsunami of 2008 and the foreclosure morass of 2010 tell us anything, it is that big companies can be grotesquely inefficient and socially irresponsible unless curbed by strong regulatory frameworks. Economies flourish best when governments set the rules and business follows. They certainly flourish if governments provide the necessary demand. The U.S. engineering sector has flourished because of its proximity to the Pentagon, not because of its lack of connection to the military; and where would the U.S. pharmaceutical sector be without federally funded research and development, and the guaranteed market provided by Medicare and Medicaid?[44] The president needs to be out there arguing for an industrial strategy that is publicly discussed and supported, to replace the politics of pork that so often in U.S. politics produces bridges to nowhere. He needs to be saying—loud and long—that public spending and public policy have a crucial role to play in the creation of long-term economic prosperity, and that such spending and policy can only come from a progressive administration, even one as cautious as his.

- The other illusion propagated by conservatives which the president needs urgently and regularly to put to bed is the one that says only the poor in America receive welfare. "The truth is that nearly half of all Americans live in a household in which someone receives government benefits, more than at any time in our history."[45] We need to be reminded of that—and of how *small* is our welfare system relative to those on offer elsewhere in the advanced industrial world—whenever the call is made to cut entitlements. The irate old-age pensioner who, in the summer of 2009, told the politicians to keep the government's hands off his Medicare, really let the cat out of the bag. What America has is an invisible welfare state[46]—a welfare state of substantial subsidies, many of which flow to the more prosperous, and some of which flow only to the rich. The biggest items in the U.S. tax code are tax relief for employer-provided health care coverage, and tax relief on the interest paid on mortgages (both prime mortgages and equity lines of credit).[47] Neither of those benefits reaches the homeless and the unemployed, those renting or those working for small companies. The great thrust of the health care reform so denigrated by conservatives is the extension of coverage to those hitherto denied it by previous illness or present poverty. That reform went along with a tax cut for 95 percent of all working Americans in 2010; but neither of those progressive truths is currently in the collective memory of the bulk of the American electorate.[48] It has been driven out by the daily drip of Republican talking points, spread far and wide by conservative media outlets. There is a progressive record of achievement and promise that the president needs urgently to articulate. If you want tax cuts that help working Americans, and tax policy that privileges the rich less than did the Bush tax cuts, only a Democratic administration will provide it—and we need to be told that again and again.

- There are other things that we need to be told over and over again. We need to be reminded that the Republican faith in unregulated markets and limited government is what got us into our present deep economic difficulties, and so cannot be expected to be the best way out of them. When Rand Paul, in his 2010 midterm acceptance speech, can baldly assert that "governments do not create jobs," he and we need to be reminded that governments can indeed create jobs, do indeed create jobs, do create jobs of value (from teachers to soldiers), and do often create jobs faster than the private sector—particularly when confidence in consumer demand is low and private businesses understandably reluctant to hire. And when Rand Paul, and many other Republicans, argue for federal budget cuts using the family budget as an analogy—when they say that families have to balance their budgets so the federal government should balance its budget, too—a progressive president has to do two immediate things. He has *not* to use the same analogy himself, because family budgets and federal budgets play different economic roles; and he has instead to argue the Keynesian case for budget deficits that can trigger economic growth and pay for themselves over the long term from the tax revenues generated by that growth. In other words, a progressive president has to go on the ideological offensive against an ideologically active conservative movement: defending the vital role of big government in periods of crisis *and* the essential role of civilized public policy in times of calm He must not let the Republicans get away with their regular assertion that markets work best when regulated least. That nonsense got us into this crisis, and it will not get us out.

- But there is more. A Democratic president with any grain of progressivism within him would tell a powerful post-war story, too. That president would challenge the mythology of the Reagan years, pointing to them not as the glory years as the Right would have them, but as the turning point from which we all now suffer.[49] It was in the Reagan years that a social settlement based on strong U.S. manufacturing performance and rising blue-collar wages was replaced by a new settlement based on growing income inequality, the outsourcing of American jobs, and the spread of a debt-based prosperity. It was in the Reagan years that the weakening of American trade unionism began the long decades of stagnant wage rates. A progressive president would not excuse the Clinton administration from responsibility for continuing that Reaganite settlement[50]—treating the Clinton presidency as the accidental beneficiary of an influx of predominantly Japanese investment funds that briefly kept U.S. firms buoyant and allowed wages slightly to rise for the first time in nearly two decades. A progressive president would draw the proper conclusion from the fragility of prosperity in even the Clinton years—and its total absence now in the wake of a financial crisis overseen by a Republican administration. He would call the country to a new settlement—a genuine New Deal—one based on greater equality in rewards, the honoring of work and family, a return to buying only what we can pay for, and the building of a stronger safety net for the weakest and most vulnerable among us.

There was a brief moment late in 2008 when the Democratic Party commanded the narrative of American politics, when deregulation was discredited and Wall Street greed was universally condemned. That moment has been allowed to pass.[51] The dominant narratives swirling around us now are once more conservative ones—that public spending is too high and out of control, that Social Security is too expensive, and the stimulus package a total waste of money. This return to conservatism is not accidental. It is consciously orchestrated and heavily funded, and it is playing to a popular common sense built up over the last three decades. The ideological terrain faced by progressives is not a level one. As Theda Skocpol and Lawrence Jacobs have observed, "it has long been well documented in survey research" that Americans are two things at once: "ideologically cautious about strong government or governmental activism," while simultaneously supportive of specific forms of government activism like Social Security or public schooling: "Americans are, in short, philosophical conservatives and operational liberals."[52] In such a cultural mix, philosophical positions will trump operational ones whenever specific policies seem to fall short, unless the conservative explanation of that shortfall is countered by a strong, deliberate, and well-formulated liberal alternative. That strong liberal rebuttal has yet to come with sufficient regularity and force from the Obama White House. Skocpol and Jacobs again:

> Why, during his honeymoon period in the first half of 2009, did President Obama not engage in sustained and nationally televised public explanations about the reasons the stimulus was structured as it was, how it differed from the Bush Wall Street bailouts, and why government spending can function to create millions of jobs? . . . Perhaps Obama and his advisors believed that . . . facts "speak for themselves" and that sharp pitched communications are inappropriate. If so, [they] failed to understand that American citizens have heard for many years a steady stream of arguments about how government spending hurts the economy and tax cuts are the only way to spur growth and create jobs. Against that prior backdrop of public beliefs and misunderstandings, the President needed to frame his overall economic recovery strategy if he wanted citizens to understand why he proposed what he did.[53]

That sharp liberal framing has been missing these last two years, but my, we need it now. In the great ideological battle between markets and politics—between the rule of money and the rule of people—civilized societies have in the end always to subordinate market forces to democratically specified social objectives. In a political culture as shaped as this has been since the 1980s by a resurgent conservatism, achieving that subordination is particularly difficult. But then if things were easy, they would already have been done. It is time, therefore, once more to push that conservatism back. This is no time to fudge the counterarguments against claims as disingenuous as those coming from the Tea Party crowd and their Republican acolytes. Rather, it is time to get the narrative back—the narrative that runs from FDR's New Deal and Lyndon Johnson's Great Society to the unfinished business of the American social revolution. The great liberal narrative of American politics will only recapture the high ground of American politics again if the White House on the one side, and all of us who care about progressive change on the other, jointly challenge on a daily basis the ubiquitous nonsense that government activism is part of the problem rather than the key to its solution. There is a vital job to be done either side of the 2012 election—arguing the case, supporting the candidates, designing the programs, rebutting the critics, implementing the policies—reconstituting that progressive movement that might yet win for our children and grandchildren a better and a stronger America than the one we currently face. This is no time to play defense. It is time for clarity and conviction. Let us hope the Obama White House gets its grove back, by being persuaded to deploy vast quantities of both.

APPENDIX 1

The Causes of the Meltdown: An Update on the Debate

The repercussions of the September 2008 financial meltdown have been both prolonged and serious, and as they have persisted, the original causes of the crisis have slipped back in time and progressively out of mind. Increasingly preoccupied with the immediate consequences of the credit crisis for employment and growth, most politicians and commentators now only rarely pause to allocate blame; leaving the rest of us—struggling daily as we are with the unemployment, home foreclosures, and tight credit that the meltdown left in its wake—ever more prone to blame our present ills on the very policy initiatives that the meltdown made necessary. We see the policies and their limited impact. We see the unemployment and the home foreclosures, and, increasingly, we treat the latter as the consequence of the former when, in truth, both have a common and an earlier cause—the meltdown itself.

Instead of bringing clarity, the passage of time is facilitating the peddling of new and misleading orthodoxies: allowing a crisis created by inadequately regulated markets to be used by conservative commentators as evidence of the need to regulate markets even less. It takes some nerve to invert reality quite as blatantly and rapidly as that, but then sections of the American Right have very strong nerves and an agenda of their own to pursue, regardless of the data. In the new conservative orthodoxy, the old list of the guilty is still there—the *Community Reinvestment Act* and politically motivated housing policy, Greenspan largesse, and the evil GSEs—but now that list is overlaid by a new one: of a Wall Street too entrepreneurial for its own good, and of a bipartisan crony capitalism that kept Washington in thrall to the bankers. There is right-wing populism out there as well as left-wing populism. The two populisms overlap in their anger with the big banks, but then diverge entirely on whether that anger is best assuaged by tightening government regulation or by retreating from government altogether.

In picking our way between these competing populisms, we are fortunate now to have more and better data on which to draw: on the role of housing policy, the GSEs, deregulation, and Wall Street in the creation of the crisis. Calm reflection is easier now partly because of the greater distance in time between our contemporary ruminations and the events on which we ruminate; but easier, too, because the crisis has triggered such a large quantity of high-level analysis written from a range of political perspectives. We have high-quality financial journalism.[1] We have high-quality academic analysis,[2] and we have high-quality investigatory inquiries and reports.[3] We also have parallel studies for linked economies like the UK.[4] They need to be our sources as we assess the quality of the new conservative orthodoxy.

The revamped conservative argument

There are some very substantial new conservative voices in play in the discussion on the financial meltdown these days—John Taylor for one and Johan Norberg for another—and some very established substantial ones: Peter J. Wallison immediately springs to mind. There are also some more idiosyncratic voices: for our purposes here, Andrew Redleaf and Richard Vigilante. Together, they make a collective and revamped conservative case.

- *Peter J. Wallison has been focused throughout the crisis on the causal role played by the GSEs, and behind them by government policy. "The current financial crisis is not, as some have said, a crisis of capitalism. It is in fact the opposite, a shattering demonstration that ill-considered government intervention in the private economy can have devastating consequences. The crisis," according to Wallison," has its roots in the U.S. government's efforts to increase homeownership, especially among minority and other underserved or low-income groups, and to do so through hidden financial subsidies rather than direct government expenditures."*[5] *The critical error here is said to be the lowering of underwriting standards and the provision of subprime mortgages encouraged by the Community Reinvestment*

Act and delivered by Fannie Mae and Freddie Mac, in particular: "Although it is difficult to prove cause and effect," Wallison had written, "it is highly likely that the lower lending standards required by the CRE influenced what banks and other lenders were willing to offer to borrowers in prime markets."[6]

- *The Taylor contribution to that case is this. The key mistakes made en route to the financial crisis by the GSEs were compounded by others made by the Federal Reserve: made by Greenspan and made by Bernanke. Departing from the sound monetary policy of the 1980s and 1990s—when his own Taylor rule applied, requiring disciplined adjustments to interest rates in line with inflation and GDP growth—the Fed was guilty from 2002 of "getting off track": guilty of running a cheap money policy that sent out the wrong signals and both encouraged and tolerated excessive risk taking. In consequence:*

. . . government actions and interventions caused, prolonged, and worsened the financial crisis. They caused it by deviating from historical precedents and principles for setting interest rates that had worked well for 20 years. They prolonged it by misdiagnosing the problems in the bank credit markets and thereby responding inappropriately, focusing on liquidity rather than risk. They made it worse by supporting certain financial institutions and their creditors and not others in an ad hoc way, without a clear and understandable framework. Although other factors were certainly in play, those government actions should be first on the list of answers to the question of what went wrong.[7]

- *It is not, therefore, a question of too little government, but of too much. The Fed drove down interest rates just as emerging economies were beginning to send capital here. There was "preemptive Keynesianism," according to Norberg, stoking the house price boom and turning the American home from "a castle" into "an ATM."*[8] *"U.S. politicians pumped up risk taking and house prices further through deductions, tax benefits for home savings accounts, and restrictions on new construction." Fannie Mae and Freddie Mac "developed the securitization of mortgages which Wall Street fell madly in love with once the credit-rating agencies—which had been given a legally protected oligopoly by the government—declared them to be safe investments." And "the Fed's safety net and the federal government's deposit insurance made banks dare to take big risks because they could privatize any gains but socialize any losses."*[9] *"The problem," Johan Norberg has recently written, "is not that we had too few regulations: on the contrary, we had too many, and above all, faulty ones."*[10]

The fundamental errors made by politicians and authorities do not mean that this crisis is entirely the fault of the government. Ordinary people, investors, and banks have made huge mistakes. Just because the central bank lowers interest rates drastically, households cannot make long-term home purchases on the assumption that the rates will remain at their low level forever. The government may wring out mortgages for households that cannot afford them, but no one is forcing anyone to buy up these mortgages . . . Anyone who is not furious about the behavior of many senior executives and traders simply cannot be aware of what they have done.[11]

- *So, on this argument, we are all to blame—not equally, of course—the government comes first, but then the rest of us get into line. And that opens the door for a conservative critique of Wall Street itself: not primarily for its greed (profit-making is, after all, the core goal of a free economy) but for its over-reliance on abstract modeling of future trends that denied the necessarily innovative and entrepreneurial dimension of successful economic activity: "judgment everywhere . . . replaced with structure and process."*[12] *Led astray by their models of "efficient markets," so the thesis runs, Wall Street came to embody the antithesis of pure capitalism: namely central and automatic economic planning. "Crony capitalists on the right and socialists on the left united as always behind their most fundamental belief, that wealth is to be captured by power and pull rather than created in the minds of men."*[13] *Andrew Redleaf and Richard Vigilante give this distortion of basic capitalist processes center-stage in their explanation of the Wall Street panic, and see in that development a threatening erosion of basic American (and Christian) values and practices. The following extract is typical:*

"If the crisis had its roots in an ideology of finance that derided judgment, denied the entrepreneur, and weakened ownership, it found its consummation in the tendency of crony-capitalist regimes, left and right alike, to encourage and exploit such weakness. Having profited politically for decades from undermining homeownership under the guise of extending it, the government diverted attention from the moral causes of this crisis. It first shielded the guilty, then actively rewarded them, and finally punished the virtuous. It was this moral failure that turned a credit crunch into the most dangerous and damaging economic crisis since the Great Depression, and even now threatens to extend the damage out for years to come."[14]

- *You might be forgiven for thinking, therefore, that if Wall Street is out of control, re-regulating it would be the sensible way forward. But no—apparently not—just the reverse, in fact. Because it was government mis-regulation of Wall Street that caused this madness, getting government as far away from Wall Street is the preferred route back to sanity. Get rid of all the hidden subsidies and protections—let the principle of moral hazard have full play—and treat banks (and mortgage companies, and overstretched home owners) exactly alike: as competitive units in an unregulated market surviving or perishing by their own virtue and actions alone. The federal government does not have the capacity to regulate finance and industry well—that was Peter J. Wallison's immediate response to the Dodd bill on financial regulation floated in 2010:*[15] *so stop pretending that it does. Such pretense only makes a bad situation worse. Norberg again:*

"The principle ought to be straightforward . . . Either a company is viable, and then it needs no government support, or it is not viable, and then it deserves no government support. Those

> *businessmen and capitalists who choose to sign a pact with the devil anyway will soon realize who is the stronger party . . . All the salvage operations and bailouts that have been implemented this time will make the problem seven times worse next time, regardless of the effect that they may have had in the short term to prevent free fall . . . Because . . . capitalism without bankruptcy is like Christianity without hell—it loses its ability to motivate people through their prudence and fears."*[16]

A liberal response

If we are going to make a reasoned response to this new and more sophisticated defense of unregulated financial markets, we need good solid data. We need data on the degree to which the crisis was caused by political pressure to extend home ownership down into the ranks of the American poor. We need data on the dissemination of subprime loans into the U.S. banking system, and the role played in that dissemination, if any, by Fannie Mae and Freddie Mac. We need to know if over-regulation, not deregulation, made the crisis worse; and we need to decide if private sector actors in general, and those on Wall Street in particular, have been unfairly singled out for criticism merely for doing their job. The data we need is as follows.

1. Housing policy: pattern and role

First, we need to establish basic data on U.S. housing policy and on the role it played—if any—in triggering the financial meltdown. So what do we know? We know two important things at least. We know that a particular set of federal policies in relation to U.S. housing policy had long been in place; and we also know that the housing policies normally singled out by conservative critics as triggers to the meltdown were at most only part of the relevant story—part of the story, and, in truth, not even the main part. The case for a re-evaluation of the role of subprime lending in the run-up to the 2008 financial collapse is as follows.

1. It is certainly the case, as Norberg and others document so well, that the federal government has long used its tax policy to encourage home ownership. From the inception of income tax in the United States, home owners have been allowed to deduct mortgage interest payments from the amount of salary then to be taxed; and that facility was extended in 1986—by a Republican president and a Democratic Congress working in tandem—to cover interest payments on second mortgages. At the same time, tax relief on other major purchases, including cars, was removed. A

decade later, a Democratic president and a Republican Congress—again working in tandem—"abolished capital gains tax on real estate (up to $500,000 for a couple) but kept it for other types of investment."[17] The result, of course, was the emergence of a new set of tax-induced incentives: incentives that sent money into the housing market and away from other investment targets, and incentives that encouraged homeowners to use second mortgage loans to finance the purchase of other consumer durables. Then add to that mixture two other things—low interest rates after 2002, and the unique U.S. legal provision that a loan taken out against a home, if defaulted, puts only the home at risk (and not the other assets of the defaulting home owner)—and you have a recipe for speculation in home ownership. And people did speculate: some taking out loans they were unlikely later to be able to pay back; others buying multiple homes to quickly sell on (to flip, as they say) or to rent out.

2. We know, too, that the U.S. housing market was long impacted by a similarly bipartisan commitment to the extension of home ownership *down* the U.S. income ladder. The much-maligned *Community Reinvestment Act* passed in 1976 required that banks receiving FDIC insurance be evaluated by their regulators to ensure that they offered credit (in ways consistent with safe and sound banking practice) to *all* communities in which they were authorized to operate. The equally maligned Department of Housing and Urban Development (HUD) was similarly committed (via the terms of reference it set Fannie Mae and Freddie Mac) to increasing the flow of mortgage funds to low and moderate income earners. And at least one major lobby organization—ACORN—made the extension of home ownership down the income chain one of its central concerns. Put those three facts together, as many conservative commentators have done, and it looks like the causes of the housing crisis are done and dusted: a veritable slam-dunk. But add some other facts, and suddenly things become less straightforward and clear. Add that the bulk of subprime loans were issued by companies *not* subject to the *Community Reinvestment Act* (CRA) (75 percent of all such loans at the peak of the lending boom) and that the preliminary staff report to the Financial Crisis Inquiry Commission reported that "loans made by CRA-regulated lenders [were] *less* likely to default than similar loans made by independent mortgage companies."[18] Add that ACORN's major role in the housing crisis was to complain loud and long about the dangers of subprime mortgages,[19] and add that HUD was still only advocating a target of 28 percent for low-income home ownership as late as 2008.[20] The CRA, HUD, and ACORN had been in play for more than 30 years when the subprime mortgage crisis broke. If they were indeed the central drivers of that crisis, then their causal impact had a long and extraordinarily slow fuse, did it not!

3. Of course, there was a subprime loan dimension to the financial crisis, and it was an important one. Many low-income families took out loans—often teaser loans—and low-income families were disproportionately affected (and still are) by the foreclosure consequences now blighting the U.S. housing market. But for the purpose of understanding the character and cause of the U.S. housing crisis, three other features of the subprime mortgage debacle need to be kept center-stage. The first is that the growth of subprime mortgages was predominantly a post–9/11 phenomenon: *its roots are recent*, even if their sprouting may have been facilitated by the character of housing finance long in place.[21] The second is that at least 34 percent of the loans that could not be paid between 2002 and 2006 were loans made to existing homeowners.[22] They were *second mortgages*, not first: taken out, not by the American poor, but by core members of the American middle class.[23] And the third and critical dimension of the subprime mortgage crisis that we need never to forget is that subprime lending and borrowing is no longer the prime cause of home foreclosures. The *prime cause now is involuntary unemployment*, triggered by the financial crisis of which subprime lending to financially challenged borrowers was initially a partial cause.
4. Even that attribution of partial causality may be too much. For as Stan Leibowitz has recently demonstrated and as Redleaf and Vigilante readily concede, "ARMs [adjustable rate mortgages], not subprimes, caused the mortgage crisis." His figures makes clear that as far back as 1998 (when data first became available), subprime foreclosure rates were highly variable over time, ebbing and flowing between 4 percent and 12 percent of all subprime loans; and that when the "subprime crisis" was being widely discussed in the media in 2007, subprime foreclosure rates were still operating within that range. For all the labeling of the crisis as one of "subprimes" (and therefore, by implication, a problem caused by pushing house ownership too far down the income ladder), "the evidence suggests very little distinction between prime and subprime loans" in terms of default performance. It was the increase in prime ARM foreclosures that was on an unprecedented scale in the run-up to the 2008 financial meltdown: "the prime ARM foreclosure rate between Q2 2005 and Q2 2006 rose by 47 percent, which is roughly twice as great as that for subprime ARMs over the same period."[24] Which means, as Redleaf and Vigilante recognized, that "the mortgage crisis was not caused by poor people."[25] The mortgage crisis happened when lower underwriting standards designed for low-income borrowers were extended to high-income borrowers as well. This was a crisis that the American middle class brought upon itself.

5. The part of the conservative critique focused on housing policy that does hold water is the critique of monetary policy. There can be no doubt that low interest rates over a lengthy period of time made it easier for people to borrow larger and larger mortgages, mortgages that then fuelled a house price rise that itself attracted even more borrowers. As Amir Khandani and his colleagues have correctly argued, "the confluence of three trends in the U.S. residential housing market—rising home prices, declining interest rates, and near-frictionless refinancing opportunities—led to vastly increased systemic risk in the financial system."[26] It was not, as some have implied, a deliberate federal policy to generate house price inflation. Rather, house price inflation appears to have emerged as an unintended consequence of a cheap money policy made possible by the influx of large amounts of foreign capital, and overseen by a Federal Reserve slow to see the dangers involved. If we wish to award the "failed leadership prize" to anyone in the run up to the 2008 financial crisis, that prize ought properly to go to Alan Greenspan, as his critics say.[27] The crisis built up on his watch and he did too little to stop it. Yet even so, his conservative critics would do well to take great care in making their case against him, for paradoxically, the inertia that wins Greenspan their negative accolade was an inertia rooted in his powerful commitment to *deregulated* financial markets—to the very level of deregulation, that is, which remains a key goal of the conservatives who now criticize him so roundly.[28]

2. Fannie, Freddie and Ginnie—The role of the GSEs

The way houses are financed differs between particular national capitalisms—in part by the degree to which ownership is privileged against renting, in part by the degree to which refinancing is easy, in part by the extent to which securitization is prevalent, and in part by the consequential ratio of mortgage debt to GDP. The U.S. housing market is very much in the liberal-market quadrant of that distribution,[29] unusual among industrialized nations for the size of its secondary mortgage market.[30] Conservative critics of over-regulation have seized on that—and on the role of the government-sponsored enterprises responsible for it—as a key element in the housing market's contribution to the financial meltdown.

So again, what do we know?

1. We know that the U.S. system for the financing of house purchases has a long history and has changed over time. We also know that government intervention—in the form of laws and institutions—has been an

important element of that system from as long ago as the 1930s, and a key trigger to those changes. Prior to the 1930s, mortgages (normally of short duration and with a high level of deposit) were provided primarily by Building and Loan Societies, and by insurance companies. We have all seen *It's a Wonderful Life* and so know that many Building (Saving) and Loans Societies (S&Ls) struggled in the 1930s. New Deal legislation created the Federal Housing Association (FHA). Immediately after the Second World War, Congress created the Veterans Housing Association (VHA). Both were federal agencies providing mortgages. The New Deal also created the Federal National Mortgage Association (Fannie Mae) to buy mortgages from the banks originating them, so long as those mortgages met the underwriting standards that Fannie Mae set. Savings and Loans were additionally protected by legislation banning commercial banks from paying interest on checking accounts.[31] Fannie Mae set tight standards—creating the so-called "conforming loans"—effectively generalizing the fully amortized 30-year fixed-rate mortgage requiring a 20 percent deposit. The result was a system of housing finance that saw house ownership rise steadily from the 1940s. It was also a system that saw house prices remain flat for an entire generation (1948–1985).

2. That system began to change from the 1960s. Fannie Mae was joined in 1968 by the Government National Mortgage Association (Ginnie Mae) as a secondary mortgage market for the VHA, and in 1970 by the Federal National Mortgage Corporation (Freddie Mac) as a secondary mortgage market for the S&Ls: and all three were semi-privatized by the late 1980s. By semi-privatized, we mean this: that they were chartered as private corporations but were given public responsibilities. They were overseen by HUD, and as government-sponsored enterprises (GSEs) carried an implicit guarantee of Treasury support, which enabled them to borrow easily and cheaply in private money markets. In legislation passed in 1992 (signed into law by the first President Bush), Fannie and Freddie were directed to send a greater proportion of their mortgages over time to low/moderate income recipients, and in 2002—under the second President Bush's *Blueprint for the American Dream*—they "committed to finance $1.1 trillion in loans to minority buyers."[32] The regulatory regime to which the GSEs were subject in the Clinton and Bush II years was no heavier than that applied to the rest of the financial system, and both major GSEs experienced accounting scandals that led to changes in leadership. Congressional pressure to tighten that regulatory regime was resisted by Democrats who feared it would reduce minority homeownership—that much of the "blame Barney Frank" thesis has merit—although the resistance was bipartisan, and was later regretted by Frank himself: "I was too late to see they were a problem," he said, "I did

see them as an important source of rental housing. I did not foresee the extent to which bad decisions . . . were causing problems."[33]

3. Parallel regulatory changes in the 1980s robbed the thrifts (the S&Ls) of their special protections in relation to depositors, so that commercial banks began to bid up deposit rates and even to play a greater role in the provision of housing finance. By 1989, more than a thousand S&Ls—trapped between rising deposit rates and their long-term fixed-rate mortgage commitments—were effectively bankrupt and had to be bailed out in 2008 fashion,[34] leaving behind a new system of housing finance. That system was marked by a shift in the sourcing of mortgages: away from S&Ls and GSE-backed sources towards private mortgage providers free of GSE constraints on the terms of the mortgages offered.[35] The new system "left an increasingly large portion of the mortgage market subject to little regulation, shifted substantial amounts of risks from lenders to borrowers, and exacerbated boom–bust cycles in housing prices."[36] It, too, brought stability and rising home ownership for a while, but now with a significant quickening in the rate of house price inflation and ultimately total systemic breakdown.
4. As a further element, securitization enters the picture. Securitization occurs when financial instruments such as loans or mortgages are pooled and sold to investors as securities that are backed by cash flows from the instruments pooled. There had been a degree of securitization of U.S. mortgages in the 1920s, which may have played its own role in the 1929 crash.[37] Securitization in the 1970s was the product of the GSEs' privatization, their way of raising money to enable them to underwrite yet more mortgage loans. Leading scholars of U.S. housing finance tend to disagree on precisely which GSE initiated securitization, while being entirely at one on the initiating role of the GSEs themselves.[38] The spread of these GSE-generated securitized mortgage packages did indeed move the U.S. house-financing system from the "lend and hold" model of the old S&Ls (in which the risk remained with the originator of the loan) to the "lend and pass on" model that played so key a role in the financial meltdown (a model in which risk is passed on to the final purchasers, and the risk-assessment process increasingly relies on agencies that specialize in that function, and whose judgment is relied upon by purchasers with no direct knowledge of the original mortgage holder's financial viability). Early on at least, because it was done cautiously, "securitization promoted the standardization of mortgage terms and underwriting requirements."[39] For there was nothing inherently subprime in securitization as a process: on the contrary, it initially spread good practice, facilitating the consolidation of the one-size-fits-all full amortized fixed-rate 30-year mortgage.[40]

5. So the GSEs did trigger securitization. That part of the critique of them is valid. But they did *not* do the two other things that turn securitization from a valuable way of stimulating the flow of credit into one creating the toxic assets that would eventually bring the U.S. credit-creating system to a total standstill. (a) They did not spread high-risk mortgage-backed securities through the American, and then later the global, system. The GSEs did not drive the banks into the acquisition of toxic assets. It was the banks themselves, hungry for investment outlets, greater market share, and enhanced profits that took themselves there, with such dire consequences for all of us, bankers and non-bankers alike.[41] (b) Nor did the GSEs—until very late in the day—lower their underwriting standards.[42] They were not the main creators of toxic assets. "The financial crisis was not primarily due to Fannie and Freddie."[43] Indeed well into the new century, the GSEs were legally "barred from making subprime, Alt-A, and jumbo loan business,"[44] which is presumably why the mortgages initially underwritten by them remained predominantly prime, and predominantly viable, throughout the crisis. It was not the GSEs who fueled the subprime crisis. It was major private financial institutions like Countrywide Financial who did that, alongside the mortgage brokers they commissioned.[45] The GSEs only came into the subprime market *after* the private institutions that dominated it ran into the predictable liquidity barriers, and came in then only because someone had to pick up the pieces. The GSEs are in problems now less because of their own fecklessness than because they took to themselves the toxic debts created by unregulated and unscrupulous mortgage lenders at the height of the house price boom.[46]

So far from making the case for the break-up of Fannie and Freddie, what their record over 50 years would rather suggest is that it is their semi-private status that needs to be changed; and, indeed, it has already been changed. The federal government now owns the GSEs—and, therefore, has the administrative capacity to shape housing finance for the future. It is a capacity it would do well to develop rather than abandon.[47] For, as the U.S. moves into its third post-war house financing system, the lesson of the past is clear. It was the regulated first system, in place from the 1930s until the early 1980s, that was the more stable. Deregulation and instability under the second system went together. As Dan Immergluck correctly put it:[48]

> Unfortunately, at the time this book goes to press, some political and ideological opponents of the GSEs are attempting to lay the principal blame for the mortgage crisis on federal investment and intervention in the mortgage marketplace via the agencies. This argument may be used to eventually privatize the bulk or all of the operations of the GSEs. The fallacy of this argument is that it was too little—not

> too much—government intervention that precipitated the problems of 2007 and 2008. In particular, the severity and spillovers of the mortgage crisis were principally due to a failure to regulate consumer mortgage markets . . . it was the damage that high-risk lenders did to housing values and overall mortgage markets that was the root of the mortgage market failure over this period.

3. Regulation or de-regulation: which was it?

In the light of Immergluck's careful and informed analysis of the U.S. mortgage market and its history, you have to be ideologically blinkered not to see the role of deregulation in laying the foundations for the 2008 financial meltdown—deregulation in at least three linked forms: deregulation of the mortgage market; deconstruction of the walls dividing the mortgage market from the rest of the financial system; and deregulation of the rest of the financial system itself.

Those who would pull the federal government out of the business of financial regulation fail to recognize that managing the currency has been a key role of the state ever since modern state-formation began in the later Middle Ages, and was a key function of the pre-modern state of ancient antiquity. Even the United States, with its much shorter history, has experienced its own share of bank collapses and associated economic downturns, precisely because the federal control of the nineteenth-century banking system was so under-developed. Indeed, one key reform triggered by the Great Depression was the *Glass-Steagall Act* of 1933 separating commercial from investment banking. That separation kept U.S. finance stable through the long post-war American growth story. Part of our modern tragedy is the way in which its removal became a key target of a financial system made prosperous by that economic growth. Mighty finance won its deregulatory battle in the decades after 1980, to the long-term detriment of the very economy that had initially made it mighty.

1. The years after 1980 certainly saw a light regulatory touch applied to the way house purchases were and are financed in the United States. The *Garn–St. Germain Act* of 1982 deregulated the S&L industry, freeing them "to venture into riskier nontraditional investments such as real estate speculation, development projects, and junk bonds;" and the lightness of the resulting federal and state oversight "facilitated fraud, overextension, and lack of prudence in investments, as well as possible criminal behavior on the part of some thrift executives."[49] Before John McCain could be named as one of the Keating 5, there had to be Charles Keating! When the resulting S&L crisis broke, Congress then eased the regulatory structure again. The 1989 *Financial Institutions Reform Recovery and*

Enforcement Act opened the way to a mortgage provision system dominated by brokers and non-depository lending institutions.

2. The deregulatory drift in the mortgage market was part of a wider retreat from regulation by state agencies––deregulation inspired by a widespread and growing consensus from the 1980s on the Reaganite need to "get government off the people's backs" in order fully to exploit the superiority of unregulated markets, especially financial ones. As Simon Johnson and James Kwak rightly record, "as banking became more complicated, more prestigious, and more lucrative, the *ideology* of Wall Street—that unfettered innovation and unregulated financial markets were good for America and the world—became the consensus position in Washington on both sides of the aisle." The political leverage which that consensus gave to leading financial institutions was truly enormous. Under Bush I and Clinton, Wall Street ruled not simply by lobbying but by "shifting the conventional wisdom in their favor, to the point where their lobbyists' talking points seemed self-evident to congressmen and administration officials."[50] So self-evident, in fact, that the separation of commercial and investment banking established by the *Glass–Steagall Act* fell victim in 1999 to Wall Street's greatest modern coup: the passage of the *Gramm–Leach–Bliley Act* that freed Wall Street banks to pursue the origination and securitization of mortgages on the grand scale.[51]
3. Compounding that set of deregulatory legislative shifts was an associated lightening of the regulatory policies still in place, and the conscious decision *not* to expand the regulatory agencies to cover the new financial instruments exploding into use each side of the new millennium. Ross Levine recently examined SEC policies towards credit-rating agencies, major investment banks, and over-the-counter derivatives, Fed policy towards credit-default swaps, and government policy towards the two big GSEs—all for the period 1996–2006. This is what he found:

> The evidence indicates that senior policymakers repeatedly designed, implemented, and maintained policies that destabilized the global financial system in the decade before the crisis. The policies incentivized financial institutions to engage in activities that generated enormous short-run profits but dramatically increased long-run fragility. Moreover, the evidence suggests that the regulatory agencies were aware of the consequences of their policies and yet chose not to modify those policies. On the whole, these policy decisions reflect neither a lack of information nor an absence of regulatory power. They represent the selection—and most importantly, the maintenance—of policies that increased financial fragility.[52]

Dean Baker clearly agrees. "Creating new agencies," he has recently argued, "is not the answer: forcing the agencies that are responsible for maintaining economic and financial stability (first and foremost the Federal Reserve Board) to do their job properly is." The Fed slept on the job, and watched the house fall down.[53] Baker calls its failure to act early in the housing bubble "perhaps the single most consequential error in economic policy in the history of the world!"[54] That may be to overstate it—but, in truth, not by much.

4. Though all the main players now concede deregulation went too far under Greenspan and Clinton/Bush II, we do well to remember that there was nothing automatic about this move to deregulate financial institutions and financial products. The deregulation was lobbied for. The consensus was consciously built. The new financial freedoms were bought. A veritable Washington–Wall Street corridor kept the voice and interests of leading financial institutions at the very center of American political power.[55] Leading bankers headed the Treasury on a regular basis. Leading bankers headed and staffed the regulatory agencies (especially the Federal Reserve Board).[56] Lobbyists were employed on the grandest of scales.[57] Nothing was left to chance. The coffers of politicians were filled with financial contributions, not least by the two main GSEs. Key senators and members of the House of Representatives were persuaded to fight battles on behalf of financial institutions based in their constituencies, and ex-members of Congress were handsomely rewarded for their previous efforts by lucrative positions on the boards of leading financial concerns. Washington was, and is, to a terrifying degree, an entirely bought town; and it is a measure of how traumatic have been the economic and social consequences of the financial meltdown that a strengthening of regulatory powers did emerge (eventually) from such corrupt corridors of power. What emerged was less than was needed. What emerged was watered down by intense defensive lobbying by Wall Street interests. But new regulations did emerge—in spite of the grip that high finance continues to hold on the thinking and policies of those who rule us.

4. Guilty finance

That banking took a hit after 2008 was a product of misbehavior prior to the collapse of the banking system in 2008. No one has gone to jail yet, and bank bonuses continue to flow, but the evidence is overwhelming. It was not over-regulation but under-regulation that led to the collapse of the system.[58] The main trigger to the financial meltdown, as we documented more fully in Chapter 10 of *Answering Back*, was recklessness, corruption, failure, greed, and arrogance at the very heart of American finance. As Michael Mayo put it to the

Financial Crisis Inquiry Commission, "the problem: banks have been an industry on steroids."

> In summary, the banking industry has been on the equivalent of steroids. performance was enhanced by excessive loan growth, loan risk, securities yields, bank leverage and consumer leverage, and conducted by bankers, accountants, regulators, government, and consumers. Side effects were ignored and there was little short-term financial incentive to slow down the process despite longer-term risks.[59]

1. There was *recklessness* aplenty, rooted in the systemic dangers associated with the widespread distribution of the new financial instruments and the toleration of ever-higher leverage ratios. Bear Stearns, for example, "had tangible equity capital of about $11 billion supporting total assets of $395 billion—a leverage ratio of 36!" That was fine in good times; but "when the market turned, it left Bear bereft of capital and willing creditors."[60] In good times if not in bad, passing risk from buyer to buyer makes perfect sense for the individual seller, but not for the system as a whole. Ultimately, risks that are passed on accumulate in the hands of those institutions that are least risk averse, which works only so long as all the risks do not come apart simultaneously. You can hedge against individual risks but not against the risk of systemic failure. Hold too much super-senior risk and, when confidence falls across the financial system as a whole, you will eventually go under, as AIG found to its cost—and, indeed, to ours.[61]
2. There was *corruption*—occasionally caught, more normally covered up[62]—and there was *failure*, particularly in the way the credit agencies responded to the volume of mortgage-backed securities whose viability they were asked to verify. Charles Gasparino was particularly critical: "If there were a group of people more universally incompetent than the SEC it would have to be the bond raters, which have missed just about every major market blow up over the past three decades."[63] It was a failure that many, including Senator Carl Levin, linked to their "inherent conflict of interest—their revenue comes from the same firms whose products they are supposed to analyze, and those firms exert pressure on rating agencies who too often put market share ahead of analytical rigor."[64] The result so often was what Bolton, Freixas and Shapiro label "the credit ratings game."[65] It certainly left some pretty startling statistics around for future bond raters to ponder: "Of AAA-rated subprime mortgage-backed securities issued in 2006, 93 percent—93 percent!—have now been downgraded to junk status."[66] These, from agencies that the SEC was explicitly prohibited from regulating by the terms of the 2006 *Rating Agency Reform Act*!

3. There was *greed*—fee-financed greed that pushed up the volume of trading and the shading of risk—greed that left the top 25 hedge fund managers in 2009 (a bad year for working Americans, after all) with an average bonus of $1 billion each: roughly equivalent to the salary bill for 680,000 teachers![67] And with the bonuses came the *arrogance*—the prize examples of which recently have all come from Goldman Sachs. Remember their CEO Lloyd Blankfein telling a London audience that investment bankers do God's work! Or again, Goldman Sachs being sued by the SEC for betting against the value of financial products they had themselves created and sold. And, of course, there was also Wall Street's blind dependence on mathematical modeling of the future and on the associated new theories of efficient markets—on which, see Appendix 2—a dependence bred in the increasingly desiccated neo-classical economics departments of America's leading universities, and generalized in their impact and speed by the power of the new communication technology.
4. It is, therefore, not entirely surprising that 2009–2010 witnessed a litany of public apologies for Wall Street excess by a string of Wall Street CEOs. Saying "sorry" has become the new Wall Street norm: but "sorry" without any sign of serious remorse, and "sorry" spoken by men (it is almost exclusively men) who continue both to practice that for which they now apologize, and lobby hard against any regulatory moves to prevent the reoccurrence of systemic breakdown.[68] Apologies we have had, but prosecutions we have not. Even Angelo Mozilo, who walked away from Countrywide Financial with a reported $140 million, settled out-of-court with the SEC for a mere $47.5 million (Bank of America picking up the rest of his total $67.5 million fine).[69] Little wonder that Richard Eskow could complain that "a banker can't get arrested in this town."[70] Not now, and not any time soon.

Finally this: if all that was at stake here were guilty men, then apologies (and prison sentences) would surely suffice. But that is not all that is at stake here. What is at stake is the necessary character of unregulated/mis-regulated financial markets. What we are living downwind of is a systemic failure of a classic kind—one in which collective *irrationality* is the product of perfectly *rational* individual behavior. This is why Greenspan ultimately failed. He failed as a regulator because of his belief that if you leave individual economic players to pursue their own self-interest in an unregulated market, the outcomes will be optimal, rational, and stable—and be all these things not just for the immediate players but for the rest of us as well. No such luck!

Why? Partly it is contextual: in a world of low interest rates, making money on riskier projects becomes ever more essential for big investment firms and their individual employees. Mainly, however, it is structural—the consequence of what JPMorgan's Peter Hancock once called "the curse of the innovation cycle."[71] Precisely because the financial industry is so internally competitive—the very condition Greenspan favored—firms cannot long garner monopoly profit (i.e., rent) on instruments they invent, because they are rapidly copied. Profits then require volume, and corporate survival requires size:[72] competitive imperatives that drive perfectly rational bankers into practices that ultimately prove disastrous. JPMorgan was initially the leader in derivatives, but not for long: by 2003, the company had lost that position to Deutsche Bank, in a year in which "Lehman Brothers, Citigroup, Bear Stearns, Credit Suisse, UBS, and Royal Bank of Scotland all fiercely ratcheted up their derivatives operations."[73] As Gillian Tett later put it:

> The story of the great credit boom and bust is not a saga that can be neatly blamed on a few greedy or evil individuals. It is a story of how an entire financial *system* went wrong as a result of flawed incentives within banks and investment funds, as well as the rating agencies; warped regulatory structures; and a lack of oversight. It is a tale best understood through the observation of human foibles, as much through economic or financial analysis. And though plenty of greedy bankers—and perhaps a few mad, or evil, ones too—play crucial parts in the drama, the tragedy of this story is that so many of those swept up in the lunacy were not acting out of deliberately bad motives. [74]

The case for financial regulation ultimately rests not on the bad apple or greedy banker theory—even though, as we have seen now in abundance, fruit does rot in the heat of avarice—but on the recognition that *without regulation what may be rational for the individual financial player will not necessarily be rational for the system as a whole.* As Senator Levin said of Goldman Sachs's unregulated synthetic financial instruments, they "became the chips in a giant casino, one that created no economic growth even when it thrived, and then helped throttle the economy when the casino collapsed."[75] Echoes here of the great John Maynard Keynes quoted earlier: "when the capital development of a country becomes a by-product of the activities of a casino, the job is likely to be ill-done."[76] Ill-done, indeed.

A final note on levels of analysis

As we saw in Chapter 6, quite where you break off your explanation of the causes of the financial meltdown ultimately turns on the depth of the analysis that satisfies you. Joseph Stiglitz rightly said, "finding root causes is like peeling back an onion. Each explanation gives rise to further questions at a deeper level."[77] Basically, you can settle at the level of the actors and the immediate causes, or you can go for the broader context of resource flows and power relationships, or you can probe deeper still, to examine the underlying logics of a capitalist system in crisis.

The proximate causes are best located by detailed financial journalism and by immediate policy analysis. Follow the people. Find the links between them. See how they slowly build up to a huge disaster. Then you get a list, looking something like this.

i. Supply of new housing is relatively flexible
ii. Tax system encourages higher leverage and flipping
iii. Legal system is swift but generous to defaulters
iv. Lenders could rely on external credit scores
v. Financial regulation did not prevent riskier lending
vi. Cash-out refinancing is inexpensive in the United States
vii. Structured finance enabled subprime and other non-conforming lending.[78]

But explaining why there was so much "structured finance" flowing around Wall Street in the first decade of the new century requires that the explanatory framework be widened, and that we probe deeper, behind the flows. Part of that money was internally generated. Part came from abroad. The internal flows (and the internal pattern of demand for them) have lots to do with growing income inequality in the post-Reagan United States: the emergence of a new stratum of the rich with money to invest, while the rest of us were working hard but seeing no significant increase in our real claim on wealth. The rich lent. We borrowed. Affluence was built on credit. The credit dried up. Recession followed. What we borrowed also came from abroad. Personal debt was matched by international debt. Economies diverged in their performance: some earned a huge overseas surplus. Others lived beyond their means. We certainly lived beyond ours, enjoying a life style that ultimately depended on the willingness of overseas investors (especially German, Japanese, and Chinese) to bring their surpluses to the United States. Some commentators found that flow functional, and a source of American power.[79] Others found such global imbalances troubling, a sign of American problems to come.[80] But either way, income inequality at home and global imbalances abroad framed the U.S. financial meltdown, and were certainly central to the wild economic ride that Wall Street took us on first in the 1990s and then after 2001.

Asking why finance should become so potent at the heart of the global system, and why some economies within that system should flourish and others not, takes us out to a still larger analysis, and to one that requires an even deeper probing of the underlying logics at play. For as Sheila Bair told the Financial Crisis Inquiry Commission, "This crisis represents the culmination of a decades-long process by which our national policies have distorted economic activity away from savings and toward consumption, away from investment in our industrial base and public infrastructure and towards housing, away from the real sectors of the economy and toward the financial sector."[81] There is a fascinating literature out there on the necessary separation of finance from industry as capitalism matures.[82] There is an equally powerful literature on the necessarily combined but uneven economic development of the global system,[83] and there is a yet third literature on the special role of hegemonic powers in global capitalism—on the costs and benefits of global economic leadership.[84] A full analysis of our contemporary condition ultimately requires us to take this final step as well. To really understand our present circumstances, there is a lot of reading that simply *has* to be done. It is time for all of us to get on with it.

APPENDIX 2

The Economics in Play[1]

To understand the crisis we need to get beyond the blame game. For at the root of the crisis was not failures of character or competence, but a failure of ideas. As Keynes famously remarked, "the ideas of economists and political philosophers, both when they are right and when they are wrong, are more powerful than is commonly supposed. Indeed the world is ruled by little else." The practices of bankers, regulators and governments, however egregious, can be traced back to the ideas of economists and philosophers. It is to the ideas of economists that we now turn, starting with those most recently in fashion. For the present crisis is, to a large extent, the fruit of the intellectual failure of the economics profession.[2]

For the non-economists reading this book, there are at least two big issues on which guidance might be particularly valuable. The first concerns the role of particular bodies of economic thought in the run-up to the financial crisis of 2008. The second concerns the current range of disagreement between economists on the causes of that crisis, and on how best to avoid its repetition. The first issue can be disposed of in reasonably quick order. The second is rather more complex.

A faith in efficient markets

There seems widespread agreement now, in much of the literature on the build up to the panic of September 2008, that one element in play was something called "the efficient market hypothesis." First formulated by Eugene Fama at the University of Chicago in 1970, the hypothesis came in three forms:

> a weak form, a semi-strong form, and a strong form. The weak form holds that future prices cannot be predicted from past prices; the semi-strong form holds that prices adjust quickly to all publicly available information (meaning that by the time you read the news in the newspaper, it is too late to make money on the news); and the strong form holds that no one has any information that can be used to predict future prices, so *market prices are always right.*[3]

In the financial institutions that dominated Wall Street, it was the strong version that came to prevail,[4] and understandably so. For if market prices are always right, particularly in financial markets, then there is no need to regulate those markets. On the contrary, financial markets and the institutions prevailing within them can be safely left—indeed, for an optimum outcome, they *must* be left—free to go wherever price signals that they should go. The fit between the efficient market hypothesis and the financial markets seemed so perfect because . . .

> underlying . . . the EMH itself is a deeper assumption. The larger, more liquid, and frictionless and fast-paced a market, and the greater its capacity for disseminating all price information to all participants at the greatest speed, and the more universally it encompasses within a single bidding system all interested buyers and sellers—*in other words, the more any market looks like modern securities markets in all their electronic and insubstantial glory*—the more likely that market is to be efficient, to get prices right, to approach the theoretically perfect market of classical theory, the market of perfect competition, perfect pricing and thus zero profits.[5]

For, if the strong version of the hypothesis holds—if "in short, financial prices are tied to economic fundamentals"—then whenever "markets rise above the levels justified by fundamentals, well-informed speculators [can be relied upon to] step in and sell until prices return to their correct levels" and "if prices fall below their true values, speculators [will] step in and buy."[6] So there is literally no danger of a speculative bubble and, therefore, no need for regulatory intervention; and any temporary bubbles that might occur because of some unexpected external trigger will be exactly that—temporary and easy to fix. Alan Greenspan made that point regularly in the run-up to the crisis of 2008, justifying his "light touch" regulatory regime to skeptics in Congress. He made it regularly, but as he reluctantly conceded in his much-cited 2008 exchange with Henry Waxman,[7] whenever he did so, unfortunately he was equally regularly wrong.

For the adverse consequences of this generalized acceptance of the validity of the strong form of the efficient market hypothesis were ultimately considerable and entirely undesirable. As Robert Skidelsky has written, the acceptance "led bankers into blind faith in their mathematical forecasting models, [and] it led governments and regulators to discount the possibility that markets could implode."[8] As the financial industry generated ever more complex financial instruments and their books became accordingly ever more difficult to read, the banks in their turn "began to develop extraordinarily complex 'black box' statistical models to measure the risks they were taking,"[9] and became dangerously over-dependent on the numbers that the models threw up. The strong version of the hypothesis was never without its critics within the academic economic community,[10] of course, and there were commentators who saw early the dangers that were building up.[11] Modern securities markets, after all, are in reality not perfect markets but "bad markets," ones that are "easily overwhelmed by information . . . because their knowledge base is so thin," and, as such, disproportionately prone "to set prices to an astonishing degree by watching—prices!"[12] But sadly, those critics were never able to stem the rising dominance of this new orthodoxy, with the result, as Alan Greenspan later conceded, that the U.S. financial system under his leadership systematically and over time triggered "the under-pricing of risk worldwide"[13] with, in 2008, truly awesome consequences.

As is widely recognized now, Alan Greenspan was a key figure in wrapping the U.S. economic policy process inside this new orthodoxy for nearly two decades; but what is less widely recognized is that he was not alone in articulating this renewed faith in the capacity of financial institutions to regulate themselves. Even before the era of Greenspan at the head of the Federal Reserve, a key generation of economists, many of them based at the University of Chicago, had spent their professional careers developing sophisticated mathematical models to guide investment decisions, in the process transforming both the discipline of economics and the way in which it was taught. Stepping back from the complexities of real economies, economists trained in the Chicago School's understanding of the discipline have been encouraged since the late 1960s to build ever more complicated mathematical models based on assumptions of individual rationality and perfect knowledge, the better to use those models both to predict real-life economic outcomes and to reinforce the message that markets work best when left undisturbed by externally imposed regulation.[14] In the hands of economists like Robert Barro and Robert Lucas, economics gathered its analytical capacity by following Milton Friedman's advice. On this view, "thinking like an economist" did not involve drawing the full complexity of daily work and consumption into the purview of the discipline. Rather, it involved deliberately retreating from that complexity by operating on what Friedman proudly declared to be "unrealistic assumptions;"[15] and there can be no more unrealistic assumptions than those of complete individual rationality based on perfect and immediately accessible knowledge of the market and its options.[16]

There was, and there remains, a politics here behind the claims for scientific status for this kind of economics, a claim which also needs to be recognized and understood. Many of the formative figures in what came to be known as the Chicago School of Economics[17] also had links to a particular private grouping—the Mont Pèlerin Society[18]—created in 1947 to counter the managed-economy mentality then prevalent in parties of the center-left and in economics departments populated by Keynesians. For there was a time when "economics was very different than it is today,"[19] a time when Keynesian orthodoxies prevailed both in academia and in government. Chicago-based economists—Milton Friedman, in particular—set out to change that orthodoxy, and by the 1970s had proved remarkably successful in that endeavor.[20] After all, we do well to remember that "the notion of financial markets as rational and self-correcting mechanisms is an invention of the last 40 years."[21] It was not commonplace before the efficient market hypothesis and the rational expectations revolution launched in Chicago. The new classical economists who effected that transformation in the content and delivery of economics now offer their discipline as a science—value-free and policy-neutral—and yet the prescriptions that necessarily follow from their way of doing economics invariably keep governments at bay and make trade unions and welfare states the prime barriers to generalized economic prosperity.[22] There is hardly much political neutrality in that, and, indeed, there could not be. For in the 30 years before the great crash of 2008, and under the influence of the Chicago School, the center of gravity of professional economics—particularly in the United States—went mathematical. It went abstract, and it went conservative.[23] It went liberal in a European rather than an American sense.[24] Not that that would have mattered much if, as Yves Smith rightly put it, "economics were merely another social science. But the fact that the discipline has so much influence over policy means that how it conducts its affairs is of vital public interest,"[25] as we have so recently discovered to our very great cost.

The fallibility of efficient markets

The crash of 2008 created a serious moment of doubt for the *rational expectations* orthodoxy and brought professional economics as a discipline into considerable disrepute. A particular paradigm met its own Waterloo, and reinvigorated its critics within the profession.[26] Lucas's "unrealistic assumptions" came in for some heavy critique—these three in particular.

- Individual actors in market relationships do not have access to full and accurate information. Nor do they automatically respond to price signals by making instrumental calculations alone. The motivations of actors are complex. Economics stands condemned as the one social science that fails to build human irrationality into its core models; and arguments about the optimum resource allocation generated by perfectly competitive and entirely unregulated markets falls foul of the reality of hidden and absent information.[27] Information asymmetry and the domination of supply by large corporations are not aberrations that serve to justify the extensive use of models of perfect competition. They are evidence that deploying the model is no longer relevant. For if all economic actors are necessarily entirely rational and equipped with perfect knowledge, then the proliferation of subprime loans through the U.S. housing market should literally not have happened. But, of course, it did. Little wonder then that fashions in economics are at last beginning to change, that behavioral economics is now a recognized part of the discipline, and that those who have long argued for more complex understandings of human motivations in economic transactions are now being honored within the profession itself—not least, as we saw with the 2002 and 2009 Nobel Prizes for Economics—the first honoring Daniel Kahneman for his work with Amos Tiersky on the psychology of choice,[28] the second honoring Elinor Ostrom for her work on the importance of social networks in avoiding the tragedy of the commons.[29]

- Markets are not, in that sense, inevitably efficient. Stock markets, in particular, are prone to error and panics, driven in moments of crisis by the loud logic of herds rather than by the quiet dictates of knowledge. The advocates of the "efficient market hypothesis" forgot their Minsky.[30] They forgot that unregulated financial markets have their own internal rhythms of development—cautious in recession, exuberant in recovery—and that that necessarily brings the dynamics of the casino into the center of the economic equation. In contrast to the conviction of efficient market theory that "markets move naturally only towards equilibrium, and that after reaching equilibrium they remain in this quiescent state until influenced by a new, unexpected, *external* event," Minsky's instability thesis "argues that financial markets can generate their own *internal* forces, causing waves of credit expansion and asset inflation followed by waves of credit contraction and asset deflation," with the result that "financial markets are not self-optimizing, or stable, and certainly do not lead towards a natural optimal resource allocation."[31] The advocates of the EMH made the mistake noted by Warren Buffett, that "observing correctly that the market was frequently efficient, they went on to conclude incorrectly that it was always efficient . . . the difference between the propositions is night and day."[32] The denouement of stock markets in the crash of 2008 re-established the relevance of the remark made by John Maynard Keynes in the 1930s and already twice quoted in this volume, that "when the capital development of a country becomes a byproduct of the activities of a casino, the job is likely to be ill done."[33]

- The broader justification for the efficient (financial) markets idea is that such markets make the "real" economy more efficient by allocating resources to where they are most needed. So it is certainly legitimate to ask what was so efficient about allocating billions of dollars in the mid-2000s to the residential housing market to enable people to buy houses that ultimately they could not afford, or to wonder what was so fundamental about the supply and demand for petroleum in 2008 that justified the price spiking at $149 per barrel for no apparent reason—with the "efficient" price soon tumbling? There was a reason of course. It was pure market speculation.[34] Advocates of the rational expectations revolution have been known to claim, as Robert Lucas did in his 2002 presidential address to the American Economic Association, that *in*voluntary unemployment was a thing of the past and that macroeconomics had solved the problems of unexpected large-scale depressions. They could claim it, but after the events of 2008–2009, in doing so they were now vulnerable to the response they had once reserved for Keynesians, namely sniggering and whispering in their audience. Because for their many critics, the one thing that the post–2008 persistence of large-scale involuntary unemployment has demonstrated beyond all reasonable doubt is that, quite contrary to Lucas's claims, macroeconomics has *not* solved "its central problem of depression–prevention" and that "the free market [is] not up to the job of creating work"[35] on the scale necessary to generate full employment.

For some commentators—particularly historians of a certain bent—all this was evidence that the status of economics needs to be watered down, and that its claim for scientific status must be rejected.[36] For others, it denoted a general propensity within economics as a profession for what Raj Patel called "Anton's blindness: an inability to see the world except in terms of unfettered markets and supply & demand, concepts so dominant in the minds of economists as necessarily to blind them to "the deeper connections between us, and [so to] distort our political choices."[37] And for yet others, particularly within the less conservative wings of the profession that was ostensibly so blind—all this was simply evidence of the need for a new paradigm in economics, one that was more sensitive to the realities of history and psychology and one that was less quick to downplay the insights provided during the last Great Depression by the writings of John Maynard Keynes.[38] For them, at least, the one good thing that might yet come out of all the human suffering created by the financial meltdown of September 2008 was "the return of the master."[39]

Keynes' second coming

So what do the new generation of Keynesian economists bring to the table? They bring a clear sense of why markets do not necessarily clear at conditions of full employment, and they bring an associated commitment to strategic government interventions—stimulus packages—that might move markets towards that more socially desirable settlement. They bring, that is, a commitment to the public management of private markets.

At the core of a Keynesian understanding, of why markets left to themselves do not automatically generate the full employment of all resources within them, is the recognition that economic life is full of *uncertainty*. As Keynes said, "[W]e have only the vaguest idea of any but the most direct consequences of our acts . . . our knowledge of the future is fluctuating, vague, and uncertain."[40] When you add to that uncertainty the fact that economic activity necessarily goes on in the medium of *time*—that there is a necessary gap between production and consumption—and that producers and consumers relate to each other through the medium of *money*, you have the framework within which to accurately place the importance of *expectations* as the motive for economic action. "Time, money and uncertainty pervade Keynesian theory—and they are what sets him apart from the free-market or classical tradition."[41] If people are pessimistic about the future, they will hold on to their money—they will exercise what Keynes termed "liquidity preference." If they are optimistic, particularly if they are entrepreneurial, they will set their money to work. It is not savings that generate investment but investment that generates savings. Shaping expectations to generate investment is the key to managing economies: shaping the expectations of investors in recessions (mobilizing their "animal spirits" as Keynes had it)[42] by injecting into what otherwise would be dormant circuits of production and exchange, public spending that will itself generate demand, income, and jobs; shaping them in times of overheated economic activity, by cutting public spending and easing the underlying inflationary pressures. Government spending, so used, does not so much absorb resources as mobilize them. It has a multiplier effect, adding cumulatively to income and demand as the money passes from hand to hand, in the process creating the tax revenue that ultimately balances out the initial injection of public money. Keynesians expect government deficits to grow in a recession. They just know that, properly managed, the recession will end and the deficits will evaporate.

Which is why now battle is seriously joined—in and around the policy-making circles in Washington, London, Berlin, and Tokyo—between a new brand of neo-Keynesian economists and an entrenched group of new classical economists. The latter remain wedded to the deregulation of markets and the use of tax cuts on the wealthy to stimulate a trickle-down effect: entrepreneurial activity that will pull people into employment, unless job creation is blocked by high payroll taxes or strong trade unions. The former remain convinced that, to avoid a lost decade in which private sector willingness to invest is delayed by the sluggishness of consumer demand in an economy beset with unemployment and foreclosures, it is imperative that governments artificially and temporarily inflate the level of activity by their own borrowing and spending.[43] If the latter can be directed to those who spend most of what they earn (the poor rather than the rich) and if the publicly funded investment can generate a strong infrastructure for future private sector competitiveness and growth, so much the better. But any kind of public spending will, in some sense, do. Military spending, welfare spending, spending on schools and roads—whatever it takes, because without it, the one thing of which we can be certain is that unemployment will persist and generalized living standards will fall.[44]

I guess I should declare an interest. I don't like the new classical economists. I think they service reactionary ends and overly privileged classes. As I wrote earlier and elsewhere, when considering varieties of growth theory and the choice between models of capitalism, it seems to me that:

> the central paradox of the modern age—in the area of growth theory and state policy, at least—would appear to be that the ideational system most dominant in policymaking circles (neoclassical economics) is the one least able to explain what is actually going on, and yet is, at the same time, the one least aware of its own limitations. It is not too much to say that many neo-liberal economists now operate—to use Gramscian terminology—as the organic intellectuals of global capitalist classes, and as the main ideologues of the existing order. Certainly, the bulk of them have reconstituted themselves as a hermetically sealed and entirely self-referential priesthood, equipped with their own holy books, mantras, catechisms, and modes of induction . . . The thought patterns into which neo-liberal economists characteristically induce their students (and into which they themselves are inextricably locked) seem to act as an effective mental sealant against any recognition of the huge and deleterious social consequences of unregulated markets, and to invite a persistent preoccupation with the exchange of commodities once produced rather than with their production per se. Indeed, when viewed from outside, many of the university departments now spawning the new generation of neo-liberal economists appear increasingly authoritarian (even potentially totalitarian) in their forms of thought and action: maintaining their credibility only by retreating into abstractionism and mathematical sophistry, shutting themselves off in the process from the scholarship and insights of the other social sciences, and proving increasingly intolerant of dissent from within their own ranks. There are some wonderful economists left, of course, networked together in schools of radical political economy; but as far as I can tell, such networks no longer set the

> intellectual agenda of mainstream economics. And to the degree that that is true, so, too, is this: that whatever else the setting of the performance of capitalist models against contemporary explanations of that performance tell us, it certainly indicates that neo-liberal growth theory is inadequate to the explanatory task and potentially dangerous in the policy process. As far as I can see, neo-liberal economics is not part of any progressive solution to the problems of capitalist models, or . . . any guide to understanding why such solutions are needed. It is actually part of the problem that the rest of us need to solve.[45]

Be that as it may, one thing at least *is* certain in this age of uncertainty. It is that this debate between schools of economists will inevitably go on. One side will go on telling us (indeed they now do so daily in the columns of *The Wall Street Journal*) that the Obama stimulus package has not reduced unemployment and, so should be abandoned. The stimulus has not worked because it was too big. It squeezed private–sector investment and job creation out of the economy it was purporting to stimulate. The other side will counter that unemployment would have been higher but for the stimulus, and would now be lower if the stimulus package had not been curtailed and internally redesigned in a vain attempt to win Republican backing. Job creation, on this counter-argument, now requires a second stimulus, not the abandonment of the first. The choice that they offer and which we, therefore, face is a stark one: between schools of economists that Paul Krugman once labeled "saltwater" and "freshwater" because of the location of the bulk of Keynesians on either coast and of the new classical economists in America's hinterland.[46]

Ideally, we would face a wider choice, for there is a deeper level of analysis that mainstream economics, and the policymaking it informs, rarely addresses. It is one that recognizes that the space for economic growth is ultimately fixed, not by economic ideas alone, but by social settlements between capitalism's contending classes, in which particular bodies of economic thought play a critical and formative part. Beneath and away from the disputes chronicled here, you can find a rich "social structures of accumulation" literature[47] that sees the heyday of post-war Keynesianism as intimately linked to the character of the immediate post-war global and internal social settlement. It is a literature which then ties the rise of the new classical economics to the contradictions of that first settlement—the stagflation of the 1970s—and to the creation of a new settlement between capital and labor (capital strong, labor weak: capital rich, labor indebted) that crashed to pieces in the financial crisis of 2008. On that argument, the progressive task before us now is bigger and even more daunting than that proposed by the new generation of Keynesian economists. It is to create a new social settlement, as well as to find a new economic paradigm.[48]

But the choice before us in the here-and-now is not that wide. What is before us, for immediate resolution, is the saltwater–freshwater clash within mainstream economics. The choice on offer is, in that sense, narrower than some of us would like, but it is a clear choice, and we have to make it. It is, in truth, the most pressing choice of the age.

Notes

Introduction

1 Paul Starr, "America's 20-Year Tug-of-War," *The American Prospect*, September 2010.

2 R. H. Tawney, discussing the electoral fortunes of the British Labour Party in the 1930s, cited in David Coates, *Answering Back* (New York: Continuum Books, 2010), 3.

3 As early as April 2010, just 15 months into the new administration, the Pew Research Center was reporting that "rather than an activist government to deal with the nation's top problems, the public now wants government reformed and growing numbers want its powers curtailed. With the exception of greater regulation of major financial institutions, there is less of an appetite for government solutions to the nation's problems—including more government control over the economy—than there was when Barack Obama first took office" (see http://people-press.org/report/606/trust-in-government).

4 Frank Rich, "Why Has He Fallen Short?" *The New York Review of Books,* August 19, 2010, 12.

5 For my view on this early in the presidency, see David Coates, *Will Obama Disappoint? Probably. Should That Surprise Us? Probably Not,* available at www.davidcoates.net/2010/02/07/will-obama-disappoint-probably-should-that-surprise-us-probably-not/

6 For the FDR wobble, see Adam Cohen, *Nothing to Fear* (New York: Penguin Books, 2009), 83–88. For Obama's, look no further that the title of the commission he established in February 2010 to examine the future financing of entitlement programs: the Bipartisan National Commission on Fiscal Responsibility and Reform.

7 For this, see David Coates, *Framing Errors in the State of the Union Address*, available at www.davidcoates.net/2010/01/31/framing-errors-in-the-state-of-the-union-address/
8 Paul Waldman, "Falling Out of Love With Obama," *The American Prospect*, July 2010 web only: available at www.prospect.org/cs/articles? article=falling_out_of_love_with_obama
9 For a full review of policy in Obama's first two years in office, see the studies commissioned by the Russell Sage Foundation, to be published in 2011 as *Reaching for a New Deal*: currently available in draft at www.russellsage.org/research/working-group-obamas-policy-agenda
10 As reported by Dan Balz in *The Washington Post*, September 21, 2010.
11 This data was in a *New York Times/CBS News* poll, reported in *The New York Times*, April 14, 2010. The role of women in the leadership of Tea Party rallies has attracted commentary and analysis since the poll was taken. See, for example, Ruth Rosen, *Why Women Dominate the Right-Wing Tea Party*, posted on Alternet.org, July 6, 2010: available at www.alternet.org/story/147436, and also reproduced in Don Hazen and Adele M. Stan (eds), *Dangerous Brew: Exposing the Tea Party's Agenda to take over America*, San Francisco, AlterNet, 2010, 151–56; and Sarah Jaffe, *Why Are There So Many Right-Wing Extremist Women?* Alternet.org, October 7, 2010: available at www.alternet.org/story/148346. For the general demographics of the Tea Party Movement, see *Dangerous Brew*, 16–26 and 30–35.
12 Technically, only a national movement in the wake of the Tea Party anti-tax rallies held on April 15, 2010, but triggered into life by Rick Santelli's widely distributed *CNBC* rant against the Obama foreclosure assistance plan, February 19, 2009. For the history of the Tea Party thus far, see Will Bunch, *The Backlash* (New York: HarperCollins, 2010).
13 The Koch brothers and Rupert Murdoch are the billionaires most cited as funders and amplifiers of the Tea Party message. For details, see Jane Mayer, "Covert Operations," *The New Yorker*, August 2010; and Adele Stan, *Tea Party Inc:, The Big Money and Powerful Elites Behind the Right-Wing's Latest Uprising*, posted on Alternet.org, October 24, 2010; available at www.alternet.org/story/148598
14 Mark Lilla, "The Tea Party Jacobins," *The New York Review of Books,* May 27, 2010, 54.
15 Data from Jamelle Bouie, posted on *Tapped*, the group blog of *The American Prospect*, September 29, 2010.
16 *CNN* data, reported in Mitchell Bard, "Krugman's Takedown of Ryan . . . ," posted on *The Huffington Post,* August 8, 2010; available at www.huffingtonpost.com/mitchell-bard/krugmans-takedown-of-ryan_b_674845.html
17 http://pewresearch.org/pubs/1701/poll-obama-muslim-christian-church-out-of-politics-political-leaders-religious
18 The thesis was discussed in all seriousness by Glenn Beck on his *Fox Channel* television program on September 15, 2010: Beck said of his earlier mistaken understanding of Obama: " . . . your gut that says, wait a minute, it's about race. No,

it's not. It's not about race. It's about colonialism, which is still the message of the left, that America is stealing the resources of the world."

19 "Incredibly, the U.S. is being ruled according to the dreams of a Luo tribesman of the 1950s. This philandering, inebriated African socialist, who raged against the world for denying him the realization of his anti-colonial ambitions, is now settling the nation's agenda through the reincarnation of his dreams in his son" (cited in Robert Parry, *This Country Just Can't Deal with Reality Any More,* posted on Alternet.org, September 16, 2010: available at www.alternet.org/story/148206).

20 Bill O'Reilly is invariably the more open and cautious of the three, willing to give credit where credit is due, and to dismiss claims that Obama is a socialist. But even he wrote this in the run-up to the midterm elections: "[T]he President believes America is fundamentally flawed, and that we need to be more progressive in our outlook to create a more just society . . . in addition, Barack Obama is an internationalist, which means he believes America does not have an 'exceptional' place in the world. He wants the United States to be humble on the international front, and if that means overemphasizing his country's mistakes, so be it" (Bill O'Reilly, *Pinheads and Patriots* (New York: HarperCollins, 2010), 87–88). For O'Reilly, Obama "cannot accurately be described as a socialist. A quasi-socialist, maybe. A Pinhead about economic matters, probably" (ibid., 129).

21 See Alexander Zaitchik, *Common Nonsense: Glenn Beck and the Triumph of Ignorance* (Holboken, NJ: Wiley, 2010).

22 Limbaugh characteristically cuts liberals less slack that does O'Reilly, in part because of his antipathy to liberals within the Republican Party (his blue-blooded country-club Republicans) and partly because he has such an apocalyptic vision of America's future under liberalism. "Not all leftists are violent," he wrote in *The Wall Street Journal* on April 23, 2010. "But most are angry. It's in their DNA. They view the culture as corrupt and capitalism as unjust." "Conservative protest," by contrast, "is motivated by a love of what America stands for." "I think we're in the middle of a disaster," he told Greta Van Susteren on air, September 27, 2010, "I think the Obama administration, the regime and its agenda, is a disaster for this country as founded . . . I think it's crunch time. I don't think this is being overstated. I don't think it's being exaggerated at all."

23 T. W. Farman and Dan Eggen, "Interest-group spending for midterm up fivefold from 2006; many sources secret," *The Washington Post*, October 4, 2010.

24 From the Conservative Book club to its members (including me!), August 24, 2010.

25 The report is at www.splcenter.org/get-informed/intelligence-report/browse-all-issues/2010/spring/rage-on-the-right

26 For the rise in physical threats to federal lawmakers, see Sari Horwitz and Ben Pershing, "Anger over health-care reform spurs rise in threats against Congress members," *The Washington Post*, April 9, 2010.

27 Adele M. Stan, "What's a Progressive to Do," in Don Hazen and Adele M. Stan, op. cit, p. 26.

Chapter 1

1 For a discussion of the causes of the meltdown, see Appendix 1.

2 See Martin Wolf, "Who Will Pick up the Thread after the Great Unwinding?" *The Financial Times*, November 23, 2007. As late as June 2007, Martin Wolf was writing of "the third item on the charge sheet: the ability of the financial brain to generate huge calamities. At present, that possibility seems remote" ("Risks and Rewards of Today's Unshackled Global Finance," *The Financial Times,* June 27, 2007). He was later to write a fascinating *mea culpa*. "I missed the details of the link between subprime loans, securitization, special investment vehicles and a meltdown in money markets . . . My mistake was to underestimate the ability of the world's premier financial institutions to sink themselves in a quagmire. But I was in good company: theirs" (*The Financial Times*, January 9, 2008). He was indeed!

3 Andrew Ross Sorkin, *Too Big to Fail* (London: Viking, 2009), 89.

4 Cited in *The Financial Times*, September 1–2, 2007.

5 Cited in *The Financial Times*, November 14, 2008.

6 With administration support, Congress actually passed legislation in February 2008 giving Fannie and Freddie permission to enter the market for "jumbo" mortgages for the first time—mortgages valued at over $417,000. "Fannie & Freddie accounted for 84% of total MBA issuance in the first quarter [of 2008]—up from 33% at the peak of the U.S. housing boom in 2006," *The Financial Times*, June 4, 2008.

7 At that point, the two GSEs were supporting $5,300 billion of mortgage credits with only $81 billion of their own capital; more than half the loans they then guaranteed had been initiated since 2005, and an indeterminate number of them broke the GSEs' previous requirement of only supporting mortgages of 80 percent loan-to-value.

8 See Peter Whoriskey, "After Bailouts, New Autoworkers Make Half as Much as Veterans in Same Plant," *The Washington Post*, July 25, 2010.

9 For the detail, see the excellent flow chart in *The Atlantic*, May 2009, 59.

10 Speaking in Mesa, Arizona, February 18, 2009.

11 Data in *The Washington Post*, September 7, 2009.

12 Tim Geitner's argument to the conference that he convened in August 2010 on the future of the GSEs. Proposals for reform should come early in 2011, between the time this book goes to press and its publication date. For developments in 2011, see www.davidcoates.net

13 For details, see Daniel Carpenter, *The Contest of Lobbies and Disciplines: Financial Politics and Regulatory Reform in the Obama Administration*, available at www.russellsage.org/research/working-group-obamas-policy-agenda

14 *The New York Times,* February 20, 2009.

15 *The Economist*, November 28, 2009. When Colonial BancGroup failed in mid-August 2009 with $25 billion in assets, it brought the number of bank failures in the United States in 2009 to more than 70 (Source: *BBC News,* August 15, 2009), The number would be more than 100 by year's end.

16 Details in *The Financial Times*, June 10, 2009.

17 In parallel moves, in December the IRS quietly issued exemptions to Citigroup and other financial institutions partially owned by the government, allowing them to retain billions in tax breaks that otherwise would fall in value as the government sold off its shares. A hidden form of subsidy, this move has the potential to cost the U.S. taxpayer more than will be regained as those shares are sold (details in *The Washington Post*, December 16, 2009).

18 *The Wall Street Journal,* January 15, 2009.

19 The plan called on the biggest four bank-holding companies to pay back at least $1 billion each in 2010. "We want our money back, and we're going to get it," the president said, and, "I urge you to cover the costs of the rescue not by sticking it to your shareholders or customers or your citizens but by rolling back bonuses" (cited in *The Financial Times,* January 15, 2010).

20 Details at www.davidcoates.net/2010/06/01/u-s-senate-finally-passes-financial-reform/ and www.davidcoates.net/2010/06/29/building-walls-or-designing-colanders-legislative-change-in-the-wake-of-the-financial-tsunami/

21 For details, see John Irons, Kathryn Edwards, and Anna Turner, *The 2009 Budget Deficit: How Did We Get Here?* (Washington, DC, The Economic Policy Institute, Issue Brief #262, August 20, 2009).

22 The figure is Josh Bivens', EPI Issue Brief #265, October 29, 2009.

23 Data in *Wall Street Journal*, October 27, 2009. The administration claimed in October 2009 that the stimulus spending had by then already saved/created 640,239 jobs (an amazingly precise figure), but the number was widely challenged and, even if correct, hardly enough. (The number for the fourth quarter was later recalibrated as nearly 600,000—by then the administration was counting only jobs *directly* created with stimulus money, not the more difficult to assess "jobs created/saved.")

24 President Obama, State of the Union Address, January 27, 2010.

25 On this, see Alan Blinder, "The Fed Is Running Low on Ammo," *The Wall Street Journal,* August 26, 2010; and Chris Giles, "That Elusive Spark," *The Financial Times*, October 6, 2010.

26 Available at www.russellsage.org/research/working-group-obamas-policy-agenda

27 Data in *The Wall Street Journal,* August 27, 2010. See also "Foreclosures Grind On," *The New York Times*, August 19, 2010; and Guhan Venkatu, *Out of the Shadows: Projected Levels of Future REO Inventory* (Federal Reserve Bank of Cleveland, October 20, 2010): available at www.clevelandfed.org

28 And was confirmed in Alan Blinder and Mark Zandi, *How the Great Recession Was Brought to an End,* July 27, 2010. Available at www.economy.com/mark-zandi/documents/End-of-Great-Recession.pdf

29 It is worth noting in passing that several of the firms heavily involved in subprime lending were also heavily involved in receiving public funds designed to redress the crisis they helped to create. (See on this the report by John Dunbar, *You Broke It, You Fix It?* Issued by The Center for Public Integrity, August 26, 2009.) The AIG bailout will no doubt go down as *the* insider deal of the crisis. On this, see William Greider, *Elizabeth Warren Uncovered What the Govt. Did to 'Rescue' AIG, and It Ain't Pretty,* posted on Alternet.org, August 9, 2010: available at www.alternet.org/story/147788

30 FDIC data, reported in the *Wall Street Journal,* November 25, 2009.
31 The figures are from FDIC chair Sheila Bair, quoted in *The Wall Street Journal*, November 25, 2009. The four biggest bank-holding companies are JPMorgan Chase, Citigroup, Bank of America, and Wells Fargo. By February 2009, the four had received $90 billion in TARP money, but by end 2008 had provided less than $15 billion in equity capital to their subsidiary banks (*The New York Times*, February 18, 2009).
32 Neil Barofsky, quoted in *BBC News*, "Key U.S. Bailout Targets Not Met," January 31, 2010.
33 Francesco Gueverra, "Banking Profits Hit Pre-crisis Levels," *The Financial Times*, September 1, 2010.
34 Alan Blinder and Mark Zandi, *How the Great Recession*. See also Robert Reich, *Aftershock* (New York: Alfred A. Knopf, 2010), 27; and Josh Bivens and Anna Turner, *Putting Public Debt in Context* (Washington, DC: Economic Policy Institute Briefing Paper #272, August 3, 2010).
35 August 2, 2010.
36 Lori Montgomery, "Report Gives Stimulus Package High Marks," *The Washington Post*, October 1, 2010.
37 Of the $275 billion set aside for investment spending in the ARRA, more than half remained unspent by July 2010 (data in *The Washington Post*, August 14, 2010). By October, 70 percent of the money had been spent.
38 The details are in *The Wall Street Journal*, August 25, 2010.
39 Total state budget deficits were predicted to reach $83.8 billion in fiscal year 2011 (*The Financial Times*, July 27, 2010).
40 Michael D. Hurd and Susann Rohwedder, *Effects of the Financial Crisis and Great Recession on American Households,* NBER Working Paper No. 16407, September 2010, 1.
41 *The Wall Street Journal,* December 31, 2009.
42 Jeffrey A. Miron, "Bailout or Bankruptcy?" *Cato Journal* 29(1), Winter 2009, 15.
43 Available at http://american.com/archive/2010/august/when-economic-policy-became-social-policy
44 *The Wall Street Journal*, September 9, 2009.
45 Jeffrey A. Miron, "Bailout or Bankruptcy?" 2.
46 Cited in *The Financial Times*, March 9, 2009.
47 Peter J. Wallison, *The Dodd-Frank Act: Creative Destruction, Destroyed*, AEI Online, August 2010: available at www.aei.org/outlook/100983
48 See, for example, Alan Greenspan, "Inflation Is the Big Threat to a Sustained Recovery," *The Financial Times*, June 26, 2009; and "Market Crisis Will Happen Again," *BBC News*, September 9, 2009.
49 Writing in *The Financial Times*, May 27, 2009. It was a view echoed by the AEI's Alan Meltzer, in "Preventing the Next Financial Crisis," *The Wall Street Journal*, October 23, 2009.
50 AEI publication, October 2009.
51 Virginia Foxx, press release, October 1, 2008.

52 Peter J. Wallison, *Republicans and Obama's New Deal*, published Friday May 21, 2010: available at www.aei.org/article/102077
53 Clashing with Princeton's Paul Krugman's call for a second stimulus package, at the World Knowledge Forum in Seoul, South Korea, as reported in *The Guardian,* October 14, 2010.
54 See for example Rea Hederman Jr. and James Sherk, *Heritage Employment Report: September's Step Back*, Heritage Foundation WebMemo 2639, October 2, 2009.
55 *The Wall Street Journal*, August 30, 2010.
56 "Encouragement of debt and spending imbalances was the equivalent of allowing undergrowth to accumulate in a forest," *The Financial Times*, September 17, 2009.
57 Reported in *The New York Times*, October 13, 2010.
58 *OECD Report on the Global Economy*, June 24, 2009: press release available at www.treasurer.gov.au/displaydocs.aspx?doc=pressreleases/2009 /078.htm&pageID=003&min=wms&Year=&DocType=0
59 The level of casuistry here would be prize winning were it not so galling. Greenspan explained current low investment levels in the U.S. economy this way in *The Financial Times*, October 7, 2010: "These shortfalls, the result of widespread private-sector anxiety over America's future, have defused much, if not most, of the impact of the administration's fiscal stimulus. *Moreover, the activism embodied in such programmes has itself stoked the degree of anxiety.*" A private sector crisis eased by public sector activity is now explained as partly caused by the activity that eased it. Remarkable!
60 Robert Reich, "Why Obama Must take on Wall Street," *The Financial Times*, January 13, 2010.
61 See the editorial, "No End in Sight," *The New York Times*, June 2, 2009; and Martin Feldstein, "How to Shore up America's Crumbling Housing Market," *The Financial Times*, May 27, 2008 (where he argues for mortgage replacement loans). For similar arguments from Joseph Stiglitz—"the best option for the country is lowering the principal"—see his *Freefall* (New York: W. W. Norton, 2010), 100.
62 See Peter S. Goodman, "U.S. Loan Effort Is Seen as Adding to Housing Woes," *The New York Times*, January 2, 2010.
63 Elizabeth Warren's report, cited in *The New York Times*, October 10, 2009.
64 Cited in David Coates, *The Foreclosure Crisis That Will Not go Away*, August 1, 2010: available at www.davidcoates.net/2010/08/01/the-foreclosure-crisis-that-will-not-go-away/
65 "Institutional strangulation consists of much more than the stoppage of policies by aggregation of veto points as designed in the U.S. Constitution. In the case of financial reform, it has *non-constitutional veto points*, including committees and cultural veto points (gender and professional finance), *strategies of partisan intransigence*, and perhaps most significantly, the *bureaucratic politics of turf and reputation*. These patterns can weaken common-interest reforms, especially in the broad arena of consumer protection" (Daniel Carpenter, "Institutional Strangulation: Bureaucratic Politics and Financial Reform in the Obama Administration," *Perspectives on Politics*, Volume 8(3), September 2010, 825).

66 James Galbraith, *Obama's Biggest Mistake: Selling Out to the Bankers*, posted on Alternet, November 7, 2010; available at www.alternet.org/story/148770
67 Ben Bernanke only just scraped through his re-nomination as Fed chairman in January 2010; and long before that, center-left critics had wanted his removal. See for example, Robert Kuttner, "The Case against Bernanke," *The Huffington Post*, January 11, 2010.
68 The flow of criticism of Geitner began early, and grew in volume over time. For a representative sample, see Dean Baker, "Geitner's Plan Will Tax Main Street to Make Wall Street Richer," *The Huffington Post*, March 31, 2009; "Geitnerism Must Go," *The Nation*, April 13, 2009; Dylan Rattifan, "The Case against Geitner," *The Huffington Post*, January 11, 2010.
69 Krugman was a persistent critic of the bank bailout strategy. "Cash for trash," he called it (*The Financial Times*, March 28, 2009). "The Big Squander," *The New York Times*, November 20, 2009.
70 For Stiglitz's critique of the bailout policy, see his "Obama's Ersatz Capitalism," *The New York Times*, April 1, 2009, which includes this. "What the Obama administration is doing is far worse than nationalization: it is ersatz capitalism, the privatizing of gains and the socializing of losses."
71 *The Huffington Post*, January 30, 2009.
72 Titles of articles posted (on *The Huffington Post*) April 7, 2009, and June 18, 2009.
73 See, for example, Robert Reich, "How Main Street Got Shafted While Wall Street Bounced Back," www.alternet.org/story/144922, posted January 5, 2010; and his "Why Obama Must Take on Wall Street."
74 The case for temporary nationalization can be found in Andrew Rosenfield, "How to Clean a Dirty Bank," *The New York Times*, April 6, 2009. For the case for more permanent ownership, see Kevin Drum, "Banks of America," *Mother Jones*, May/June 2009; and Fred Moseley, "Time for Permanent Nationalization," *Dollars & Sense*, March/April 2009.
75 "Where the Obama administration did go wrong, in my opinion, was in the *way* it bailed out the banking system. It helped the banks . . . by supplying them with cheap money and relieving them of some of their bad assets. This was a purely political decision: on a strictly economic calculation it would have been better to inject new equity into the balance sheets of the banks. But this would have given the government effective control of a large part of the banking system. The Obama administration considered that politically unacceptable because it would have been called nationalization and socialism. The decision to bail out the banks without exerting government control over their balance sheets backfired and caused a serious political backlash" (George Soros, "The Real Damage to the Economy," *The New York Review of Books,* November 11, 2010, 16).
76 Paul Krugman, "The World As He Finds It," *The New York Times,* November 14, 2010.
77 As Paul Krugman later recalled, "As I pointed out in February 2009, the CBO was predicting a $2.9 trillion hole in the economy over the next two years; an $800 billion, partly consisting of tax cuts that would have happened anyway, just wasn't up to the task of filling that hole" (*The New York Times*, September 2, 2010).

Likewise Joseph Stiglitz, "In the end, the Obama administration's stimulus made a big difference—but it should have been bigger and better designed" (*Freefall,* 62).

78 See John Nichols, "Bernanke Is a Drag on the Economy and Democrats," *The Nation,* January 27, 2010.

79 See Dean Baker, "The Green Shoots Are Dead: We Need a Third Stimulus," *The Guardian Unlimited,* July 6, 2009; Robert Kuttner, "Three Reasons Why We Need An Economic Wake-Up Call," *AlterNet.org,* posted July 7, 2009; Robert Reich, "Americans Are Jobless and Scared: The Government Must Spend More Money to Kick-start Our Economy," AlterNet.org, posted October 5, 2009; and Charlie Cooper, "Stimulus, Schmimulus—We Need Jobs to Build a Sustainable Economy," *The Huffington Post,* December 31, 2009.

80 See Paul Krugman, "Too Little of a Good Thing," *The New York Times,* November 2, 2009; and his "Free to Lose," *The New York Times,* November 13, 2009.

81 No less a person than Christina Romer, chair of the president's Council of Economic Advisers, admitted in January 2010 that the unemployment numbers remained a disappointment and that the United States needed to pump more money into job creation and aid to the unemployed (cited in the *Wall Street Journal,* January 11, 2010). She was not alone. The list of prestigious economists arguing for a third stimulus grew rapidly through the winter of 2009–2010 as unemployment dug in at 10 percent and the dangers of a jobless recovery became more and more evident. (For the program many of them required, see Ross Eisenbrey, *The Plan to End the Jobs Crisis,* Washington, DC: The Economic Policy Institute, Policy Memorandum #152, October 20, 2009.)

82 Paul Krugman, "Hey, Small Spender," *The New York Times,* October 10, 2010.

83 Paul Krugman, "Falling into the Chasm," *The New York Times,* October 24, 2010.

84 *The Financial Times,* September 1, 2010.

85 Paul Krugman, "The March of the Peacocks," *The New York Times,* January 29, 2010.

86 President Obama, State of the Union Address, January 27, 2010.

Chapter 2

1 See E. P. Thompson, "The Moral Economy of the English Crowd in the Eighteenth Century," in his *Customs in Common* (London: The Merlin Press, 1991), 185–258.

2 John Maynard Keynes, *The General Theory of Employment, Interest and Money* (London: Macmillan, 1936), 383.

3 For a recent general presentation of this case, see Andrew Bernstein, *The Capitalist Manifesto: The Historic, Economic and Philosophical Case for Laissez-faire* (Lanham, MD: University Press of America, 2005).

4 As a percentage of the living standards of the core capitalisms (North America, Western Europe, Australia, and New Zealand) in 1988, Southern Europe scored 74.8 ,South Korea 20.2 and Latin America 12.1. Only Japan's GNP/capita was higher, at 117.9 (Giovanni Arrighi, "World Income Inequalities and the Future of Socialism," *New Left Review* 198, March/April 1993, 45).

5 As Peter Berger put it, "Industrial capitalism has generated the greatest productive power in human history, to date no other socioeconomic system has been able to generate comparable productive power . . . advanced industrial capitalism has generated, and continues to generate, the highest material standard of living for large masses of people in human history," in *The Capitalist Revolution* (New York: Basic Books, 1986), 36, 43. A decade earlier, the self-proclaimed neo-conservative Irving Kristol had restricted capitalism to two cheers, lauding it but denying it the third cheer because its "prosperity is not equally shared" (*Two Cheers for Capitalism*, New York: Basic Books, 1978, x).

6 Arrighi, "World Income," 53.

7 See Hans Breitenbach, Tom Burden, and David Coates, *Features of a Viable Socialism* (London: Harvester, 1990), 18.

8 Robert A. Degan, *The Triumph of Capitalism* (New Brunswick: Transaction Publishers, 2008), xi.

9 For the argument, see Milton Friedman, "The Power of the Market" in his *Free to Choose* (New York: Houghton Mifflin Harcourt, 1990).

10 Adam Smith, *The Wealth of Nations* (1776) Book IV, ii, 456.

11 Kristol, *Two Cheers*, xi.

12 Milton Friedman, "The Line We Dare Not Cross," *Encounter,* November 1976, 11.

13 Ibid., 11.

14 See Guinevere Nell, James Sherk, and Paul L. Winfree, *Free Market Philanthropy: The Social Aspect of Entrepreneurship* (Heritage Foundation, Center for Data Analysis, CDA08–07, September 16, 2008).

15 The quotations and arguments of this paragraph are taken from Martin Wolf, "The Morality of the Market," *Foreign Policy,* Issue 138, September/October 2003.

16 That capacity for innovation is even perhaps limited by patent law. For the debate on this, see James Bessen and Michael J. Meurer, "Of Patents and Property," *Regulation*, Winter 2008–2009, 18–26; and Andrew Grossman, *Promoting Innovation with Patent Reform*, The Heritage Foundation, January 16, 2009.

17 Hence the furious resistance to the *Employee Free Choice Act* in 2009. See Newt Gingrich's claim that "card check could cost 600,000 jobs in its first year," in his *Dancing to Big Labor's Tune* (Human Events website, March 11, 2009).

18 In the immediate wake of the Enron Scandal and the passing of the *Sarbanes-Oxley Act*, the CEO of Sun Microsystems rejected the new regulations as draining of shareholder value. The CEO of JPMorgan Chase warned that it might "damage what's made Wall Street great, and what's made this country great," (cited in *The Financial Times*, October 10, 2002). More recently, the president of the Czech Republic made a similar point, from an Eastern European perspective. "Our historical experience gives us a clear instruction: we always need more of markets and less of government intervention . . . The best thing to do now would be temporarily to weaken, if not repeal, various labor, environmental, social, health and other 'standards', because they block rational human activity more than anything else" (*The Financial Times,* January 7, 2009).

19 "There is no increase in what Keynesians refer to as aggregate demand since every dollar that is spent on a stimulus package is a dollar that the government must first borrow from private credit markets. Keynesianism doesn't boost national income, it merely redistributes it" (Daniel Mitchell, *Spending Is Not Stimulus,* Cato Institute Tax and Budget Bulletin, No. 5, February 2009, 2).

20 "Not only has adherence to Keynes's principles not averted the current economic disaster, it has greatly contributed to causing it. The Keynesian desire to manage aggregate demand, ignoring the long-run costs, pushed Alan Greenspan and Ben Bernanke to keep interest rates low in 2002, fueling excessive consumption by the household sector and excessive risk-taking by the financial sector. More importantly, it has been the Keynesian training of our policy-makers that has led them to ignore the role that incentives play in economic decisions" (Luigi Zingales, debating with Brad DeLong on *The Economist* website, March 10, 2009).

21 For this, see Brian M. Reidl, *Why Government Spending Does Not Stimulate Economic Growth* (Heritage Foundation Backgrounder No. 2208, November 12 2008).

22 Ayn Rand's novel *Atlas Shrugged* is currently much favored by intellectuals at the Cato Institute and by editorial writers at *The Wall Street Journal.* Ron Paul is also much in vogue among young Republicans disenchanted with the previous Bush administration.

23 Friedman, *Free to Choose,* 3. For a recent restatement of the more conventional tolerance of limited government, see Brett Shaefer, *How The Scope of Government Shapes the Wealth of Nations*, Heritage Lecture #925, March 7, 2006.

24 Extracts from the text of the letter, "With All Due Respect, Mr. President, That Is Not True," signed by 100 non-Keynesian economists and published by the Cato Institute in *The Wall Street Journal*, January 2009.

25 "The United States is the freest nation on earth. It happens to be also the richest nation as well. These two facts are no coincidence. Somehow freedom on the one hand and progress in the economic and human spheres on the other hand seem to go together" (Walter E. Williams, *America: A Minority Viewpoint*, Stanford University: Hoover Institution Press, 1982, i).

26 A. Lindbeck, "What Is Wrong with the West European Economies?" *The World Economy*, 8(2) (1985), 153–70.

27 Radio interview, November 4, 2005.

28 George W. Bush, press conference, October 11, 2006.

29 See Gary Becker and Kevin Murphy, "Do Not Let the 'Cure' Destroy Capitalism," *The Financial Times*, March 20, 2009.

30 Newt Gingrich sarcastically congratulated Obama on a highly successful first 100 days in office, "successfully moving to a European model of government control." (On the website of *Human Events*, April 29, 2009.)

31 *Join the Conservative Underground,* Human Events website, April 29, 2009.

32 For this as a general feature of popular conservatism these days, see David Coates, *Answering Back* (New York: Continuum Books, 2010), 15–27.

33 "The Obama administration falls squarely into the increased competition camp with respect to all three markets. Health care reform ... financial regulation reform ... energy reform ... All three will increase transparency and competition," in

Christine E. Weller, *Obama's Pro-Market Economics* (Washington, DC: Center for American Progress, July 15, 2010).

34 Apparently also a third time, in a posthumously published history of astronomy, in which he spoke of "the invisible hand of Jupiter" (I am grateful to Justin Fox, writing in *Time*, April 5, 2010, for this piece of erudition!)

35 John Kay, *The Truth About Markets* (London: Penguin, 2004), 184.

36 Patricia Werhane, *Adam Smith and His Legacy for Modern Capitalism* (New York: Oxford University Press, 1991), 7. As she notes (viii), Smith was fully aware that "pursuing one's private interests . . . may contribute to, the public good, but only under specific conditions in which economic liberty operates in the context of prudence, cooperation, a level playing field of competition, and within a well-defined framework of justice."

37 Rashida Hussein, *Hard Lessons for Hard Times: The Perils of Remembering Adam Smith's Wealth of Nations and Forgetting his Theory of Moral Sentiments*, paper delivered at the 2010 APSA Annual Meeting, 5.

38 "Whenever the regulation . . . is in favor of the workmen, it is always just and equitable; but it is sometimes otherwise when in favor of the masters." Adam Smith, *An Inquiry into the Nature and Causes of the Wealth of Nations* (Indianapolis: Library Classics, 1976 (originally 1776)), 157–58.

39 The argument and quotations here are from Karen I. Vaughn, "Invisible Hand," in John Eatwell, Murray Milgate, and Peter Newman (eds), *The New Palgrave: A Dictionary of Economics* (New York: W.W. Norton, 2001).

40 For the general argument, see Ha-Joon Chang, "Breaking the Mould: An Institutionalist Political Economy Alternative to the Neo-liberal Theory of the Market and the State," *Cambridge Journal of Economics* 26 (2002), 539–59.

41 Seeing things so firmly through a market lens that you can only give them a market value is called 'Anton's blindness" or "anosogosia" by Ray Patel in his excellent, *The Value of Nothing* (New York: Picador, 2009), 20–24. For more on this, see Appendix 2.

42 The issue is wonderfully explored in Debra Satz, *Why Some Things Should Not Be For Sale* (Oxford: Oxford University Press, 2010). The fluid construction of the boundary line between the private and the public is thoughtfully explored in Andrew Stark, *Drawing the Line* (Washington, DC: Brookings Institution Press, 2010). It is noteworthy that there was generalized outrage in October 2010 at the decision of the South Fulton fire department *not* to put out the house fire of someone who had failed to pay his annual surcharge for their services (details in *The New York Times*, October 6, 2010).

43 Two very accessible examples are Kenneth J. Arrow, "Problems Mount in Application of Free Market Economic Theory," *The Guardian*, January 4, 1994; and Joseph Stiglitz, "There Is No Invisible Hand," *The Guardian*, December 20, 2002.

44 Smith was no fan of large (joint stock) companies. On this, see Werhane, *Adam Smith*, 164. For an argument that Smith's work applies particularly badly to modern finance, see Philip Augur, "Adam Smith's Hidden Hand Is Vanishing," *The Financial Times*, March 14, 2007.

45 This thesis is developed in full in William Lazonick, *Business Organization and the Myth of the Market Economy* (Cambridge: Cambridge University Press, 1991).

46 There is a whole new discipline of "behavioral economics" addressed to this, exploring the interface between economic and psychology. In 2002, the Nobel Prize for Economics went to two leading figures in this new discipline, one an economist, the other a psychologist. See also Robert Schiller, "A Failure to Control the Animal Spirits," *The Financial Times*, March 9, 2009. For more on this, see Appendix 2.

47 For a guide to the rich literature on markets and socialism, see Brietenbach et al., *Viable Socialism*.

48 On this, see Euclid Tsakalotos, "Competitive Equilibrium and the Social Ethos: Understanding the Inegalitarian Dynamics of Liberal Market Economies," *Politics and Society*, 35(3) (September 2007), 427–46.

49 The 2010 BP-generated oil spill in the Gulf of Mexico will no doubt become one of the most cited examples of this danger. Strange then that more extreme elements in the anti-regulatory wing of the Republican Party should have been so quick to apologize—not to the American people for the easing of regulations on deep-water drilling under the Bush administration—but to BP for the way the Obama administration had criticized it and made it pay for the cleanup! (See, for example, Representative Joe Barton, the ranking Republican member of the House Energy Committee, quoted in *The Washington Post*, June 22, 2010.)

50 For a general historical survey, see Richard Kozul-Wright, "The Myth of Anglo-Saxon Capitalism: Reconstructing the History of the American State," in H. J. Chang and B. Rowthorn (eds), *The Role of the State in Economic Change* (Oxford: Oxford University Press, 1995); and David Coates, *Models of Capitalism* (Cambridge: Polity Press, 2000), 201–10. For the latest figures, see Stephen Slivinski, *The Corporate Welfare State: How the Federal Government Subsidizes U.S. Businesses* (Cato Institute Policy Analysis 592, May 14, 2007); Brian Reidl, *How Farm Subsidies Harm Taxpayers, Consumers and Farmers Too* (Heritage Foundation Backgrounder No. 2043, June 19, 2007); George Monbiot, "The Free Market Preachers Have Long Practiced State Welfare for the Rich," *The Guardian*, September 30, 2008; and Clyde Prestowitz, *The Betrayal of American Prosperity* (New York: Free Press, 2010), 269–70. Slivinski estimates that in 2006 the federal government spent $92 billion in subsidies, much of it going to big companies. The $92 billion included $21 billion to the farming sector, two-thirds of which went to agribusiness. All this *before* the 2008–2009 bailout of the banks.

51 Adam Smith's state was very active in *creating* the conditions for capitalism, by suppressing resistance to the new political economy of the market. On this, see Michael Perelman, *Classical Political Economy: Primitive Accumulation and the Social Division of Labor* (Totowa, NJ: Rowman and Allenhead, 1983).

52 The case is well made in Stephanie Greenwood (ed.), *10 Excellent Reasons Not To Hate Taxes* (New York: The New Press, 2007).

53 For the general case for industrial policy, see "Industrial Policy: introduction" in David Coates (ed.), *Industrial Policy in Britain* (London: Macmillan, 1996), 3–30.

For the United States, see Jeff Madrick, *The Case for Big Government* (Princeton: Princeton University Press, 2009); and Lawrence D. Brown and Lawrence R. Jacobs, *The Private Abuse of the Public Interest* (Chicago: University of Chicago Press, 2008).

54 For the rebuttal of the nonsense about FDR extending the Depression, see the evidence given to the Economic Policy Subcommittee of the Senate Committee on Banking, Housing and Urban Affairs (March 31, 2009) by Christina D. Romer, James K. Galbraith, and Lee E. Ohanian. (I am grateful to Dr. Mike Lawlor for these references.) More accessible may be Hale Steward, *The Great Depression,* posted on *The Huffington Post*, December 31, 2008, and January 2, 2009; or Paul Krugman, "Franklin Delano Obama?" *The New York Times*, November 10, 2008.

55 On this, see Appendix 2.

56 The case is extremely well put in "Why Keynesian Economics is Best," in Will Hutton, *The State We're In* (London: Jonathan Cape, 1994).

57 The title of a much-cited essay by Milton Friedman in *Encounter*, November 1976 (see this chapter note 12).

58 Joseph Shaanan called this "the darker side" of the freedom to profit so central to the American story, and as such in need of restraint since "the danger, if it is not too late already, is the loss of democracy." Joseph Shaanan, *Economic Freedom and the American Dream* (New York: Palgrave Macmillan, 2010), 3, 197. Many critics of the Supreme Court judgment in *Citizens United* currently echo that sentiment.

59 For a fully statement of this argument, see Coates, *Answering Back*, 121–24.

60 Bo Rothstein, "Marxism, Institutional Analysis and Working Class Power: The Swedish Case," *Politics and Society*, 18(3) (1990), 325.

61 David Coates, "Labour Power and International Competitiveness: A Critique of Ruling Orthodoxies," in Leo Panitch and Colin Leys (eds), *Global Capitalism Versus Democracy: Socialist Register 1999* (London: The Merlin Press, 1999), 131.

62 David Coates , "The Question of Trade Union Power," in David Coates and Gordon Johnston (eds), *Socialist Arguments* (London: Martin Robertson, 1983), 58–62; David Coates, *The Context of British Politics* (London: Hutchinson, 1984), 88–91.

63 For the argument that the term "market" acts as a "veil" over class power, see Paul Stiles, *Is The American Dream Killing You? How "The Market" Rules Our Lives* (New York: HarperCollins, 2005), 98–101. As he says (101), "you have the give the Market credit—it is one hell of a liar."

64 The argument here follows the "social structures of accumulation" literature as found, for example, in David Gordon, "Chickens Home to Roost: From Prosperity to Stagnation in the Post-war U.S. Economy," in M. Bernstein and D. E. Adler (eds), *Understanding American Economic Decline* (Cambridge: Cambridge University Press, 1994), 34–76.

65 For the different fate of the minimum wage in the two periods, see Larry Bartels, *Unequal Democracy: The Political Economy of the New Gilded Age* (Russell Sage Foundation: University of Princeton Press, 2008), 223–51.

66 On this, see Coates, *Answering Back*, chapter 10; and here, Appendix 1.

67 For the more positive take on U.S. labor unions, see R. B. Freeman and J. L. Medoff, *What Do Unions Do?* (New York: Basic Books, 1984); and Lawrence Mishel and Pauline Voos (eds), *Unions and Competitiveness* (New York: M.E. Sharpe, 1992). It is worth asking: if trade unions are so bad for international competitiveness, how are we to explain the continuing economic international strength of the highly unionized German economy? For an answer, see Coates, *Models of Capitalism*, chapter 4.
68 On this, see also the later chapter on trade: and Arrighi, *World Income*.
69 For a radical critique of the existing distribution of pay and bonuses, and of the myths perpetrated to defend that distribution, see the NEF report, *A Bit Rich: Calculating the Real Value to Society of Different Professions* (London: The New Economic Foundation, January 2009).
70 "The substantial increases in senior executive compensation since the early 1990s—many given to executives irrespective of their contribution to the creation of shareholder value—far exceed the additional resources companies have devoted to CSR [corporate social responsibility] over a similar time period." David Vogel, *The Market for Virtue: The Potential and Limits of Corporate Social Responsibility* (Washington, DC: Brookings Institution Press, 2005), 14.
71 For a list of Wall Street fines in the two years after 9/11, see Stiles, *American Dream*, 183; for a list of recent corporate scandals, see 189–90; in charitable organizations, see 198.
72 For a systematic study of how these external forces interact with market constraints, see David Vogel, *Market for Virtue*.
73 See Rebecca M. Blank and William McGurn, *Is the Market Moral: A Dialogue on Religion, Economics and Justice* (Washington, DC: Brookings Institution Press, 2004).
74 For the argument in detail, see William J. Baumol, "(Almost) Perfect Competition (Contestability) and Business Ethics," in William Baumol and Sue Anne Batey Blackman, *Perfect Markets and Easy Virtue: Business Ethics and the Invisible Hand* (Cambridge, MA: Blackwell, 199)1; or Paul Stiles, *American Dream*, 173–204. For David Vogel's more nuanced argument that the drivers are both external and internal, and that there is a need for greater external pressure (civil and governmental) see *Market for Virtue*, 3, 173.
75 It is significant in this respect that Nicholas Sarkozy, president of France, should have established the International Commission on the Measurement of Economic Performance and Social Progress, chaired by Joseph Stiglitz and advised by Amartya Sen. The Commission's 292 page report, published in 2009, proposed, among other things, a income- and consumption-focused measure of material well-being.
76 Speaking in 1968, cited in Jeff Maddrick, *Big Government*, 29.
77 Raymond Plant, "Social Limits to Markets," *Economic Affairs* (August/September 1987), 18.
78 Plant, "Social Limits," 19.
79 Peter Saunders, *Capitalism: A Social Audit* (Milton Keynes: Open University Press, 1995), 80.

80 There is now a growing literature on the economics of happiness. See for example Bruno S. Frey and Alois Stutzer (eds), *Happiness and Economics* (Princeton: Princeton University Press, 2002); and Richard Layard, *Happiness: Lessons from a New Science* (London: Penguin, 2005). For a more accessible if much more conservative take on the same issues, see Arthur C. Brooks, *Gross National Happiness: How Happiness Matters for America—And How We Can Get More of It* (New York: Basic Books, 2008).

81 For the strongest argument that the two are incompatible, see Stiles, *American Dream*. For the counter argument, see Brooks, *Gross National Happiness*.

82 OECD, *Society at a Glance: OECD Social Indicators, 2009*, 121.

83 The conflicting data is in Brooks, *Gross National Happiness*, 14–15; and in Robert Lane, *The Loss of Happiness in Market Democracies* (New Haven: Yale University Press, 2001), 20. The Brooks data suffers from its immersion in a free-market frame that has American workers choosing to work long hours because they so value job satisfaction, and one that discounts the impact of economic inequality on happiness. Pity!

84 The average annual hours worked in the United States in 2006 were 1,804, as against 1,436 for Germany, 1,564 for France, 1,669 for the United Kingdom, and 1,784 for Japan. That makes 368 hours difference each year between the United States and Germany—that's the equivalent of almost ten extra 40-hour weeks! (The data is in Lawrence Mishel, Jared Bernstein and Heidi Shierholz, *The State of Working America 2008/9*, Ithaca: ILR Press, 2009, 365.)

85 For stress and American capitalism right now, see Stiles, *American Dream*, 35–50, 263. For capitalism in general and over time, see Barbara Ehrenreich, *Dancing in the Streets: A History of Collective Joy* (London: Granta, 2007). For recent trends in the quality of work, broadly downwards, see Francis Green, *Demanding Work: The Paradox of Job Quality in the Affluent Economy* (Princeton: Princeton University Press, 2006).

86 The twice-poor numbered 91.1 million in the United States in 2007 (Mishel et al., *Working America*, 301).

87 "In 1965, U.S. CEOs in major companies earned 24 times more than the average worker: this ratio grew to 298 at the end of the recovery in 2000, then fell due to the stock market decline in the early 2000s and recovered to 275 in 2007" (Ibid., 9).

88 This was abundantly clear, too, in the Bush administration's Labor Department and OHSA. The Wages and Hours Division of the Labor Department, for example, had 750 investigators for a labor force of 130 million. In 1941, the figures had been 1,800 to cover 15.5 million eligible workers (*The Nation*, April 27, 2009, 6). When tested by undercover work by the GAO, the Division mishandled 9 of the 10 cases brought! (*The New York Times*, March 25, 2009).

89 "In addition to soaring inequality and insecurity, laissez-faire policies have produced a range of social poisons: rising greed and envy, rampant fraud and dishonesty, failing trust between Americans, and a crisis of ethics in nearly every institution in American life ... A long-overdue conversation about how unchecked markets can distort and damage American society has begun" (David Callaghan, "The Moral Market," *Democracy*, 13 (Summer 2009)).

90 On this, see Norton Garfinkle, *The American Dream versus The Gospel of Wealth: The Fight for a Productive Middle-Class Economy* (New Haven: Yale University Press, 2006).

91 In a genuinely epochal moment before the House Committee on Oversight and Government Reform, October 23, 2008. What was it that Dorothy said when she landed in Oz? "Toto, I've a feeling we're not in Kansas anymore." That kind of moment.

Chapter 3

1 In an October 2010 *NBC/Wall Street Journal* poll, 53 percent of those surveyed said that free trade agreements hurt the United States. The equivalent figure in 1999 had been 32 percent (details in *The Wall Street Journal,* October 4, 2010). For growing global public unease with the pace of globalization, see the details of the 2008 BBC poll at www.worldpublicopinion.org/pipa/articles/btglobalization-tradera/ 446.php?lb=btgl&pnt=446&nid=&id=

2 The WTO reported 83 new trade restricting measures from 24 countries and the EU in the three months to July 2009, twice as many as the trade-liberating measures introduced in the same period (see *The Financial Times*, July 2, 2009). Lest we forget, this is true even for the United States. The Obama stimulus package included "buy American" requirements that discriminated even against NAFTA partner Canada, and this was but the most recent in a long line of protectionist measures that favored both distressed industries (like steel) and profitable ones (especially agriculture). The United States industrialized behind tariffs against cheaper foreign products (initially British) from the War of 1812 to the *Smoot-Hawley Act* of 1930. (For a succinct history of U.S. tariffs, see John Steele Gordon, "Look Who's Afraid of Free Trade," *Commentary*, 25(2) (February 2008), 20–25.)

3 For the argument that all twentieth-century progressive presidents (from Wilson to Clinton) were free-traders, and properly so, see Ed Gresser, *Freedom from Want* (Brooklyn, NY: Soft Skull Press, 2007).

4 We will leave Pat Buchanan to put his own protectionist case. See, for example, *Fair Trade and Funny Math* posted on his website February 27, 2007.

5 Robert Krol, *Trade, Protectionism, and the U.S. Economy: Examining the Evidence* (Washington, DC: Cato Institute Trade Briefing Paper No. 28, September 16, 2008), 3.

6 The source here is Philip Levy, *Trade Truths for Turbulent Times* (Washington, DC: AEI website, posted February 20, 2007).

7 For this refutation of the "development of under-development" thesis, see Peter Saunders, *Capitalism: A Social Audit* (Milton Keynes: Open University Press, 1995), 36–51; and P. Berger, *The Capitalist Revolution* (New York: Basic Books, 1984), 115–39.

8 For the argument that competition is the great spur to innovation, and innovation to productivity, see W. J. Baumol, *The Free Market Innovation Machine* (Princeton: Princeton University Press, 2002). Baumol treats "competition, innovation and foreign trade as mutual stimuli" (287–88).

9 Daniel T. Griswold, *WTO Report Card: America's Economic Stake in Open Trade* (Washington, DC: Cato Trade Briefing Paper, April 3, 2000), 4.
10 For a critique, see Johan Norberg, *In Defense of Global Capitalism* (Washington, DC: Cato Institute, 2003), 158–60.
11 See, for example, Glenn Hubbard, "Outsourcing Is Good for America," *The Financial Times,* March 24, 2004, 15.
12 "Trade does, as critics stress, mean painful adjustment for those affected, as well as shifts in the rewards for different workers. Yet this is just as true of productivity. Information technology destroyed the jobs of armies of clerks and raised the wages of educated workers relative to those of less educated workers. But it had no deleterious effect on employment. Between 7 and 8 percent of U.S. private jobs are lost every quarter. But employment has still increased. Neither rising productivity nor growing imports will undermine overall employment, provided the labor market is flexible" (Martin Wolf, "Why Trade Is Not Bad for the American Job Market," *The Financial Times*, February 25, 2004, 13).
13 Griswold, *WTO Report Card*, 5.
14 Ibid.
15 The data is in Griswold, *WTO Report Card*, 7.
16 Ibid., 8.
17 Cited in Griswold, *WTO Report Card*, 8.
18 Robert Lawrence and Robert Litan, *Globaphobia: The Wrong Debate Over Trade Policy* (Washington, DC: Brookings Institution website, posted July 16, 2008), 3.
19 Anthony Kim, *Economic Pessimism: No Excuse for Protectionism* (Washington, DC: Heritage Foundation WebMemo No. 1883, April 4, 2008), 2.
20 The general case is made in Gresser, *Freedom From Want.*
21 Ibid., 10.
22 This in Ambassador Terry Miller, *Free Trade: Media Should Include Facts with Opinion Polls* (Heritage Foundation WebMemo No. 1670, October 18, 2007), 1.
23 The data is from Scott Bradford, Paul Grieco, and Gary Hufbauer, "The Payoff to America from Globalisation," *The World Economy,* 29(7) (July 2006), 893.
24 "Since 1990, the share of U.S. GDP that Americans have earned abroad through exports of goods and services and earnings on foreign investments has jumped from 12 percent to 17.4 percent . . . the highest ratio of exports to GDP in our history . . . Three quarters of the world's spending power and 96 percent of its people live outside the United States. This represents a huge potential market for U.S. producers" (Dan Griswold, before the House Small Business Committee, U.S. Congress, June 19, 2008).
25 Daniel Griswold, *America's Record Trade Deficit: A Symbol of Economic Strength* (Washington, DC: Cato Trade Policy Analysis No. 12, February 9, 2001), 9. "Trade critics . . . wrongly assume that every import from China displaces domestic production, eliminating jobs in the economy. In reality, much of what we import from China . . . substitutes for imports from other low-wage producers. Another sizeable portion of our imports consists of intermediate inputs, which are then assembled into U.S.-made products by American manufacturers."

26 On this, see Daniel Griswold, *America's Record Trade Deficit*; and John H. Makin, *America's External Balances* (AEI Economic Outlook, August 2006).
27 Ibid., 16.
28 Bradford et al., "The Payoff to America," 893.
29 *Cato Handbook for the 108th Congress* (Washington, DC: Cato Institute, December 2007), 611.
30 For the argument that tariffs hit wages, particularly the wages of the poor, see Gresser, *Freedom From Want*, 173–75.
31 Daniel Griswold, *"Shipping Jobs Overseas" or Reaching New Customers? Why Congress Should Not Tax Reinvested Earnings Abroad* (Cato Free Trade Bulletin No. 36, January 13, 2009).
32 Michael Bloomberg, "America Must Resist Protectionism," *The Financial Times*, December 12, 2007.
33 "Are the poorest of the poor suffering from the excessive attention of beastly transnational corporations and greedy foreign buyers? The answer is clearly no. The world's poorest people are at the margins of domestic economies that are themselves at the margin of the world economy. To ascribe their plight to globalization is to confuse the disease with the cure" (Martin Wolf, "Spreading the World's Wealth," *The Financial Times*, December 20, 2000).
34 Norberg, *Global Capitalism*, 25.
35 Ibid. 13.
36 For the list, see Norberg, *Global Capitalism*, 25–59, 72–89.
37 See, for example, Brink Lindsey, *The Trade Front: Combating Terrorism with Open Markets* (Washington, DC: Cato Trade Policy Analysis No. 24, August 5 2003).
38 Norberg, *Global Capitalism*, 56.
39 Tim Kane, *Free Trade Is Dead, Long Live Free Trade* (Washington, DC: Heritage Foundation WebMemo No. 1409, March 27, 2007), 3.
40 Jagdish Bhagwati, *In Defense of Globalization* (New York: Oxford University Press, 2004), 11.
41 Jagdish Bhagwati, *Free Trade Today* (Princeton, NJ: Princeton University Press, 2002), 52–57.
42 Peter Mandelson, quoted in *The Guardian*, September 7, 2005, 12.
43 Thomas L. Friedman, *The World Is Flat* (New York: Farrar, Straus and Giroux, 2006), 374.
44 Indur M. Goklany, *The Improving State of the World* (Washington, DC: Cato Institute, 2007), 71, 72, 77.
45 Daniella Markheim, *Free Trade: The Fairest Trade Policy for America* (Heritage Foundation WebMemo 2169, December 12, 2008), 2.
46 Matt Miller, "Liberalism's Moral Crisis on Trade," *The Washington Post*, October 7, 2010.
47 See Francisco Rodríguez and Dani Rodrik, *Trade Policy and Economic Growth: A Skeptic's Guide to the Cross-National Evidence* (NBER Working Paper 7081, April 1999); Anne Harrison and Gordon Hanson, *Who Gains From Trade Reform*

(NBER Working Paper 6915, January 1999); Athanasios Vamvakidis, "How Robust Is the Growth–Openness Connection? Historical Evidence," *Journal of Economic Growth* 7 (2002), 57–80; and Joseph Stiglitz and Andrew Charlton, *Fair Trade For All* (Oxford: Oxford University Press, 2005), 23–36.

48 Net job growth in the U.S. private sector July 1999–July 2009 was a meager 121,000 in a labor force of 109 million, an annual growth rate for the decade of 0.01 percent (*New York Times*, August 8, 2009).

49 The best source for wage data is the Economic Policy Institute's bi-annually produced *The State of Working America*. As we will see in more detail in Chapter 5, the inflation-adjusted income of the median American family actually fell between 2000 and 2009, by 4.8 percent!

50 Quotation from the press release for the latest Demos report on credit card use, available at: www.demos.org/press.cfm?currentarticle ID=C1AA23D3–3FF4–6-C82–5011CF28174638DB. On this, see also the important essay by Johnna Montgomerie, "Neoliberalism and the Making of Subprime Borrowers," in Martijn Konings (ed.), *The Great Credit Crash* (London:Verso, 2010), 103–18.

51 David Coates, *A Liberal Took Kit* (Westport, CT: Praeger-Greenwood, 2007), 149–50.

52 For the argument that those advocating free trade exaggerate the gains to the U.S. consumer and low-ball the costs of trade liberalization by omitting its general adverse impact on wage growth, see L. Josh Bivens, *The Marketing of Economic History: Inflating the Importance of Trade Liberalization* (Washington, DC: Economic Policy Institute Issue Brief 238, December 17, 2007). See also his *Who Gains from Trade* (EPI Working Paper, December 17, 2007); and his *Everyone Wins Except Most of Us* (Washington, DC: EPI 2008).

53 L. Josh Bivens, *Everyone Wins*.

54 L. Josh Bivens, *Trade, Jobs and Wages: Are the Public's Worries about Globalization Justified?* (Washington, DC: Economic Policy Institute Issue Brief 244, May 6, 2008), 3.

55 Paul Krugman, "Trouble with Trade," *The New York Times*, December 28, 2007.

56 On this distinction, see Bob Rowthorn, "Deindustrialisation in Britain," in R. Martin and B. Rowthorn (eds), *The Geography of Deindustrialisation* (London: Macmillan, 1986), 1–30; and R. Rowthorn and John Wells, *Deindustrialization of Foreign Trade* (Cambridge: Cambridge University Press, 1987); See also David Coates, *The Question of UK Decline* (Hemel Hempstead: Harvester Wheatsheaf, 1994), 11–12; and David Coates and John Hillard (eds), *UK Economic Decline: Key Texts* (Hemel Hempstead: Harvester Wheatsheaf, 1995), 11–14.

57 Josh Bivens, *Shifting Blame for Manufacturing Job Loss* (Washington, DC: Economic Policy Institute Briefing Paper, 2003).

58 "(the value of imports rose from 21 percent to 82 percent of domestic manufacturing output between 1979 and 2006), and it now exports the near-majority of domestic production (the value of exports rose from 21 percent to 43 percent of domestic output over the same period) . . . Manufactured imports and exports constituted over 60 percent of total trade in 2006 and over 85 percent of the total deficit" (Bivens, *Everybody Wins*, 13).

59 This was certainly the key finding in the Cornell University report commissioned by the U.S. Trade Deficit Review Commission in May 2000: that "international trade and investment policies, combined with ineffective labor laws, have created a climate that has emboldened employers to threaten to close, or actually to close their plants to avoid unionization . . . as expected, Mexico was the country most often mentioned in plant closing threats" (Kate Bronfenbrender, *Uneasy Terrain: The Impact of Capital Mobility on Workers, Wages, and Union Organizing* (Cornell University, September 6, 2000), vi–vii).

60 Janet Ceglowski and Stephen Golub, "Just How Low Are China's Labor Costs?" *The World Economy* (2007), 611.

61 Robert E. Scott, *The China Trade Toll* (Washington, DC: Economic Policy Institute Briefing Paper 219, July 30, 2008), 1–2. He holds Wal-Mart personally responsible for nearly 200,000 U.S. job losses between 2001 and 2006 (Robert E. Scott, *The Wal-Mart Effect*, Issue Brief 235, June 25, 2007).

62 "The U.S. trade deficit with China has surged over the past two decades . . . from $10 billion in 1990 to $266 billion in 2008, although it fell to $227 billion in 2009 . . . larger than the *combined* U.S. trade deficits with OPEC, the 27 nations that make up the European Union . . . Mexico, Japan and Canada (together they totaled $225 billion)" (Wayne Morrison, *China-U.S. Trade Issues*, Congressional Research Service, July 29, 2010, 7). The United States' main export to China is currently scrap metal and waste products!

63 Robert E. Scott, *NAFTA'S Legacy* (Washington, DC: Economic Policy Institute Briefing Paper 173, September 28, 2006).

64 From nearly zero in 1991, U.S. overseas debt grew to $811 billion in 2006, 6.1 percent of GDP. It is expected to rise to 10–12 percent of GDP if present trends continue.

65 Owen Herrnstadt, *Offsets and the Lack of a Comprehensive U.S. Policy* (Washington, DC: Economic Policy Institute Briefing Paper 201, April 17, 2008).

66 See A. B. Atkinson and A. Brandolini, "On Data: A Case Study of the Evolution of Income Inequality Across Time and Across Countries," *Cambridge Journal of Economics*, 33(2), May 2009, 381–404.

67 Larry Elliott, "World Poverty Reduced by Growth in India and China," *The Guardian*, April 16, 2007. For more general information, see Christian E. Weller, Robert E. Smith, and Adam S. Hersh, *The Unremarkable Record of Liberalized Trade* (Washington, DC: Economic Policy Institute, 2001).

68 See Marcia Clemmit, *Global Food Crisis* (Washington, DC: *CQ Researcher* 18(24), June 27, 2007); and essays on "The Crisis in Agriculture and Food," *Monthly Review*, 61(3), July–August 2009.

69 This in Sabrina Dewan, *Wage Inequality Is a Global Challenge* (Washington, DC: Center For American Progress, December 3, 2008).

70 *Growth Isn't Working: The Uneven Distribution of Benefits and Costs from Economic Growth* (New Economics Foundation website, February 22, 2006).

71 John Isbister, *Promises Not Kept: Poverty and the Betrayal of Third World Development* (Bloomfield, CT: Kumarian Press, 2003), 19.

72 See G. Arrighi, "World Income Inequalities and the Future of Socialism," *New Left Review* 189, September–October 1991, 39–65.

73 Goran Therborn, "Meanings, Mechanisms, Patterns and Forces: An Introduction," in his edited *Inequalities of the World* (London: Verso, 2006), 37–38.
74 Commenting on the Doha round of trade talks, Robert Wade wrote this: "The developed countries are insistent that developing countries make big cuts in protection on non-agricultural imports . . . Most developing countries face serious dangers of de-industrialization if they accept the basic terms of this negotiation. They risk becoming more specialized than at present in the production of primary commodities and simple labor-intensive products, and even less diversified in the production of more complex, rich country goods" (*The Guardian*, July 6, 2006).
75 See David Harvey, *A Brief History of Neo-Liberalism* (Oxford: Oxford University Press, 2005); and James Petras and Henry Veltmeyer, *Imperialism in the Twenty-First Century* (London: Zed Books, 2001).
76 This is the central thesis of Paul Dunkerley's *Free Trade* (London: Zed Books, 2004). For an excellent summary of anti-free trade arguments, see 225–29.
77 For a pithy overview of contemporary capitalism and its history, see James Fulcher, *Capitalism: A Very Short Introduction* (Oxford: Oxford University Press, 2004).
78 Not that U.S. companies then export their foreign-made produce back to the United States. "Close to 90 percent of the goods and services produced by U.S.-owned affiliates abroad are sold to customers either in the host country or exported to consumers in third world countries outside the United States." Daniel Griswold, *"Shipping Jobs Overseas."*
79 On this, see David Coates, *Seen from Below: Labor in the Story of Capitalism*, available at www.davidcoates.net/publications/non-fiction/global-capitalism/
80 This quotation is from chapter 5, "The Globalization of Labor" in the IMF's 2007 *World Economic Outlook*, as reported in *The Financial Times* April 5, 2007. For the argument that "the large increase in the developed world's labor supply . . . is the major underlying cause of the global macroeconomic imbalances that led to the great recession," see Ravi Jagannathan, Mudit Kapoor, and Ernst Schaumburg, *Why Are We In A Recession? The Financial Crisis Is The Symptom Not the Disease* (NBER Working Paper 15404, October 2009).
81 For the literature critiquing the Friedman thesis, see *Cambridge Journal of Regions, Economy and Society*, 1(3), November 2008; and John Gray "The World Is Round," *New York Review of Books,* August 11, 2005.
82 See Martin Wolf, *Fixing Global Finance* (Baltimore, MD: John Hopkins University Press, 2009); and Robert Skidelsky, "The World Finance Crisis and the American Mission," *New York Review of Books* LVI(12), July 16–August 12 2009, 31–33.
83 For details, see Ha-Joon Chang, Gabriel Palma, and D. Hugh Whittaker (eds), *Financial Liberalization and the Asian Crisis* (Basingstoke: Palgrave, 2001).
84 Elliott, *World Poverty*.
85 Dani Rodrik, quoted in *The Guardian*, December 12, 2005.
86 Rodrik, quoted in *The Guardian*, December 12, 2005.
87 For the argument that, contrary to the conventional wisdom, ISI in Latin America failed because its capital markets were too *open* rather than because their import markets were too closed, see Stiglitz and Charlton, *Fair Trade for All*, 22.

88 Carlos Salas, *Between Unemployment and Insecurity in Mexico: NAFTA Enters Its Second Decade* (EPI Briefing Paper 173, September 28, 2006), 42.
89 Tim Weiner, "Free Trade Accord at 10: Growing Pains Are Clear," *The New York Times*, December 27, 2003, 5.
90 Athanasios Vamvakidis, "How Robust Is the Growth-Openness Connection? Historical Evidence," *Journal of Economic Growth*, 7 (2002), 60.
91 Ha-Joon Chang, "Kicking Away the Ladder: Neoliberals Rewrite History," *Monthly Review*, January 2003, 10; and 'Kicking Away the Ladder: An Unofficial History of Capitalism, Especially in Britain and the United States," *Challenge*, 45(5), September/October 2002, 63–97. This thesis is more fully developed in his *Kicking Away the Ladder: Development Strategy in Historical Perspective* (London: Anthem Press, 2002); *Bad Samaritans: The Myth of Free Trade and the Secret History of Capitalism* (New York: Bloomsbury Press, 2008), 40–64; and Ha-Joon Chang and Robert Rowthorn (eds), *The Role of the State in Economic Change* (Oxford: Oxford University Press, 1995).
92 Chang, "Kicking Away the Ladder," 58.
93 Krugman, "Divided Over Trade," *The New York Times*, May 14, 2007.
94 Dan Roberts and Edward Luce, writing in *The Financial Times*, August 20, 2003, 11.
95 Colin Hines, 'Globalization Is Not Like Gravity," *The Guardian*, April 25, 2005.
96 Dani Rodrik, "The Cheerleaders' Threat to Global Trade," *The Financial Times*, March 27, 2007.
97 Ray Marshall, "Foreword," in Paulo Paiva, Ray Marshall, and Robert H. Wilson (eds), *Labor in the Americas* (Austin: University of Texas, 2007), xx.
98 For the general case for international labor standards, see Werner Sengenberger and Frank Wilkinson, "Globalization and Labour Standards," in Jonathan Michie and John Grieve Smith (eds), *Managing the Global Economy* (Oxford: Oxford University Press, 1995), 111–34. For the argument that labor standards have to empower third world workers in their domestic as well as export sectors—and particularly women workers—see Naila Kabeer, "Labor Standards, Women's Rights, Basic Needs: Challenges to Collective Action in a Globalizing World," in Lourdes Benaria and Savitri Bisnath (eds), *Global Tensions: Challenges and Opportunities in the World Economy* (New York: Routledge, 2004), 173–92.
99 See Christian E. Weller and Stephen Zucconi, *Labor Rights Can Be Good Trade Policy* (Washington, DC: Center for American Progress, September 2008). The Obama administration made clear (August 2010) that it would enforce a new set of worker protections in the revised free trade agreement with South Korea it is keen to have enacted. (Similar promises accompanied the enactment of NAFTA!)
100 André Reynauld and Jean-Pierre Vidal, *Labour Standards and International Competitiveness* (Cheltenham, UK: Edward Elgar, 1998); Bivens, *Everyone Wins*, 80–82.
101 Ray Marshall, "Foreword."
102 The House of Representatives passed the *Currency Reform for Fair Trade Act* in September 2010, which, if passed by the Senate and signed by the president, would mandate the Department of Commerce to take note of a foreign country's currency interventions when deciding whether its trade practices were fair.

103 Chang, *Bad Samaritans*, 84.
104 For this, see Peter Orzag and Michael Deich, *Growth, Opportunity and Prosperity in a Globalizing Economy* (Washington, DC: The Hamilton Project, Brookings Institution, July 2006), 10; and the ILO Report, *A Fair Globalization: Creating Opportunities for All* (Geneva: ILO, 2007).
105 On this, see Harriet Lamb, "Fair Trade versus Free Trade," in Frank Trentmann (ed.), *Is Free Trade Fair Trade?* (London: The Smith Institute, 2009), 72–83; and David Ransom, *The No-Nonsense Guide to Fair Trade* (Oxford: The New Internationalist Press, 2006).
106 The case has been put many times, and will be discussed again in Chapter 6. For the latest, see Ha-Joon Chang, *23 Things They Don't Tell You About Capitalism* (London: Allen Lane, 2010), 88–101, 257–59.

Chapter 4

1 In his 2007 State of the Union Address, when he first spoke of the United States being "addicted to oil," especially foreign oil, and set new goals for fuel efficiency and the development of alternatives.
2 In 2006, Schwarzenegger even went so far as to sign a groundbreaking agreement with the UK to fight global warming: the 12th largest carbon emitter making a deal—sidestepping the Bush administration—with another of the world's leading carbon emitters.
3 These were not intended as empty promises: on the contrary, as the president-elect designed his White House team in January 2009, he appointed an environmental "czar" (Carol Browner), promising a "new level of coordination across the government, and my personal engagement as president" on energy and climate policy (cited in *The Washington Post*, January 7, 2009).
4 First in a speech in Oregon, May 12, 2008.
5 Specifically, ten of the largest companies—including Alcoa and GE—members of the U.S. Climate Action Partnership, which in January 2007 urged George W. Bush to adopt a system of mandatory caps on greenhouse gas emissions designed to cut them by 30 percent by 2022 (details in *Financial Times*, January 22, 2007).
6 The biggest example of this came in April 2007 in a report written by 11 retired U.S. generals. For details, see Mark Turner and Fiona Harvey, "Climate Change a threat to world security, retired U.S. generals warn," *Financial Times*, April 17, 2007.
7 For details, see National Resources Defense Council, *Legislative Facts*, May 2008: available at www.nrdc.org/policy. The bill failed in the Senate in June 2008, blocked by a Republican filibuster.
8 The full story is in Judith A. Layzer's report for the Russell Sage Foundation, *Cold Front: How the Recession Stalled Obama's Clean-Energy Agenda,* available at www.russellsage.org/research/working-group-obamas-policy-agenda

9 If signed into law, the act would require U.S. emissions to decline by 17 percent by 2020. The vote was 219:212, with 44 Democrats voting against and nine Republicans voting for.
10 For the negative knock-on effects of the absence of energy legislation on the U.S. role in the November 2010 Cancun conference, see Juliet Eilperin, "U.S. plays conflicted role in global climate debate," *The Washington Post*, November 1, 2010.
11 Cited in Sebastian Maloby, "Al Gore's Unlikely Helpers," *The Washington Post*, May 22, 2006.
12 Rush Limbaugh, "Know Our Enemy," *The Limbaugh Letter*, 16(1), January 2007.
13 Rush Limbaugh, "Bono Praises 'Father Al,'" January 25, 2008: available at www.rushlimbaugh.com/home/daily/site
14 Cited in Paul Krugman, "Betraying the Planet," *The New York Times*, June 29, 2009.
15 Thomas Sewell, *Green Bigots Versus Human Beings*, May 24, 2001.
16 Fred Singer, *Unstoppable Global Warming* (Lanham, MD: Rowman and Littlefield, 2007), 251.
17 See, for example, Kesten C. Green and J. Scott Armstrong, *Global Warming: Experts' Opinions Versus Scientific Forecasts* (National Center for Policy Analysis Policy Report No. 308, February 2008); David R. Legates, *Breaking the Hockey Stick* (National Center for Policy Analysis "Brief Analysis" No. 478, July 2004); and Ronald J. Rychlak, *Understanding Visual Exhibits in the Global Warming Debate* (The Heartland Institute, March 2008).
18 Richard Lindzen, "Climate of Fear," *Wall Street Journal*, April 12, 2006.
19 Cited in Center for American Progress, *Talking Points*, February 8, 2007.
20 "The report's first table of figures—inserted by the IPCC bureaucrats after the scientists had finalized the draft and without their consent . . . the result of this dishonest political tampering with the science was that the sum of the four items in the offending table was more than twice the IPCC's published total" (Christopher Monckton, *Dishonest Political Tampering with the Science on Global Warming*, posted on the website of "Frontiers of Freedom," December 11, 2007: available at http://ff.org).
21 S. Fred Singer, *Nature, Not Human Activity, Rules the Climate* (Chicago: The Heartland Institute, 2008), iv.
22 Steven Hayward, "Cooled Down," *Pittsburgh Tribune Review*, February 6, 2005, 4: available at www.pittsburghlive.com/x/pittsburghtrib/print_300191.html
23 For details, see the House of Commons Science and Technology Committee, *The Disclosure of Data from the Climate Research Unit at the University of East Anglia*, Report HC 387–1, published by The Stationery Office Limited, London, March 31, 2010.
24 *Global Warming Censored*, a special report from the Business and Media Institute, Media Research Center 2008.
25 Lindzen, "Climate of Fear."
26 See in particular Lawrence Solomon, *The Deniers* (Richard Vigilante Books, 2008).
27 Cited in Hayward, "Cooled Down," 5.

28 This, in a lecture to the Marshall Institute, December 1, 2004, available on request from rlindzen@mit.edu.
29 Denis Bray and Simon Shackley, *The Social Simulation of the Public Perception of Weather Events and their Effect upon the Development of Belief in Anthropogenic Climate Change* (Tyndall Centre for Climate Change Research, Working Paper 58, September 2004).
30 The quotation is from *The Australian*, April 23, 2008, cited in Deroy Murdoch, "Chill Out on Climate Hysteria," *National Review Online,* May 2, 2008: available at http://article.nationalreview.com/print
31 Bjorn Lomborg, *Cool It: The Skeptical Environmentalist's Guide to Global Warming* (New York: Alfred A. Knopf, 2007).
32 For the argument that global warming will make the UK a better place to live—a "Northern Arcadia"—see Marek Kohn, *Turned Out Nice* (London: Faber, 2009).
33 National Center for Policy Analysis, *Brief Analysis No 516*, May 19, 2005, 2.
34 Lomborg, *Cool It*, 41.
35 Quoted in *The New York Times*, June 2, 2007.
36 Kintzen, "Climate of Fear."
37 *Climate Issues and Questions* (George C. Marshall Institute, 2004), 4. Also, see Singer, 105–06.
38 *Climate Science and Policy: Making the Connection* (George C. Marshall Institute, 2001), 3.
39 Hayward, *Cool Down*, 2. For a full discussion, see *Climate Issues and Questions*, 17–20.
40 Kesten C. Green and J. Scott Armstrong, "Global Warming: Forecasts by Scientists Versus Scientific Forecasts," *Energy and Environment*, 18 (2007), 997.
41 NCPA *Brief Analysis 516*, 1.
42 William Gray, *Global Warming and Hurricanes* (*icecap.us/docs/change/GlobalWarming%26HurricanePaper.pdf*) Support for this view came from the *Copenhagen Consensus* of polled economists (details in Lomborg, *Cool It*, 44).
43 Gray, *Global Warming*.
44 H. Svenmark and E Friis-Christensen, "Variation in Cosmic Ray Flux and Global Cloud Cover—A Missing Link in the Solar Climate relationship," *Journal of Atmospheric Solar-terrestrial Physics,* 59 (1997).
45 Fred Singer, *Global Warming: Man-made or Natural?* (Texas Public Policy Foundation, Center for Economic Freedom, September 2007), 4.
46 This in his *The Way Things Ought To Be* (New York: Simon and Schuster, 1993), 155: written when the thinning of the ozone layer was the top climate-debate concern.
47 See Iain Murray, *The Really Inconvenient Truth* (Washington, DC: Regnery Publishing, 2008), 3.
48 See for example, Deborah Corey Barners, *Al Gore's Carbon Crusade: The Money and Connections Behind It* (Capital Research Center, Foundation Watch, August 2007).
49 For details, see Marcus Baram, "An Inconvenient Verdict for Al Gore," *ABC News,* October 12, 2007: available at http://abcnews.go.com/print?id=3719791; Murray, *Inconvenient Truth*, 7–12; and Lomborg, *Cool It*, 53–112.

50 These from John Stossel, *A Convenient Lie*, Townhall.com July 5, 2006; George Landrith, *Climate Change: Fabricating the Numbers*, Frontiers of Freedom, October 3, 2007: available at http://ff.org
51 See, for example, Christine Hall, *Does Al Gore Need to Go on an Energy Diet?* (Competitive Enterprise Institute, May 24, 2006: at http://cei.org).
52 See, for example, Ben Lieberman, *Beware of Cap and Trade Climate Bills* (Heritage Foundation webmemo 1723, December 6, 2007); and Brett Schaefer and Ben Lieberman, *The U.S. Must Be Resolute to Avoid Harmful Consequences of the Bali Global Warming Conference* (Heritage Foundation webmemo 1759, December 21, 2007).
53 Human Events, *Urgent Cap and Trade Alert,* July 9, 2009. And they are not alone in thinking this: the U.S. Department of Energy predicted in 2000 that meeting the Kyoto standard would raise gas prices 52 percent and electricity prices 86 percent, cutting personal disposable income by 2.5 percent and GDP by 4.2 percent. (This in H. Sterling Burnett, *Reality and Climate Change Policy*, National Center for Policy Analysis Brief Analysis No. 367, August 15, 2001, 2.)
54 William W. Beach and Shanea Watkins, *Paying More at the Pump* (The Heritage Foundation webmemo 1729, December 10, 2007).
55 Ben Lieberman, *The EPA's Prudent Response to Massachusetts v. EPA* (Heritage Foundation webmemo 1870, March 28, 2008), 2.
56 Ben Lieberman, *The True Costs of EPA Global Warming Regulation* (Heritage Foundation webmemo 2213, November 24, 2008).
57 Nicolas Loris and Ben Lieberman, *EPA Should Not Increase the Ozone Regulation Burden* (Heritage Foundation webmemo 1827, February 26, 2008).
58 The phrase is Patrick Michaels, in his "Carbon Copies," *American Spectator* (online), February 27, 2008.
59 The John Locke Foundation, *A Wind Power Primer*, Spotlight No. 345, March 7, 2008.
60 Ben Lieberman, *Time for Second Thoughts on the Ethanol Mandate* (Heritage Foundation webmemo 1879, April 2, 2008); and David Biello, "Biofuels Are Bad for Feeding People and Combating Climate Change," *Scientific American*, February 7, 2008: available at www.sciam.com/article
61 Kenneth P. Green, *Obama's "Green Jobs" Plan Will Not Work* (AEI: On the Issues, November 2008).
62 Ben Lieberman, *Green Stimulus: Tying Economic Package to Energy and Environment Plan Is Not Workable* (Heritage Foundation webmemo No. 2245, January 26, 2009).
63 David W. Kreutzer, *The Economic Case for Drilling Oil Reserves* (Heritage Foundation webmemo 2093, October 1, 2008), 2.
64 This in Jack Spencer, *Nuclear Power Critical to Meeting President's Greenhouse Gas Objectives* (Heritage Foundation webmemo 1898, April 18, 2008).
65 "The chief drivers of [environmental] improvement are economic growth, constantly increasing resource efficiency, technological innovation in pollution control, and the deepening of environmental values among the American public. Government regulation has played a central role, to be sure, but in the grand

scheme of things is a lagging indicator of change, and often achieves results at needlessly high cost. Were it not for rising affluence and technological innovation, regulation would have the same effect as King Canute commanding the tides" (Steven Hayward, *Index of Leading Environmental Indicators,* AEI, 2008), 1.

66 Indur Goklany, *The Improving State of the World* (Washington, DC: Cato Institute, 2007), 326.

67 For the full case, see Stuart Butler and Kim Holmes, *Twelve Principles to Guide U.S. Energy Policy* (Heritage Foundation webmemo 2046, June 26, 2007); and Steve Milloy, *Green Hell* (Washington, DC: Regnery Publishing, 2009).

68 On this, see Fiona Harvey, "Lingering clouds," *The Financial Times*, August 30, 2010.

69 Alan L. Leshner, "Don't let the climate doubters fool you," *The Washington Post*, December 9, 2009.

70 Reported in *The Guardian*, July 7, 2009.

71 Juliet Eilperin, "Debate on Climate shifts to Issue of Irreparable Change," *Washington Post*, January 29, 2006, A01.

72 On their numbers, see Singer, *Unstoppable Global Warming*, 123–24.

73 "Here's the short version of everything you need to know about global warming. First, the consensus of the scientific community has moved from skepticism to near-unanimous acceptance of the evidence of an artificial greenhouse effect." Greg Easterbrook, "Case Closed: The Debate about Global Warming is Over," *Issues in Global Governance* 3, June 2006.

74 Quoted in *The Financial Times*, October 31, 2006.

75 From his keynote address to an emergency conference of 2,500 climate experts from 80 countries, Copenhagen, March 2009: quoted in *The Guardian,* March 13, 2009.

76 A report supervised by the chief scientist to the World Bank and launched at the Royal Society in London, March 30, 2005. Data here from *The Guardian*, March 30, 2005.

77 Details at http://edition.cnn.com/2009/WORLD/europe/05/29/annan.climate.change.human/

78 Details at http://hdr.undp.org/en/reports/global/hdr2010, and *The Guardian*, November 4, 2010.

79 Ibid.

80 Details in *The Wall Street Journal*, July 6, 2010. After carefully reviewing IPCC findings and procedures, the Inter-Academy Council (IAC), an Amsterdam-based organization of the world's science academies, reported in August 2010 that "*the process used by the Intergovernmental Panel on Climate Change to produce its periodic assessment reports has been successful overall*, but IPCC needs to fundamentally reform its management structure and strengthen its procedures to handle ever larger and increasingly complex climate assessments as well as the more intense public scrutiny coming from a world grappling with how best to respond to climate change."

81 Reported in the Center for American Progress Talking Points for May 29, 2007: *Blocking Progress on Climate Change.*

82 Scientists at the Mauna Loa Observatory in Hawaii, reported in *The Guardian*, May 13, 2008.
83 Details in *The Financial Times*, July 29, 2010, and August 28, 2010.
84 For an excellent survey of legislative achievements and remaining tasks, see Carol Browner and Gary Guzy, "Today's Healthy Air Choice: Addressing Key Elements in the Approach to Air Quality," in John A. Riggs (ed.), *Tackling the Critical Conundrum* (Aspen Institute, 2004), 11–18.
85 On this, see Steven Hayward, *Index of Leading Environmental Indicators* (AEI, 2008); Joel Schwartz, "Clearing the Air," *Regulation* (Summer 2003), 22–29.
86 An ecological footprint is measured by the resources consumed per head in particular economies. The U.S. figure for 2003 (at 9.6) was more than twice that of the EU (4.8), and both figures were higher than the world average (2.23) or the figure that would guarantee ecological sustainability over time. The U.S. ecological deficit was second only to Brazil, at 4.8 (data from The WWF's *Living Planet Report,* 2006, 3).
87 CQ Researcher, *Climate Change,* 16(4) (January 2006), 80. China produces 14.8 percent and the EU 14 percent.
88 *A Global Warming Primer,* available at http://www.ncpa.org/pub/a-global-warming-primer, 17. The figures for the UK, Japan, and Germany are all under 10 tons/head.
89 Environmental health, air pollution, water resources, biodiversity and habitat, productive natural resources, and climate change: available at http://epi.yale.edu
90 But not Belgium, that ranked 57th. China, India, and Australia all ranked lower than the United States.
91 See, for example, George Monbiot, "There is climate change censorship—and it is deniers who dish it out," *The Guardian*, April 10, 2007, 27. On the general issue of politics distorting science, see CQ Researcher, *Science and Politics*, 14(28), August 20, 2004.
92 Possibly the most notable example was that of Philip A. Cooney, whose intervention in a large number of government climate reports, always playing down evidence of a human role, was exposed in the *New York Times.* On this, see Thomas L. Friedman, "How Many Scientists?" *New York Times*, March 28, 2007. For other cases, see Juliet Eilperin, "Cheney's Staff Cut Testimony on Warning," *Washington Post*, July 9, 2008.
93 Ian Sample, "Scientists offered cash to dispute climate study," *The Guardian*, February 2, 2007, 2: citing a letter from the AEI visiting scholar Kenneth Green. The AEI is partially funded by ExxonMobil.
94 Speaking at the Delhi Sustainable Development Summit in January 2007, the then-UK Energy Secretary proposed a 3D energy revolution: demand management (more efficient cars, houses, appliances), de-carbonization (using alternative fuels and capturing and storing carbon emissions), and de-centralization of power sources. www.davidmiliband.info/archive/defra/defra_07_02.html
95 Conservative leader David Cameron spent 2008 urging the UK electorate to "vote blue, go green" (In Europe, "red" is the left-wing color, "blue" the right!).

96 "Under the ETS, EU countries get national allocations which they then parcel out to over 11,500 factories in five dirty industries. Companies can and sell allocations among themselves, and they can also buy "certified emission reductions" from developing countries to meet their caps through Kyoto's 'clean development mechanism'" (*The Economist*, December 5, 2009, special report, 12).

97 Lobbying from European business eventually softened the deal, to avoid "carbon leaking"—the loss of jobs from the EU to less-regulated countries—hence the EU's interest in a post-Kyoto full global regulated system.

98 A very problematic solution even in relation to land, disregarding as it does the capacity of farmers to recognize the problem themselves and take appropriate voluntary collective action.

99 If you doubt this as a general truth, read W. J. Baumol and S. Blackman, *Perfect Markets and Easy Virtue* (Cambridge, MS: Blackwell, 1991). If you doubt it as a local empiric, read the NRDC's *Issues: Global Warming*, where they argue that "voluntary efforts won't work . . . we need mandatory limits on carbon dioxide . . . the federal government has relied on voluntary measures to address global warming since the creation of the first President Bush's National Energy Strategy in 1989. Yet this approach has clearly failed to reduce emissions of carbon dioxide . . . between 1990 and 2003, U.S. carbon dioxide emissions increased by 17 percent [and] from electric power production increased by 26 percent, twice as fast as emissions from the rest of the economy": at www.nrdc.org/globalWarming/fmandatory.asp

100 See Frank S. Arnold, *Environmental Protection: Is It Bad for the Economy?* (Environmental Law Institute Report, July 1999) for the argument that "there is no evidence that U.S. environmental regulation causes large-scale plant closures and job losses, that it impairs our international competitiveness, or that it encourages companies to flee to nations with more lax environmental protection requirements" (1).

101 See in particular, James O'Connor, "The Second Contradiction of Capitalism," in T. Benton (ed.), *The Greening of Marxism* (New York: Guildford Press, 1996); and John Bellamy Foster, Brett Clark, and Richard York, *The Ecological Rift: Capitalism's War on the Earth* (New York: Monthly Review Press, 2010). For the view that the problem is less capitalism than industrialization, and that "there is no Green energy mix that can sustain industrialization in a world of high and rising human numbers," see John Gray, *False Dawn* (London: Granta, 2009), xxiv.

102 The New Economic Foundation publishes a regular calculation of what they call "ecological debt day": the day at which the UK begins living beyond its environmental means by consuming more natural resources than it can replace. The day moves forward each year—in 2007, it was April 15. In 1961, it had been July 9 (NEF, *The UK Interdependence Report* (NEF, 2007). As Timothy Gorton Ash put it, "There is the inescapable dilemma that this planet cannot sustain six-and-a-half billion people living like today's middle-class consumers in its rich north" (*The Guardian,* February 22, 2007, 31).

103 In a remarkable set of essays edited by Leo Panitch and Colin Leys, *Coming to Terms With Nature; The Socialist Register 2007* (Merlin Press, 2007): see in particular, 254–72.

104 See Thomas Freidman, *Hot, Flat and Crowded* (New York: Farrar, Straus and Giroux, 2008), 164.
105 For details, see NRDC, *Oil and Energy: A Responsible Energy Plan for America*; available at www.nrdc.org/air/energy/rep/execsum.asp
106 For details, see Jason Furman et al., *An Economic Strategy to Address Climate Change and Promote Energy Security* (The Hamilton Project, September 2007).
107 For details, see Robert Pollin et al., *Green Recovery* (Center for American Progress and the Political Economy Research Institute, University of Massachusetts-Amherst, September 2008); Robert Pollin, "Doing the Recovery Right," *The Nation,* February 16, 2009; "The Green Challenge: Special Report," *The American Prospect*, April 2009; and Kit Batten et al., *Investing in a Green Economy* (Center for American Progress, June 2008).
108 For details, see *The New Apollo Program*: http://apolloalliance.org/apollo-14
109 For details, see George Sterzinger, *Energizing Prosperity: Renewable Energy and Re-industrialization* (EPI Discussion Paper, Agenda for Shared Prosperity, February 13, 2008).
110 Ibid., 157–58.
111 The full details are on the website *Obama for America* at www.barackobama.com/pdf/factsheet_energy_speech_080308.pdf
112 These included Nobel Prize-winning physicist Steven Chu as Energy Secretary, Lisa Jackson to head the EPA, Nancy Sutley to head the White House Council on Environmental Policy, Todd Stern to lead climate negotiations, and Harvard Physicist John Holden to direct the White House Office of Science and Technology Policy. The "Green Team" reference is from the *The New York Times* editorial, December 13, 2008.
113 Details in *The Financial Times*, May 20, 2009.
114 Joshua Green, "Better Luck This Time," *The Atlantic*, July/August 2009, 84.
115 For a more upbeat assessment of the potential of wind power, see NRDC *Wind Power*: www.nrde.org/are/energy/renewables/wind.asp
116 Including the Sierra Club, Greenpeace, and Friends of the Earth.
117 Professor John Beddington, quoted in *The Guardian,* March 7, 2008.
118 Lawrence Summers, "We need to bring climate idealism down to earth," *Financial Times*, April 30, 2007, 11. See also the same source, April 26, 2007, for material on fraud.
119 See, for example, Alexander Zaitchik, *The Dark Side of Climate Change*, posted on Alternet.org, July 10, 2009: available at www.alternet.org/story/141081; or Charles Konanoff, "Senate Climate Bill Dies—Does the Environment Win?" *The Nation*, July 28, 2010.
120 Energy drawn from the recycling of agricultural waste and landfills: for the case, see NRDC, *Biomass Energy*: available at www.nrdc.org/air/energy/renewables/biomass.asp
121 For the data, see Josh Bivens, John Irons, and Ethan Pollack, *Green Investment and the Labor Market* (Washington, DC: Economic Policy Institute, Issue Brief #253, April 7, 2009).
122 This is Thomas Friedman at his very best. See "Going Cheney on Climate," *The New York Times*, December 9, 2009. Included there is this: "When I see a problem

that has even a one percent probability of occurring and is 'irreversible' and potentially 'catastrophic,' I buy insurance. That is what taking climate change seriously is all about."

Chapter 5

1 Documented in Peter Beinhart, *The Icarus Syndrome: A History of American Hubris* (New York: HarperCollins, 2010).
2 "America continues to be qualitatively different. To reiterate, exceptionalism is a two-edged phenomenon; it does not mean better. This country is an outlier" Seymour Martin Lipset, *American Exceptionalism: A Double-Edged Sword* (New York: W.W. Norton, 1996), 26.
3 Cited in Lipset, *American Exceptionalism*, 31.
4 Ibid., 31.
5 The title of a 1960s collection of Lipset's writings on American uniqueness, this one was republished by Transaction Publishers in 2003.
6 On the absence of a socialist, or indeed even an independent, Labor Party, in the United States, see Lipset, *American Exceptionalism*, 77–109; Seymour Martin Lipset, "American Exceptionalism Reaffirmed," in Bryon Shaffer (ed.), *Is America Different?* (Oxford: Oxford University Press, 1991), 1–45; and Seymour Martin Lipset and Gary Marks, *It Didn't Happen Here: Why Socialism Failed in the United States* (New York: W.W. Norton, 2000).
7 Lipset, *American Exceptionalism*, 72.
8 Ibid., 63.
9 Olaf Gersemann, *Cowboy Capitalism: European Myths, American Reality* (Washington, DC: Cato Institute, 2004).
10 See, for example, Benjamin M. Friedman, "The Economic System," in Peter H. Schuck and James Q. Wilson (eds), *Understanding America: The Anatomy of an Exceptional Nation* (New York: Public Affairs, 2008), 87–119.
11 On this, see Assar Lindbeck, "What Is Wrong with the West European Economies?" *The World Economy*, 8 (June 1985), 153–70.
12 Ibid., 2–3.
13 Martin Wolf, "European Corporatism Needs to Embrace Market-Led Change," *The Financial Times*, January 24, 2007.
14 Peter H. Schuck and James Q. Wilson, "Looking Back," in their *Understanding America*, 643.
15 Ibid., 643.
16 Ibid., 643.
17 Rush Limbaugh, "Liberals and the Violence Card," *The Wall Street Journal*, April 23, 2010.
18 Thomas F. Madden, *Empires of Trust: How Rome Built—and America is Building—a New World* (New York: Dutton, 2008), 12.
19 Ibid., 67.
20 Ibid., 14.

21 Ibid., 192.
22 Ibid., 9.
23 Ibid., 297.
24 See, for example, Robert Kagan, "The Benevolent Empire," *Foreign Policy* No. 111 (Summer 1998), 24–35; Kimberley Kagan, "Hegemony, Not Empire," *The Weekly Standard*, May 6, 2002; and Niall Ferguson, *Colossus: The Price of America's Empire* (New York: Penguin, 2004).
25 Mancur Olson, *The Rise and Decline of Nations: Economic Growth, Stagflation and Social Rigidities* (New Haven: Yale University Press, 1982). This thesis is common among economists of a neoclassical persuasion, and informs the work of many growth accountants, including that of the original giant in the field, Edward Denison. For a discussion of Olson and growth accounting, see David Coates, "Paradigms of Explanation," in his edited volume, *Varieties of Capitalism, Varieties of Approaches* (Houndsmill: Palgrave Macmillan, 2005), 4–9.
26 Rush Limbaugh, "This Isn't About Immigration. It's About Advancing Liberalism, Seizing Power & Hurting America," transcript of his radio show, April 11, 2006.
27 With Geoffrey Hodgson, it is not the contention here "that the tradition of American exceptionalism is the sole or even the principal cause of the things that have 'gone wrong' in American political life and foreign policy." Rather, the contention is, like his, that we would all do well to look "with a skeptical and humble eye at the many and subtle dangers of self-praise." Geoffrey Hodgson, *The Myth of American Exceptionalism* (Yale: Yale University Press, 2009), xvii. See also John Kingdon, *America the Unusual* (New York: Worth Publishers, 1998); and Bryon Schaffer (ed.), *Is America Different: A New Look at American Exceptionalism* (Oxford: Oxford University Press, 1991).
28 On the danger, this from Hodgson: "Such claims are dangerous because they are the soil in which unreal and hubris assumptions of the American destiny have grown" (*Myth of American Exceptionalism*, 16).
29 Ibid., 130.
30 To quote Richard Young, "My contention is that Lipset's analysis obscures the historical reality that during the American republic's first half century (1787–1837), the economic success and political stability of the United States depended upon the dispossession of Native Americans and the enslavement of African Americans" (Richard Young, *American Exceptionalism as a Truly Double-Edged Sword: Anglo-America as a Contract State and a Predatory State*, paper, APSA, September 1999).
31 Paul Smith, *Primitive America: The Ideology of Capitalist Democracy* (Minneapolis: University of Minnesota Press, 2007), xi.
32 "The American Negro has the great advantage of never having believed that collection of myths to which white Americans cling: that their ancestors were all freedom-loving heroes, that they were born in the greatest country the world has ever seen, or that Americans are invincible in battle and wise in peace, that Americans have always dealt honorably with Mexicans and Indians and all other neighbors or inferiors, that American men are the world's most direct and virile, that American women are pure. Negroes know far more about white Americans than that." James Baldwin, *The Fire Next Time* (New York: Dial Press, 1963), 115.

33 For details of the literature on this, see Chapter 2, note 50.
34 Stephen Slivinski, *The Corporate Welfare State: How the Federal Government Subsidizes U.S. Business* (Cato Institute: Policy Analysis No. 592, May 14, 2007), 1.
35 Graham Adams Jr., *The Age of Industrial Violence 1910–1915* (New York: Columbia University Press, 1966).
36 Occasionally good people remember. See, for example, E. J. Dionne, 'When Unions Mattered, Prosperity Was Shared," *The Washington Post*, September 6, 2010.
37 There is, of course, an extensive literature on the failures of the American Left, stretching all the way back to Marx and Engels, and to Werner Sombart's 1913 classic, *Why There Is No Socialism in the United States*. See in particular Lipset and Marks, *It Didn't Happen Here*; Ira Katznelson, *Working Class Formation* (Princeton: Princeton University Press, 1986); Rick Halpern (ed.), *American Exceptionalism: U.S. Working Class Formation in an International Context* (New York: St. Martin's Press, 1997); and Mike Davis, *Prisoners of the American Dream* (London: Verso, 1999).
38 Lawrence Mishel, Jared Bernstein, and Heidi Shierholz, *The State of Working America 2008/9* (Washington, DC: Economic Policy Institute, 2008), 361.
39 As Harold Meyerson put it, "The Great Recession has taken a far greater toll on our nation's workers than on workers in similar countries, even those whose economies have dipped more steeply than ours . . . only a purblind ideologue could miss the pattern here. American employers—more than employers in other nations and more than American employers in earlier downturns—have imposed the costs of the recession and, increasingly, the costs of doing business, on their workers, and kept for themselves damn near all the proceeds from doing business" (*The Washington Post*, September 6, 2010).
40 John Miller, "What's In a Name," *Dollars and Sense*, July/August 2009, 14.
41 640,000 jobs lost in North America, as against 354,000 in Europe and 244,000 in Asia Pacific (ILO figures reported in *The Financial Times*, October 14, 2009).
42 Data in *The Washington Post*, September 9, 2010. The full report is available at www.weforum.org/en/initiatives/gcp/Global%20Competitiveness%20Report/index.htm.
43 I am grateful to Mary Beth Morrissey for this data.
44 Mark Weisbrot, "Myths About U.S. Economic Model May Not Survive the World Recession," *The Guardian Unlimited*, August 14, 2009.
45 Mishel et al., *State of Working America*, 365.
46 See Judy Heymann, Alison Earle, and Jeffrey Hayes, *The Work, Family and Equity Index: How Does the United States Measure Up?* (Montreal, The Institute for Health and Social Policy, 2007).
47 *The Global State of Workers' Rights: Free Labor in a Hostile World* (Washington, DC: Freedom House, August 26, 2010), 51.
48 There is now an extensive comparative literature emphasizing European strengths, much of it produced during the Bush years. See, for example, Will Hutton, *A Declaration of Interdependence: Why America Should Join the World* (New York: Norton, 2002); Jeremy Rifkin, *The European Dream* (New York:

Penguin, 2004); Mark Leonard, *Why Europe Will Run the Twenty-First Century* (New York: Public Affairs, 2005); Jeffrey Kopstein and Sven Steinmo (eds), *Growing Apart: America and Europe in the Twenty-First Century* (Cambridge, UK: Cambridge University Press, 2008); and Thomas Geoghegan, *Were You Born on the Wrong Continent?* (New York: The New Press, 2010). For an intellectual counterweight to those who see difference, see Peter Baldwin, *The Narcissism of Minor Differences: How America and Europe are Alike* (New York: Oxford University Press, 2009). For an intellectual counterweight to those who see European superiority, see Alberto Alesina and Frencesco Giavazzi, *The Future of Europe: Reform or Decline* (Cambridge: The MIT Press, 2006).

49 Before any of us point the finger of unemployment at Germany, saying that its job creation record since 1990 does not stand comparison with that of the United States, it is worth remembering that West Germany spent the 1990s incorporating 17 million East Germans and an entirely uncompetitive East German industrial system into its social market model, and did so with remarkable speed and generosity. Had the United States had such a task, unemployment rates here would no doubt also have exploded.

50 Jo Blanden, Paul Gregg, and Stephen Machin, *Intergenerational Mobility in Europe and North America* (London: The Sutton Trust, April 2005).

51 Gillian Tett, "Money Is Moving East—and the Bankers Will Follow," *The Financial Times*, December 17, 2009.

52 Clive Crook, "America's Human Capital Is Tested," *The Financial Times,* July 7, 2008.

53 Data in *The New York Times*, November 14, 2007.

54 "In fourth grade, American children are ahead of almost everyone in the world. By the eighth grade they are even and by 12th grade they are seriously behind" (Byron Wein, "America's Decline Will Not Be Easily Reversed," *The Financial Times*, August 11, 2008).

55 The OECD's Program for International Student Assessment (PISA) was first administered to 15-year-olds in 2000, and subsequently in 2003, 2006, and 2009. In 2000, U.S. 15-year-olds earned 493 out of 1,000 on the math scale, putting them 18th out of the 27 countries then participating. By 2006, they were only scoring 474 out of 1000, and ranked 25th out of the 30 countries then reviewed. Scores on reading and science similarly fell! (OECD *Education at a Glance 2008*; and Andrew Coulson, "All Americans Left Behind", *TCSdaily.com*, December 13, 2007).

56 Data from report by Center for Labor Market Studies, Northeastern University Boston (CNN .com).

57 On this, see Francis Green and David Ashton, *Education, Training and the Global Economy* (Cheltenham, UK: Edward Elgar, 1996): and D. Finegold and D. Soskice, "The Failure of Training in Britain: Analysis and Prescription," *Oxford Review of Economic Policy*, 4(3) (1988), 21–53.

58 David Mason, *The End of the American Century* (Lanhan: Rowman and Littlefield, 2009), 1.

59 Thomas Friedman, *The World is Flat* (New York: Farrar, Straus and Giroux, 2005); Arianna Huffington, *Third World America* (New York: Crown Publishing Group, 2010).
60 *Rising Above the Gathering Storm Revisited: Rapidly Approaching Category 5*: available at www.nap.edu/catalog.php?record_id=12999.
61 Charles Vest, former M.I.T. president, reporting on *Rising Above the Gathering Storm Revisited*: cited by Thomas Friedman in *The New York Times,* October 26, 2010.
62 CRS Report for Congress, *America COMPETES Act: Programs, Funding and Selected Issues*, January 22, 2008, 11–12.
63 Mason, *End of American Century*, 81.
64 Nina Fedoroff, Condelessa Rice's science and technology adviser, cited in *The Washington Post,* May 29, 2008.
65 Thomas Friedman, "Facts and Folly," *The New York Times*, March 29, 2006.
66 CRS Report, *America COMPETES*, 7.
67 Richard J. Elkus Jr., *Winner Takes All: How Competitiveness Shapes the Fate of Nations* (New York: Basic Books, 2008), 11, 13.
68 www.weforum.org/en/initiatives/gcp/Global%20Competitiveness%20Report/index.htm
69 For the general critique, see Will Hutton, *The State We're In* (London: Jonathan Cape, 1994).
70 For the UK story, see David Coates, *The Question of UK Decline: The Economy, State and Society* (Hemel Hempstead, UK: Harvester-Wheatsheaf, 1994), 151–67.
71 Mason, *End of American Century*, p. 16.
72 Ibid., xix.
73 Jeffrey Sachs, "America Has Passed on the Baton," *The Financial Times*, September 30, 2009.
74 Interviewed by Terrence McNally and posted on Alternet.org, September 6, 2010: available at http://alternet.org/story/148094. See also Andrew Bacevich, *The Limits of Power: The End of American Exceptionalism* (New York: Henry Holt, 2008).
75 The numbers come from Chalmers Johnson, *Three Good Reasons to Liquidate Our Empire and 10 Ways to Do It*, posted on Alternet.org, July 31, 2009. For the full argument, see the trilogy by Johnson: *Blowback* (2000); *Sorrows of Empire* (2004), and *Nemesis* (2008).
76 The latest example being the $60 billion deal with the Saudi regime selling F-115 fighters and assorted military helicopters, to reinforce an ally against an Iranian regime disliked in Washington.
77 See, for example, Samuel Bowles and Arjun Jayadev, *Garrison America*, Economists Voice, www.bepress.com/ev, March 2007; also Bowles et al., *Beyond the Wasteland* (Garden City, NY: Anchor Press/DoubleDay, 1983).
78 On this, see David Coates, *Models of Capitalism* (Cambridge: Polity, 2000), 203–10.
79 Chalmers Johnson, *Dismantling the Empire; America's Best Hope* (New York: Henry Holt, 2010), 129.

80 Speaking in the House of Representatives, May 21, 2010.

81 The U.S. defense budget for fiscal 2008 was $623 billion. The nearest "big spender" was China, at $65 billion—just a tenth of the U.S. expenditure. Total global military expenditures for 2004 were $1,100 billion with the United States included, but less than half that ($500 billion) if the United States was left out. "Defense-related spending for fiscal 2008 exceeded $1 trillion for the first time in history . . . The defense budget for fiscal 2008 was the largest since World War II" (Chalmers, *Dismantling the Empire*, 137, 141).

82 For fascinating and scholarly discussion of this, see Andrei S. Morkovits, *Uncouth Nation: Why Europe Dislikes America* (Princeton: Princeton University Press, 2007); and Andrew Kohut and Bruce Stokes, *America Against the World* (New York: Henry Holt, 2007).

83 Johnson, *737 US Military Bases = Global Empire*, Alternert.org, February 19, 2007.

84 National Intelligence Council, *Global Trends 2025: A Transformed World*, November 2008, iv.

85 There is now a considerable academic literature on the similarities and differences of the various "empires." For competing views, see, Patrick Karl O'Brien and Armand Cleese (eds), *Two Hegemonies: Britain 1846–1914 and the United States 1941–2001* (Aldershot, UK: Ashgate, 2002); Niall Ferguson, "Hegemony or Empire," *Foreign Affairs* 85(2) (2003); Michael Cox, "Empire, Imperialism and the Bush Doctrine," *Review of International Studies* 30 (2004); and Vaclav Smil, *Why America Is Not a New Rome* (Cambridge, MA: The MIT Press, 2010).

86 For a powerful essay on the degradation of American culture, see Chris Hedges, *Empire of Illusion: The End of Literacy and the Triumph of Spectacle* (New York: Nation Books, 2009).

87 Mason, *End of American Century*, xiii.

88 Johnson, *Three Good Reasons*.

89 I am not alone in thinking this. See, for example, the Amped Status Report, *The Critical Unraveling of American Society*, at http://ampedstatus.com/the-critical-unraveling-of-us-society

90 Mishel et al., *State of Working America*, 357.

91 That was 44 million Americans in total. If you factor in food stamps and other anti-poverty programs, 8 million of those poor Americans just escape the poverty line; but remember, it is a national poverty line. It doesn't allow for the higher cost of housing in urban American, or other regional variations in costs of living. It is also a very low poverty threshold, nowhere near the 60 percent of median income used as the measure of poverty in Western Europe. For the argument that the figures understate the true level of poverty, see David McGraw, *That 'Official' Poverty Rate? It's Much Worse Than You Think,* posted on alternet.org, September 23, 2010: available at www.alternet.org/story/148255.

92 *The Wall Street Journal,* September 17, 2010.

93 www.alternet.org/story/144388, posted December 5, 2009.

94 In conversation with Amy Goodman, posted on Alternet.org, September 15, 2010: available at www.alternet.org/story/148192

95 Amy Goodman, opening the same interview.

96 For details, see Peter N. Stearns, *From Alienation to Addiction: Modern American Work in Global Historical Perspective* (Boulder: Paradigm Publishers, 2008), 139–60; and Francis Green, *Demanding Work: The Paradox of Job Quality in the Affluent Economy* (Princeton: Princeton University Press, 2006).
97 Rifkin, *European Dream*, 30. See also Peter McClelland and Peter Tobin, *American Dream Dying: The Changing Economic Lot of the Least Advantaged* (Lanham, MD: Rowman and Littlefield, 2009).
98 For a similar view, see William Grieber, *Come Home America* (New York: Rodale, 2009).
99 Quoted in Reich, September 25, 2008, 38.

Chapter 6

1 This has long been the view of the editors of *Monthly Review*, best captured most recently in John Bellamy Foster and Fred Magdoff, *The Great Financial Crisis* (New York: Monthly Review Press, 2009).
2 The clearest arguments currently available on the impact of the tendency of the rate of profit to fall can be found in Robert Brenner, "That Hissing? It's the Sound of Bubblenomics Deflating," *The Guardian*, September 27, 2007; and his "What Is Good for Goldman Sachs Is Good for America: The Origins of the Present Crisis," the prologue to the Portuguese version of his *Economics of Global Turbulence* (Akal, 2009).
3 See Leo Panitch and Martijn Konings (eds), *American Empire and the Political Economy of Global Finance* (New York: Palgrave Macmillan, 2008); Leo Panitch and Martijn Konings, "Myths of Neoliberal Deregulation," *New Left Review* 57 (May–June, 2009), 67–83; and Greg Albo, Sam Gindin, and Leo Panitch, *In and Out of Crisis* (Oakland, CA: PM Press, 2010).
4 Martin Wolf, "Why Britain Has to Curb Finance," *The Financial Times*, May 22, 2009. There is a lovely note on Martin Wolf in Arianne Huffington's *Third World America* (New York: Crown Publishers, 2010), 28. "When the chief economics commentator at the *Financial Times* is sounding like the second coming of Karl Marx, you know that things have gotten out of hand."
5 Simon Johnson, "The Quiet Coup, *The Atlantic* (May 2009), 49; Martin Wolf, "Cutting Back Financial Capitalism Is America's Big Test," *The Financial Times*, April 15, 2009.
6 Panitch and Konings, "Myths of Neoliberal Deregulation," 73, 74.
7 Clyde Prestowitz, *The Betrayal of American Prosperity* (New York: Free Press, 2010), 271–72.
8 For the latest data on U.S. personal and international debt, see updates to Ronald Aronica and Mtetwa Ramdoo, *The World Is Flat*? (Tampa: Meghan-Kiffer Press, 2008): available at www.mkpress.com/Flat
9 Robert Reich, *Aftershock* (New York: Alfred A. Knopf, 2010), 76.
10 Sherle Schwenninger, "Redoing Globalization," *The Nation* (January 12/19, 2009), 30.

11 See, for example, Geitner's largely unsuccessful attempt to persuade surplus economies to reflate their exchange rates and levels of internal demand, to bring current account surpluses down to approximately 4 percent of GDP, in negotiations at the G-20 summit, October 2010.
12 Joseph Stiglitz, *Freefall* (New York: W. W. Norton, 2010), 187.
13 Thomas Friedman, "The Fat Lady Has Sung," *The New York Times*, February 21, 2010.
14 Arianna Huffington, *Third World America*, 28.
15 There are votes to be won here. The poll in *The Washington Post* immediately before the midterm elections found "a majority of Americans . . . worried about making their mortgages or rent payments" (*The Washington Post*, October 28, 2010).
16 The movement of power is all the wrong way during this foreclosure crisis. Banks worried about their Wall Street standing are left free to decide when/how to end a moratorium caused by their sloppy procedures, and even to pick up taxation powers at local level, as though we were moving back to the kind of tax farming that helped trigger the French Revolution! On the big banks as modern tax farmers, see Fred Schulte and Ben Protess, "Wall Street Is the New Tax Collector," posted on alternet.org, October 18, 2010: available at http://www.alternet.org/story/148537
17 The Obama administration's failure to see beyond the immediate effects of the foreclosure moratorium led it to resist the moratorium being generalized—another classic case of a crisis wasted. On this, see Shaun Donovan, U.S. Secretary for Housing and Urban Development, arguing that "a national blanket moratorium on all foreclosed sales would do far more harm than good—hurting homeowners and homebuyers alike when foreclosed homes make up 25 percent of home sales." "How We Can Really Help Families," posted on HuffPost, October 18, 2010: available at www.huffingtonpost.com/shaun-donovan/how-we-can-really-help-fa_b_765528.html?utm_source=DailyBrief&utm_campaign=101810&utm_medium=email&utm_content=BlogEntry&utm_term=Daily+Brief
18 Ibid.
19 Economic Policy Institute, *American Jobs Plan* (Washington, DC: EPI, 2009).
20 For the data on the "costs" of poverty, see Richard Wilkinson and Kate Pickett, *The Spirit Level: Why Equality is Better for Everyone* (London: Penguin Books, 2010).
21 See, for example, William Gruber, "The Future of the American Dream: Imagining an Economy That Puts People First," *The Nation* (May 25, 2009), 116.
22 *The American Prospect* ran two reports on how to tackle poverty in Obama's America: in the September and October 2009 editions. Both reports are well worth seeking out and reflecting upon.
23 Reich, *Aftershock*, 3–4.
24 Dorian Warren, "The American Labor Movement in the Age of Obama," *Perspectives on Politics*, 8(3) (September 2010), 849.
25 For details, see Kate Bronfenbrenner, *No Holds Barred: The Intensification of Employer Opposition to Organizing* (Washington, DC: Economic Policy Institute, Briefing

Paper #235, May 20, 2009). On the effectiveness of the new attack on public sector wages, see Lisa Rein and Ed O'Keefe, "New Post Poll Finds Negativity towards Federal Workers," *The Washington Post*, October 18, 2010.

26 For details, see *Jobs Well Done; What the Obama Administration Can Do for American Workers Right Now,* the report by Demos published in *The American Prospect*, October 2010.

27 "Many countries use special tax holidays, capital grants and other financial incentives essentially to bribe global companies to locate factories, labs and headquarters facilities within their borders. This practice has often resulted in in the off-shoring of otherwise competitive U.S.-based production and the loss of good U.S. jobs" (Prestowitz, *The Betrayal*, 293).

28 As Robert Kuttner put it: "We need a radically different approach to trade, so that the global trading system has a single set of rules rather than a maze of double standards; and . . . we need standards to differentiate legitimate development policy from predation, as well as buffers to protect our legitimate interests when other nations pursue predatory policies" (*The American Prospect*, January/February 2010, A9.)

29 As Clyde Prestowitz said, "The truth is that governments cannot avoid industrial policies. The only question is whether such choices and policies will be guided by some overarching strategy and principles or solely by idiosyncrasy and political trade-offs" (*The Betrayal*, 287).

30 See Prestowitz, *The Betrayal*, 27–31, 255; and Robert E. Scott, *The Importance of Manufacturing* (Washington, DC: Economic Policy Institute Briefing Paper #211, February 13, 2008).

31 The case is well put by Arianna Huffington, *Third World America*, 182.

32 Richard Elkus, among others, is full of suggestions for the route that such a policy should take: a national strategy for competiveness through strong leadership at the highest levels of government, bringing together key leaders from each involved section of industry and higher education; analyzing long-term strengths and weaknesses with policy designed rapidly to correct the latter; easing of anti-trust laws to allow vital industrial cooperation and joint ventures; not picking winners and losers, but locating what is lacking in the nation's strategic technologies, products, and markets, the better to fill the gaps. In his model, dollar depreciation, socialized health costs, and fair trade laws are also vital requirements for the rebuilding of an effective manufacturing base. Richard J. Elkus Jr., *Winner Takes All: How Competitiveness Shapes the Fate of Nations* (New York: Basic Books, 2008).

33 Jeffrey Sachs has criticized both Bush and Obama; "Neither would do what America needs and China is doing better: investing for the future through serious attention to sustainable energy, cutting-edge infrastructure, enhanced labour force skills and the promotion of international development through the export of infrastructure" (*The Financial Times*, July 22, 2010).

34 The Prestowitz program is laid out in *The Betrayal of American Prosperity,* 295–303.

35 For details, see *The American Prospect* report, "Made in the USA: Reviving American Manufacturing Before It Is Too Late," in the January/February 2010 issue.

36 *Three Good Reasons,* Chalmers Johnson, "Three Good Reasons to Liquidate Our Empire," posted *on Huffington Post*, July 30, 2009: available at http://www.huffingtonpost.com/chalmers-johnson/three-good-reasons-to-liq_b_247758.html
37 Op.cit, p. 187.
38 This data is from the American Friends Service Committee, mailed out October 2010.
39 As Hacker and Pierson put it, "Gridlock is not neutral . . . stalemate in Washington leads to a slow and steady deterioration of governance—deterioration that is at the heart of our present economic crisis . . . it corrodes public faith in the ability of government to address problems" (in *The American Prospect,* November 2010, 19–20).
40 "The far more important fact, for progressive purposes, is simply this: the system is rigged, and it's rigged against us. Sure, presidents can pretty easily pass tax cuts for the wealthy and powerful corporations. They can start whatever wars they wish . . . But what they cannot do, even with supermajorities in both houses of Congress behind them, is pass the kind of transformative progressive legislation that Obama promised in his 2008 presidential campaign," Eric Alterman, "Kabuki Democracy: Why a Progressive Presidency Is Impossible, For Now," *The Nation* (August 30/September 6, 2010), 12.
41 Though only as the most recent chapter in what Jacob Hacker and Paul Pierson correctly label as a "thirty year war" in their *Winner-Take-All Politics* (New York: Simon and Schuster, 2010), 6.
42 For details, see Stephanie Kirschgaessner, "The Pay Poll People," *The Financial Times*, October 22, 2010. "According to FEC data, only 32 percent of groups paying for election ads are disclosing the names of their donors. By comparison, in the 2006 midterm, 97 percent disclosed; in 2008, almost half disclosed." Robert Reich, "The Secret Big-Money Takeover of America," *The Huffington Post,* October 8, 2010: available at www.huffingtonpost.com/robert-reich/the-secret-bigmoneytakeo_b_754938.html?utm_source=DailyBrief&utm_campaign=100810&utm_medium=email&utm_content=BlogEntry).
43 The Republican Party press conferences immediately after the midterm elections made it clear that the newly elected House Speaker, and the newly elected Republican senators, expected the White House to completely adopt the Republican program; but the president continued to insist that he would seek bipartisan agreement wherever possible. For a first judgment on the limits of that strategy, see www.davidcoates.net/2010/11/04/the-morning-after-the-day-before/
44 "The first step on the way out of our present predicament should be to reread our own history. And not only to reread it, but to broadcast and promote it to diverse audiences so that a wide crosssection of leaders and ordinary citizens understand the complex and subtle interaction between the government and the private sector that has always underpinned American success," Prestowitz, *The Betrayal*, 285–6).
45 Including 41.3 million Americans receiving food stamps in June 2010, 9.7 million receiving unemployment benefits, and 19 million due to receive federal subsidies on their purchase of health care by 2019 (Sara Murray, "Obstacle to Deficit Cutting: A Nation on Entitlements," *The Wall Street Journal,* September 15, 2010).

46 Suzanne Mettler has called it "the submerged state," in her "Reconstituting the Submerged State: The Challenges of Social Policy Reform in the Obama Era," *Perspectives on Politics*, 8(3) (September 2010), 803–24.
47 Ibid., table 1, 806.
48 "Indeed, a good chunk of the country believes it has been saddled by this administration with tax hikes. Back in mid-February, a full 24 percent of respondents to a *CBS News/New York Times* poll said that their taxes had increased under Obama. Fifty-three percent said they had stayed the same. Only 12 percent thought their taxes had gone down" (Sam Stein, "Tax Day Fact Check: Most Americans Got A Tax Cut This Year," posted on *The Huffington Post*, April 15, 2010: available at www.huffingtonpost.com/2010/04/15/tax-day-2010-protesters-i_n_538556.html
49 On this, see William Kleinknecht, *The Man Who Sold the World: Ronald Reagan and the Betrayal of Main Street America* (New York: Nation Books, 2009); and Judith Stein, *Pivotal Decade: How the United States Traded Factories for Finance in the Seventies* (New Haven: Princeton University Press, 2010).
50 The current vulnerability of blue-collar voters to Tea Party arguments needs to be traced back to "the failure of liberals to defend the interests of working men and women as our manufacturing sector was dismantled, labor unions were destroyed and social services were slashed" (Chris Hedges, "Our Menace Isn't Insane Right Wingers," posted on alternet.org, on September 13, 2010, and available at www.alternet.org/story/148173
51 "Alas, though, instead of making nation-building in America his overarching narrative and then fitting health care, energy, educational reform, infrastructure, competitiveness and deficit reduction under that rubric, the president has pursued each separately. This made each initiative appear to be just some stand-alone liberal obsession to pay off a Democratic constituency—not an essential ingredient of a nation-building strategy—and, therefore, they have proved to be easily obstructed, picked off or delegitimized by opponents and lobbyists" (Thomas Friedman, *The Fat Lady Has Sung*).
52 Theda Skocpol and Lawrence Jacobs, *Reaching for a New Deal*, prepared for the Russell Sage Foundation, October 2010, and available at www.russellsage.org/research/working-group-obamas-policy-agenda
53 Ibid., 47–48.

Appendix 1

1 Including Charles R. Morris, *The Trillion Dollar Meltdown: Easy Money, High Rollers and the Great Credit Crash* (New York: PublicAffairs, 2008); Paul Muolo and Mathew Padilla, *Chain of Blame: How Wall Street Caused the Mortgage and Credit Crisis* (Hoboken, NJ: John Wiley, 2008); Paul Mason, *Meltdown: The End of the Age of Greed* (London: Verso, 2009); Les Leopold, *The Looting of America* (White River Junction: Chelsea Green Publishing, 2009); Charles Gasparino, *The Sellout: How Three Decades*

of Wall Street Greed and Government Mismanagement Destroyed the Global Financial System (New York: HarperCollins, 2009); Andrew Ross Sorkin, *Too Big to Fail* (New York: Viking, 2009); Gillian Tett, *Fool's Gold* (New York: Simon and Schuster, 2009); Nomi Prins, *It Takes a Pillage; Behind the Bailouts, Bonuses and Backroom Deals from Washington to Wall Street* (Hoboken: John Wiley, 2009); William D. Cohan, *House of Cards: A Tale of Hubris and Wretched Excess on Wall Street,* (Knopf Doubleday Publishing 2009); Simon Johnson and James Kwak, *13 Bankers* (New York: Pantheon Books, 2010); Dean Baker, *Plunder and Thunder: The Rise and Fall of the Bubble Economy* (Sausalito, CA: Polipoint Press, 2009); Dean Baker, *False Profits: Recovering from the Bubble Economy* (Sausalito, CA: Polipoint Press, 2010); Michael Lewis, *The Big Short: Inside the Doomsday Machine* (New York: W. W. Norton, 2010); Jonathan Tasini, *The Audacity of Greed* (Brooklyn: IG Publishing, 2009); Johan Norberg, *Financial Fiasco: How America's Infatuation with Homeownership and Easy Money Created the Economic Crisis* (Washington, DC: Cato Institute, 2009); Andrew Redleaf and Richard Vigilante, *Panic: The Betrayal of Capitalism by Wall Street and Washington* (Washington DC Richard Vigilante Books, 2010); Fred Magdoff and Michael D. Yates, *The ABC of the Economic Crisis: What Working People Need to Know* (New York: Monthly Review Press, 2009).

2 Including Herman M. Schwartz, *Subprime Nation* (Ithaca: Cornell University Press, 2009); Carmen Reinhart and Kenneth Rogoff, *This Time It's Different: Eight Centuries of Financial Folly* (Princeton: Princeton University Press, 2009); Gerald F. Davis, *Managed by the Markets: How Finance Reshaped America* (Oxford: Oxford University Press, 2009); Richard A. Posner, *A Failure of Capitalism* (Cambridge: Harvard University Press, 2009); Joseph Stiglitz, *Freefall: America, Free Markets, and the Sinking of the American Economy* (New York: W. W. Norton, 2010); Dan Immergluck, *Foreclosed: High-Risk Lending, Deregulation and the Undermining of America's Mortgage Market* (Ithaca: Cornell University Press, 2009); Robert Skidelsky, *Keynes: The Return of the Master* (New York: PublicAffairs, 2009); Martin Wolf, *Fixing Global Finance* (Baltimore: The John Hopkins University Press, 2010); Richard Wolff, *Capitalism Hits the Fan* (Northampton: Olive Branch Press, 2010); Howard J. Sherman, *The Roller Coaster Economy* (Armonk, NY: M. E. Sharpe, 2010); and my favorite, Martijn Konings (ed.), *The Great Credit Crash* (London: Verso, 2010). See also the special edition of *Comparative European Politics* 6 (2008) for essays by Mark Blyth, and by Herman Schwartz and Leonard Seabrooke; Richard K. Greene and Susan M. Wachter, "The American Mortgage in Historical and International Context," *Journal of European Perspectives* 19(4) (Fall 2005); Paul Langley, "Securitizing Suburbia: The Transformation of Anglo-American Housing Finance," *Competition and Change* 10(3) (September 2006); and NBIR Working Papers No's 14712, 15283, 15362, 15573, 15650, 15956, and 02138.

3 Including the 2,200-page report on the collapse of Lehman Brothers by the court-appointed examiner Anton Valukas (March 2010); and the ongoing evidence to the Financial Crisis Inquiry Commission (chaired by Phil Angelides).

4 See Graham Turner, *The Credit Crunch: Housing Bubbles, Globalization and the Worldwide Economic Crisis* (London: Pluto Press, 2008); Robert Peston, *Who Runs Britain?* (London: Hodder & Stoughton, 2008); Larry Elliott and Dan Atkinson, *The Gods That*

Failed: How the Financial Elite Have Gambled away Our Futures (London: Vintage, 2009); Alex Brummer, *The Crunch: How Greed and Incompetence Sparked the Credit Crisis* (London: Random House Business Books, 2009); John Lanchester, *Whoops!* (London: Penguin, 2010); Andrew Gamble, *The Spectre at the Feast: Capitalist Crisis and the Politics of Recession* (London: Palgrave Macmillan, 2009); James Brassett, Lena Rethel, and Matthew Watson, "Special Section on the Political Economy of the Subprime Crisis in Britain," *The British Journal of Politics and International Relations* 11(3) (August 2009).

5 Peter J. Wallison, *Government Policies and the Financial Crisis*, AEI Online, November 2008, available at: www.aei.org/outlook/299015
6 Peter J. Wallison, "The True Origins of the Financial Crisis," *The American Spectator*, February 2009, 24.
7 John B. Taylor, *The Financial Crisis and the Policy Responses, Evidence to the Financial Crisis Inquiry Commission*, November 2008, 10: see also his NBIR Working Paper 02138 (January 2009).
8 Norberg, *Financial Fiasco*, 6.
9 Ibid., 134–35.
10 Ibid., 134.
11 Ibid., 15–16.
12 Redleaf and Vigilante, *Panic*, 7–8.
13 Ibid., 10.
14 Ibid., 244–45.
15 "There are many reasons to oppose [the bill]. The simplest and clearest is that the FDIC is completely unequipped by experience to handle the failure of a giant nonbank financial institution" (Peter J. Wallison and David Skeel, "The Dodd Bill: Bailouts Forever," *The Wall Street Journal,* April 7, 2010, A15).
16 Norberg, *Financial Fiasco*, 137–38, 141, 143. "Here is the quickest way to determine whether you are operating in an honest capitalist system or a corrupt imitation thereof: check the bankruptcy rate. For most of the last hundred years, the United States has had both the strongest economy and the highest bankruptcy rate of any reasonably large developed nation. By contrast, the old Soviet union had a bankruptcy rate of essentially zero" (Redleaf and Vigilante, *Panic*, 196).
17 Ibid., 6.
18 For this, see the Financial Crisis Inquiry Commission Preliminary Staff Report, *The CRA and the Mortgage Crisis*, April 7, 2010, 7. As Dean Baker said, "The other myth that requires debunking is that banks issued junk mortgages because of pressure to comply with the *Community Reinvestment Act*. This myth is unfounded no matter how you look at it . . . the CRA had almost nothing to do with the explosion of subprime and Alt-A loans during this period" (Baker, *False Profits*, 30). As Joseph Stiglitz likewise reported, "Default rates on CRA lending were actually comparable to other areas of lending—showing that lending, if done well, does not pose greater risks" (*Freefall*, 10). The often-cited defense of CRA-motivated lending by Janet Yellen, the president of the Federal Reserve Bank of San Francisco, is cited in full in Immergluck, *Foreclosed*, 162–63; see also David

Coates, *Answering Back: Liberal Responses to Conservative Arguments* (New York: Continuum Books, 2010), 246; and Konings, *Great Credit Crash*, 96–98, 138).

19 For the general campaign against ACORN, see Peter Dreier and Christopher R. Martin, "How ACORN Was Framed: Political Controversy and Media Agenda Setting," *Perspectives on Politics*, 8(3) (September 2010), 761–92.

20 The data (and data sources) for this are in Coates, *Answering Back*, 245–46, 268–69.

21 "In 2001, newly-originated subprime, Alt-A, and home equity lines (second mortgages) totaled $330 billion and amounted to 15 percent of all new residential mortgages. Just three years later . . . these mortgages accounted for almost $1.1 trillion in new loans and 37 percent of residential mortgages. Their volume peaked in 2006 when they reached $1.4 trillion and 48 percent of new residential mortgages" (Ronald D. Utt, "The Subprime Mortgage Market Collapse. A Primer on the Causes and Possible Solutions," The Heritage Foundation, *Backgrounder* No. 2127, April 22, 2008).

22 The figure is from Atif and Sufi (see footnote 20). "The first peak in cash-out refinancing occurs in 1998Q4, when volume surpasses $100 billion for the first time. Although the volume in the following 9 quarters (1999Q1 to 2001Q1) was less than $100 billion per quarter, the average value of cash-out refinancing per quarter was $204 billion in the subsequent 30 quarters (2001Q2 to 2008Q3), far exceeding the average value in the preceding 41 quarters from 1991Q1 to 2001Q1 . . . During this period [1991Q1 to 2008Q1] homeowners extracted $6,720 billion in equity. These figures suggest that equity extractions represent a non-trivial portion of outstanding mortgages, and the risk transferred from homeowners to the financial sector due to these extractions may have had a significant impact on the overall risk exposure of this sector to real-estate prices" (Amir Khandani, Andrew Lo, and Robert Merton, *Systemic Risk and the Refinancing Ratchet Effect*, NBER Working Paper 15362, September 2009, 11, 14).

23 Atif Mian and Amir Sufi similarly conclude from their research that "borrowing against the increase in home equity by existing homeowners [was] responsible for a significant fraction of both the sharp rise in U.S. household leverage from 2002 to 2006 and the increase in defaults from 2006 to 2008" (*House Prices, Home Equity-Based Borrowing, and the US Household Leverage Crisis*, NBER Working Paper 15283, August 2009).

24 "Why the confusion? Why then did virtually everyone report that the mortgage crisis began with subprime loans? One possibility is that the subprime story provided an easy scapegoat: subprime lenders. Another is that markets with private securitization of mortgages tended to have a disproportionately large share of subprime loans and that these were the securities being downgraded by the rating agencies and receiving most of the attention. A third possibility is that because the total number of subprime foreclosures was larger than the number of prime foreclosures early in the mortgage crisis (the subprime share peaked at 58 percent in Q2 2007 although it was down to 33 percent by Q2 2009), analysts simplemindedly rounded the subprime share up to one and rounded the prime share down to zero. The truth is probably a combination of these factors although, being of a cynical bent, I put more weight on the first possibility" (this, and the quotes, in

Stan J. Liebowitz, "ARMs, Not Sub-primes, Caused the Mortgage Crisis," *The Economists' Voice*, November 2009: www.bepress.com/ev).

25 Ibid., 140.

26 Ibid., 1.

27 Greenspan was particularly criticized when appearing before the Financial Crisis Inquiry commission, though at that juncture his main interlocutor was Brooksley Born, who when heading the Commodity Futures Trading commission in the late 1990s had called for greater oversight of the new financial instruments, only to be overruled by Greenspan and others.

28 For Alan Greenspan's defense of his role in the run-up to the financial crisis, see his *The Crisis*, a research paper from The Brookings Institution, March 2010.

29 For this, see Herman Schwartz and Leonard Seabrooke, "Varieties of Residential Capitalism in the International Political Economy: Old Welfare States and the New Politics of Housing," *Comparative European Politics* 6 (2008), 244.

30 The U.S. secondary mortgage market is the biggest in the world, containing $5.37 *trillion* of securitized mortgage loans in 2005, and an additional $4.48 trillion held as "whole loans"—secondary market sales which are not securitized. Most European countries now have some secondary mortgage market, largely concentrated in the UK, but the total EU volume was only €244.6 *billion* in 2006. Australia is next, with $126 billion (HUD, *Mortgage Securitization: Lessons for Emerging Markets*, July 2007, 4).

31 "Pundits used to describe the life of a banker at a savings and loan institution . . . by the code 3–6–3. It signified 'issue savings deposit at three percent, lend them out on 30-year house mortgages at six percent, and be on the golf course by three o'clock'" (Jan Kregel, *Changes in the U.S. Financial System and the Subprime Crisis*, Working paper No. 530 (The Levy Economics Institute, 2008), 40).

32 Johnson and Kawk, *13 Bankers*, 145.

33 Cited in *The Washington Post*, October 12, 2010. For the full story, see Helen Thompson, "The Political Origins of the Financial Crisis: The Domestic and International Politics of Fannie Mae and Freddie Mac," *Political Quarterly*, 80(1) (January–March 2009), 17–24.

34 On the bailout of the S&Ls, see David Glasberg and Dan Skidmore, *Corporate Welfare Policy and the Welfare State; Bank Deregulation and the Savings and Loans Bail-out* (New York: Aldine De Gruyter, 1997); and Stephen Pizzo, Mary Fricker, and Paul Muolo, *Inside Job: the Looting of America's Savings and Loans* (New York: McGraw Hill, 1989).

35 In 1955, S&L-provided mortgages made up 37.6 percent of the total; mortgages from life insurance companies, 22.6 percent; from commercial banks, 16.6 percent; GSE mortgages, 4.1 percent; and individuals and others, 20.1 percent. By 2000, the equivalent figures were 10.6 percent, 3.5 percent, 24.4 percent, 41.7 percent, and 19.7 percent. By 2007, the GSE share had dropped to 34.6 percent and privately issued mortgages had risen by more than 10 points (to 30.7 percent) (Utt, "Subprime Mortgage," 8).

36 Immergluck, *Foreclosed*, 17.

37 William N. Goetzmann and Frank Newman, *Securitization in the 1920s*, NBER Working Paper 15650 (January 2010); and Eugene N. White, *Lessons from the Great*

American Real Estate Boom and Bust of the 1920s, NBER Working Paper 15573 (December 2009).

38 "Mortgage securitization has often been portrayed as a private-sector financial innovation. Yet it was . . . Ginnie Mae, the federal agency that facilitates the purchase of FHA loans, that issued the first residential mortgage-backed securities (RMBS) in 1970, guaranteeing interest and principal payments on pools of FHA- and Veteran Administration-insured mortgages." (Immergluck, *Foreclosed*, 35). "Fannie Mae and Salomon Brothers essentially invented the modern MBS market in 1981 and also pioneered the overseas selling of these securities. Freddie Mac invented the collaterized mortgage obligation (CMO), a derivative that slices up principal and interest payments into different tranches so that investors can buy bonds with maturities and returns that vary from the underlying individual mortgages in 1983" (Schwartz, *Subprime Nation*, 102).

39 Immergluck, *Foreclosed*, 40.

40 "In the 1990s, the GSEs did not relax their credit standards dramatically and, at least in their direct lending activities, did not appear to engage in the sort of high-risk lending practices in which the emerging subprime lenders were engaging" (ibid., 63).

41 On the role of JPMorgan staffers in the creation of credit derivatives, on the lines of "slice and dice" mortgages, see Gillian Tett, *Fool's Gold*, 52–56, 95–98.

42 "Although there was some easing of standards in the conforming market, especially in the GSEs' extended programs and the FHA's seller-financed downpayment program, it was minor compared with the one that occurred in the rest of the market. Arrear rates on the GSEs' single-family home portfolio have risen a great deal recently, but this only started in the second half of 2007 . . . Likewise, the increase in arrear rates on FHA mortgages has been fairly mild." Luci Ellis, *The Housing Meltdown: Why Did It Happen in the United States?* (Bank of International Settlements, Working Paper No. 259, September 2008), 14. The data are graphed by Immergluck (*Foreclosed*, 136); and confirmed in testimony before Congress in April 2010. (See *The Wall Street Journal*, April 10–11, 2010.)

43 Johnson and Kwak, *13 Bankers*, 144.

44 Mark Zandi, *Financial Shock* (Saddle River, NJ: Pearson Education, 2009), 42. In consequence, their share of the mortgage market fell rapidly after 2003 "because the loans being made violated their underwriting standards and because the Wall Street banks were so eager to get their hands on those loans" (Johnson and Kwak, *13 Bankers*, 145). It was this that brought Fannie Mae in June 2005 to what, in an internal document, its then-head Donald Mudd termed "a strategic crossroads," after which the GSE did engage in heavier investment in the subprime and alternative mortgage markets. (This came clear only later, in evidence to Henry Waxman's Oversight Committee, reported in *The Financial Times*, December 10, 2008.)

45 "During the peak of the housing boom in 2005, the nation's 30 largest institutions accounted for half of all the loans originated . . . Countrywide topped the list, originating more than 1 million loans worth almost a quarter-trillion dollars that year" (Johnson and Kwak, *13 Bankers*, 104).

46 So it is true that "by 2007 Agency MBS accounted for one-half of an outstanding U.S. mortgage debt of roughly $10 trillion, split 5:4 between Fannie Mae and Freddie Mac. A further one-quarter of the outstanding mortgage debt was privately securitized, and the last on-quarter resided with the lending institution as a discrete loan" (ibid., 104).

47 "If they are to exist going forward, Fannie and Freddie should be 100 percent government owned, and the government should simply issue mortgages to the population of the United States directly since this is essentially what is already happening today, without the added burden of supporting a privately funded, and arguably insolvent, capital structure" (J. Kyle Bass, written evidence to the Financial Crisis Inquiry Commission, January 13, 2010, 6).

48 Ibid., 5.

49 Glasberg and Skidmore, Corporate Welfare Policy, 40.

50 Ibid., 5–6.

51 Nomi Prins was particularly exercised by this. "You may get tired," she wrote, "of my beating this dead horse, but you have to believe me: the horse totally deserves it. I cannot overstate the value of Glass-Steagall. If it had not been repealed a decade ago, our current banking system meltdown would not have occurred" (*It Takes a Pillage*, 141).

52 Ross Levine, *An Autopsy of the U.S. Financial System*, NBER Working Paper No. 15956 (April 2010), 2.

53 And it is not as though Greenspan and Bernanke were not warned. They were, as early as 2003 at the BIS meeting in Wyoming. For details, see Tett, *Fool's Gold*, 153–54. On Geitner's greater pragmatism on these matters, see ibid., 156–60.

54 Baker, *False Profits*, 7. For chapter and verse on the Fed failure, and the failure of other regulators, see Johnson and Kwak, *13 Bankers*, 143–50.

55 Simon Johnston labeled it "The Quiet Coup" in a widely cited piece in *The Atlantic Monthly*, May 2009. For the rise of U.S. finance, see Gerald F. Davis, *Managed by the Markets: How Finance Reshaped America* (Oxford: Oxford University Press, 2009); and John Bellamy Foster and Hannah Holleman, "The Financial Power Elite," *Monthly Review*, 62(1) (May 2010), 1–19.

56 For a particularly egregious example, see Greg Kaufmann, "Friedmanism at the Fed: How Former New York Fed Chair Stephen Friedman Made a Bundle on the AIG Bailout," *The Nation*, March 15, 2010. Dean Baker likened the internal construction of the Fed "to the pharmaceutical industry picking members of the Food and Drug Administration" (*False Profits*, 9).

57 "As of October 2009, 1,537 lobbyists representing financial institutions, other businesses, and industry groups had registered to work on financial regulation proposals before Congress—outnumbering by 25 to one the lobbyists representing consumer groups, unions, and other supporters of stronger regulation. Even Citigroup, 34 percent owned by the government, hired 46 lobbyists of its own. In the first nine months of 2009, the industry spent $344 million on lobbying" (Johnson and Kwak, *13 Bankers*, 192). For more details, see Deniz Igan, Pracci Mishra, and Thierry Tressel, *A Fistful of Dollars: Lobbying and the Financial Crisis* (IMF Working Paper WP/09/287, December 2009).

58 As Michael Barr told Congress, in the housing sector "the worst and most widespread abuses occurred in the institutions with *the least* federal oversight," while it was "lax supervision, supervisory neglect, lack of transparency and conflicts of interest" that combined to undermine the viability of the U.S. financial system (in evidence to the House of Representative's Committee on Oversight and Government Reform, November 14, 2008; also cited by Joshua Holland on alternet.org, October 10, 2010, available at www.alternet.org/story/148454).
59 Managing Director and Financial Services Analyst, Calyon Securities (USA), Inc: Evidence, January 13, 2010.
60 John Cassidy, "Lessons from the Collapse of Bear Stearns," *The Financial Times*, March 15, 2010.
61 For this core weakness in the system, see Tett, *Fool's Gold*, 70, 215.
62 See, for example, Gasparino, *The Sellout*, 178-87, on the Spritzer inquiry into Citigroup CEO Sandy Weill; and the report of the court-appointed bankruptcy examiner Anton Valukas into balance sheet manipulation at Lehman Brothers in the weeks before its collapse.
63 Ibid., 496.
64 Senator Carl Levine, "Wall Street and the Financial Crisis: The Role of Investment Banks," posted on *The Huffington Post*, April 27, 2010.
65 NBER Working Paper No. 14712, February 2009.
66 Paul Krugman, "Berating the Raters," *The New York Times*, April 26, 2010.
67 The calculation of Les Leopold, posted on Alternet.org on April 10, 2010: as www.alternet.org/story/146402/. The full details are in Trevor Ganshaw, *Hedge Funds Humbled* (New York: McGraw Hill, 2010), 13–16.
68 Prudential Financial, for example, sent $2 million to the U.S. Chamber of Commerce to help fund its campaign against strong financial regulation. General Motors, while still partly government owned, formed a political action committee and funded Republican Minority Leader Mitch McConnell (details in *The New York Times*, October 17, 2010, and *The Washington Post*, October 24, 2010).
69 Details in *The New York Times*, October 15, 2010.
70 *The Huffington Post,* August 5, 2010.
71 Referenced in Tett, *Fool's Gold*, 20.
72 For the way in which unregulated competition generated mega-banks that then dominated the entire economy, see Johnson and Kwak, *13 Bankers*, 59–61.
73 Tett, *Fool's Gold*, 93.
74 Ibid., x.
75 Carl Levine, "Wall Street," 3.
76 *The General Theory of Employment, Interest and Money* (London: Macmillan, 1936), 142.
77 Stiglitz, *Freefall* xvii.
78 Ellis, *Housing Meltdown*, v.
79 By far the most complex of the Pollyannish arguments is Herman Schwartz's hugely impressive study of what he called the *Subprime Nation* (Schwartz, *Subprime Nation*). See also his "Structured Finance for Financed Structures: American Economic Power Before and After the Global Financial Crisis," in Konings, *Great*

Credit Crash, 173–97. The less *sophisticated* academic and policy circle optimism is well documented in Carmen Reinhart and Kenneth Rogoff's equally valuable *This Time Is Different: Eight Centuries of Financial Folly* (Princeton: Princeton University Press, 2009), 208–14.

80 Martin Wolf is among the more important commentators holding this view. As he wrote in the updated version of his *Fixing Global Finance*, "My view, then, is that the United States has been as much the victim of decisions made by others as the author of its own misfortunes. That is a desperately unpopular view—in the United States, because it is easier for most Americans to accept that they are incompetent than that they are impotent, and in the rest of the world, because it is far easier to accept that the United States is guilty than that others share the responsibility. But the principal argument of this book is that the crisis is a global predicament explained by decisions—and frailties—across the globe" (*Fixing Global Finance*, 207).

81 Sheila Bair, Chairman, FDIC, written evidence, January 14, 2010, 50.

82 Start with Giovanni Arrighi, *The Long Twentieth Century* (London: Verso, 2010).

83 Start with David Harvey, *The Enigma of Capital and the Crises of Capitalism* (London: Profile Books, 2010).

84 Start with Leo Panitch and Martijn Konings (eds), *American Empire and the Political Economy of Global Finance* (Houndmills: Palgrave Macmillan, 2008).

Appendix 2

1 I would like acknowledge here a considerable debt to two honored colleagues, from whose writings and conversation I have learned much about the recent history of economics as discipline: Don Frey and Michael Lawlor. Neither, of course, bears any responsibility for what is written here. It is rather that, without their erudition and generous sharing of thoughts, I would not have had the courage to begin writing at all! I thank them both.

2 Robert Skidelsky, *Keynes: The Return of the Master* (New York: PublicAffairs, 2009), 28.

3 Simon Johnson and James Kawk, *13 Bankers* (New York: Pantheon Books, 2010), 68. Emphases added. The story told here is told in greater detail in John Quiggen, *Zombie Economics* (Princeton: Princeton University Press, 2010); and in Clyde Prestowitz, *The Betrayal of American Prosperity* (New York: Free Press, 2010), 112–59.

4 Indeed, "by the 1980s, many M.B.A. students were being taught that the efficient market hypothesis was a description of reality." John Cassidy, *How Markets Fail* (New York: Farrar, Straus and Giroux, 2009), 96. See also Joseph Stiglitz, *Freefall: America, Free Markets and the Sinking of the World Economy* (New York: W. W. Norton & Co, 2010), 265–66.

5 Andrew Redleaf and Richard Vigilante, *Panic* (Richard Vigilante Books, 2010), 106.

6 Cassidy, *How Markets Fail*, 86.

7 For the exchange between them, see David Coates, *Answering Back* (New York: Continuum Books, 2010), 256. The key exchange was this. *Waxman*: You had the authority to prevent irresponsible lending practices that led to the subprime loan crisis. You were advised to do so by many. Do you feel that your ideology pushed you to make decisions you wish you had not made?

Greenspan: Yes, I've found a flaw. I don't know how significant or permanent it is. But I've been very distressed by that fact.
Waxman: Were you wrong?
Greenspan: Partially.

8 Robert Skidelsky, "How to Rebuild a Shamed Subject," *The Financial Times*, August 6, 2009.
9 Redleaf and Vigiliante, *Panic*, 171.
10 Johnson and Kwak cite work by Stiglitz, Schiller, Summers, DeLong, and Waldman (*13 Bankers*, 69–70), some of whom, of course, have also been major policy players.
11 Primarily Robert Schiller, and also *The Financial Times's* Gillian Tett. For their prescience, see Yves Smith, *Econned* (New York: Palgrave Macmillan, 2010), 9–15. Cassidy adds Stiglitz, Grossman, and Benoit Mandelbrot to that list (*How Markets Fail*, 93–96), saying this: "'Modern finance was the official religion,' Mandelbrot later recalled, 'my hypothesis contradicted it; and I was about as welcome in the established church of economics as a heretical Arian at the Council of Nicene'" (96). We should add also at least one Chicago-based economist, the brave Raghuram Rajan, who broke ranks at the 2005 symposium honoring Alan Greenspan to warn of a financial meltdown to come. See also Rajan and Zingales, *Saving Capitalism from the Capitalists* (Princeton: Princeton University Press, 2004).
12 Redleafe and Vigilante, *Panic*, 119.
13 Cited in Skidelsky, "How to Rebuild a Shamed Subject."
14 For the persistence of this way of thinking in most U.S. economics Ph.D. programs, see Cassidy, *How Markets Fail*, 105–07.
15 This was Friedman's advice to the profession in 1953, cited in detail in Smith, *Econned*, 47–48.
16 Or, as Todd Buchholz put it, "freaky assumptions such as instantaneously adjusting markets and superhuman capacities to absorb information," in *New Ideas from Dead Economists* (New York: Penguin/Plume, 1990), 297.
17 For an overview by Michael Fitzgerald, see: http://magazine.uchicago.edu/0910/features/chicago_schooled.shtml
18 For details, see Philip Mirowski, "The Neo-liberal Thought Collective," *Renewal* 17(4) (2009), 26–36.
19 Smith, *Econned*, 34. For a history of this transformation, see Roger Backhouse, "Economists and the Rise of Neo-liberalism," *Renewal* 17(4) (2009), 17–25.
20 One of the key figures in the new economics—Robert Lucas—is widely quoted as observing in 1980 that "one cannot find good under-forty economists who identify themselves or their work as Keynesian . . . At research seminars, people don't take Keynesian theorizing seriously anymore; the audience starts to whisper or giggle to one another." Cited in Robert Pollin's review of John Cassidy's book,

"Return of Reality-Based Economics," *Monthly Review* 62(4) (September 2010), 5. The fuller quote is in Cassidy, *How Markets Fail*, 97).

21 Cassidy, *How Markets Fail*, 36.

22 Lucas famously argued that changes in monetary policy could have no real impact on output or employment because actors would respond to the announcement of such policy changes by altering their own behavior, nullifying the effect. This was his "policy ineffectiveness proposition" that so directly challenged Keynesianism.

23 As Skidelsky said, "[I]n economics, there are many respectable economists who would not accept what I describe . . . as the central beliefs of the profession. Mostly, though, they are isolated figures in their department, usually of an older age group" ("How to Rebuild a Shamed Subject," 29).

24 As the Mont Pèlerin Society puts it on its website in a footnote to its Aims, "Note: Here, 'liberal' is used in its European sense, broadly epitomized by a preference for minimal and dispersed government, rather than in its current American sense which indicates the opposite preference for an extension and concentration of governmental powers."

25 Smith, *Econned*, 38.

26 See in particular, Paul Omerod, "The Current Crisis and the Culpability of Macroeconomic Theory," *21st Century Society* 5(1) (February 2010), 5–18.

27 It is important to note that there grew up in economics in the post-1970 era a prestigious literature on "the economics of information." In fact, many so-called "New Keynesians" based their arguments for unemployment on this literature. Joseph Stiglitz won the Nobel Prize in Economics based on contributions to this literature. Larry Summers, George Akerlof, and Michael Spence are economists of this school. The bigger point, though, is that this literature, while widely influential, did not change the core beliefs and methods of economics, or provide it with a widespread alternative paradigm. "New Keynesianism" tried to show that even if one used the rational expectation hypothesis and the fancy mathematics of "New Classicism," there were informational asymmetries between firms and workers that could account for "involuntary unemployment." In trying so hard to be so rational and mathematical, in order to be respectable economists, they ended by satisfying no one. The New Classicals ignored them and the Old Keynesians rightly did not feel they needed their arguments to be convinced of the possible reality of involuntary unemployment" (Mike Lawlor, in private correspondence with the author).

28 The details are in Cassidy, *How Markets Fail*, 192–204; Buchholz, *New Ideas*, 299–303; and Ellen Ruppell Shell, *Cheap: The High Cost of Discount Culture* (New York: The Penguin Press, 2009), 60–65.

29 For Joseph Stiglitz's own work on hidden information and other necessary market imperfections, see his *Freefall*, 238–60. He wrote this in *The Guardian*, December 20, 2002: "Last year's laureates emphasized that different market participants have different (and imperfect) information, and these symmetries in information have a profound impact on how an economy functions. In particular, last year's laureates implied that *markets were not, in general, efficient*; that were was an important role for government to play. Adam Smith's invisible hand—the idea that free

markets lead to efficiency as if guided by unseen forces—is invisible, at least in part, because it is not there." He was, of course, one of those laureates.

30 Hyman Minsky (1919–1996), professor of economics at Washington University in St. Louis. For a critical application of his approach to the current crisis, see Gary A. Dymski, "Why the Subprime Crisis Is Different: A Minskyian Approach," *Cambridge Journal of Economics* 34 (2010), 239–55. For a superb overview and critique of Minsky's work, see Thomas Palley, "The Limits of Minsky's Hypothesis" and John Bellamy Foster and Robert McChesney, "Listen Keynesians, It's the System," both in *Monthly Review* 61(11) (April 2010), 28–58.

31 George Cooper, *The Origin of Financial Crises* (New York: Vintage Books, 2008), 13.

32 Cited in John Kay, "Markets after the Age of Efficiency," *The Financial Times*, October 7, 2009.

33 Cited in Will Hutton, *The State We're In* (London: Jonathan Cape, 1994), 243.

34 I am grateful to Don Frey for this observation.

35 The title of an article arguing that, by Mort Zuckerman in *The Financial Times*, October 19, 2009.

36 See for example Gideon Rachman, 'Sweep Economists off Their Throne," *The Financial Times*, September 6, 2010, and Philip Mirowski, "The Great Mortification: Economists' Responses to Crisis of 2007—(and counting)," *The Hedgehog Review* 12(3) (Summer 2010). Likewise, Yves Smith: "Is it fair to attack economists? To a large degree, yes. The specialty has done itself and the wider world considerable damage through its pursuit of a misguided, overly ambitious goal of putting itself on a scientific footing. But rather than create greater understanding, the result is Potemkin science, all facade and no substance . . . the widespread acceptance of the phony precepts of financial economics and neoclassical economics helped bring about the financial crisis by endorsing policies and practices that allowed financial firms to exploit customers, shareholders and taxpayers on a scale hitherto only seen in banana republics" (*Econned*, 19, 21–22).

37 Ray Patel, *The Value of Nothing: How to Reshape Market Society and Redefine Democracy* (New York: Picador, 2009), 22.

38 Joseph Stiglitz, for one, has argued the case for a new paradigm: see his "Needed: A New Economic Paradigm," *The Financial Times*, August 20, 2010.

39 The title of the book by Robert Skidelsky published by Public Affairs in 2009; and of the review article by Andrew Gamble in *The New Statesman*, September 3, 2009.

40 Cited in Hutton, *The State We're In*, 239.

41 Ibid., 241.

42 John Llewellyn, "Only Keynes' Animal Spirits Can Intoxicate Our Hung-over Economies," *The Observer*, August 22, 2010.

43 "The sudden increase in public debt is a direct and automatic response to the recession that was driven by the rapid decrease in private debt that followed the bursting of the housing bubble. A failure to accommodate the recession-induced decline in private debt with rising public debt would have resulted in a much harsher economic downturn." Josh Bivens and Anna Turner, *Putting Public Debt in*

Context (Washington, DC: Economic Policy Institute Briefing Paper #272, August 3, 2010).

44 Keynes argument about the value of paying people to dig holes in roads is reproduced in Buchholz, *New Ideas*, 222. James Galbraith wrote a powerful essay "In Defense of Deficits," in *The Nation,* March 22, 2010.

45 David Coates, "Conclusion" in David Coates (ed.), *Varieties of Capitalism, Varieties of Approaches* (London: Palgrave, 2005), 269.

46 Paul Krugman, "How Did Economists Get It So Wrong?" *The New York Times*, September 9, 2009. Skidelsky, more prosaically, labels the two schools "New Classicals and New Keynesians" ("How to Rebuild a Shamed Subject," 29).

47 For the latest version, see Terence McDonough, Michael Reich and David M. Kotz (eds), *Contemporary Capitalism and Its Crises: Social Structures of Accumulation Theory for the 21st Century* (Cambridge, UK: Cambridge University Press, 2010). For an alternative but equally structurally focused view, see also Greg Albo, Sam Gindin, and Leo Panitch, *In and Out of Crisis: The Global Financial Meltdown and Left Alternatives* (Oakland, CA: PM Press, 2010).

48 This case is made more fully in Chapter 6.

Author Index

Adams, Graham 121
Angle, Sharon 8
Avery, Dennis 94

Bacevich, Andrew 134
Bair, Sheila 177–8
Baker, Dean 172–3
Barro, Robert 27, 181
Beck, Glen 8
Bernanke, Ben 22, 31, 162
Bhagwati, Jagdish 68
Bivens, Josh 71
Blankfein, Lloyd 175
Bloomberg, Michael 66
Brown, Paul 92
Buffett, Warren 183
Bush, George W. 13

Cameron, David 28
Chang, Ha-Joon 87
Chapman, Phil 94
Cline, William 64
Clinton, Bill 158, 173

Degan, Robert 36
De Soto, Hernando 82

Elkus, Richard 131, 154, 228 n. 32
Emanuel, Rahm 155
Eskow, Richard 175

Fama, Eugene 180
Frank, Barney 26, 27, 168–9
Friedman, Milton 40, 46, 49, 181, 182
Friedman, Thomas 68, 109–10, 129, 148

Galbraith, James 30
Galbraith, J. K. 126
Gasparino, Charles 174
Geitner, Timothy 4, 22, 31
Gersemann, Olaf 116–17
Gingrich, Newt 7–8
Goklany, Indur 68–9
Gore, Al 89, 92, 95, 96
Gray, John 133
Gray, William 95

Grayson, Alan 136
Green, Joshua 111
Greenspan, Alan 27, 28, 31, 160, 162, 167, 173, 175, 180, 195 n. 59
Griswold, Dan 64

Hancock, Peter 175
Hannity, Sean 8
Hayward, Steven 93
Hodgson, Geoffrey 120
Hoover, J. Edgar 122
Huffington, Arianna 31, 129, 149, 154

Immergluck, Dan 170–1
Inholfe, James 91–2
Isbister, John 75

Jacobs, Lawrence 158–9
Johnson, Chalmers 134, 136, 137–8, 154
Johnson, Lyndon 55, 159
Johnson, Simon 172

Kahneman, Daniel 183
Keynes, John Maynard 33, 35, 40, 176, 180, 183–4, 185
Khandani, Amir 167
Konings, Martijn 144
Krol, Robert 61
Krugman, Paul 31, 64, 71, 85, 196 n. 77
Kwak, James 172

Lane, Robert 56
Leibowitz, Stan 233 n.24
Levin, Senator Carl 174, 176
Levine, Ross 172
Lieberman, Ben 97
Limbaugh, David 10
Limbaugh, Rush 8, 92, 95, 118, 119, 191 n. 22
Lintzen, Richard 93, 94
Lipset, Seymour Martin 115–16, 117, 122
Lomborg, Bjorn 94
Lucas, Robert 181, 184

McCain , John 90, 98
Madden, Thomas 118
Marx, Karl 78, 81
Mason, David 129, 133, 137
Merkel, Angela 22, 28, 107
Miller, Joe 8
Miller, Matt 69
Minsky, Hyman 183
Mozilo, Angelo 175

Norberg, Johan 82, 161, 162–3, 164

Obama, Barack 2, 3, 4, 7, 16, 29, 91, 110, 118–19, 134
O'Donnell, Christine 9
Olson, Mancur 119
O'Reilly, Bill 8, 191 n.20
Ostrom, Elinor 183

Panayotakis, Costas 108
Panitch, Leo 144
Patel, Raj 184
Paul, Rand 8, 26, 157
Paulson, Henry 13
Perot, Ross 64
Prestowitz, Clyde 145, 154

Reagan, Ronald 35, 52, 158
Redleaf, Andrew 161, 163, 166
Reich, Robert 29, 147, 152
Ricardo, David 61, 68
Rich, Frank 3
Rifkin, Jeremy 139
Rodrik, Dani 86
Roosevelt, Franklin Delano 31, 33, 40, 134, 159
Roosevelt, Theodore 104
Ryan, Paul 9

Sachs, Jeffrey 133, 154
Sarkozy, Nicholas 28, 107
Saunders, Peter 55
Schumpeter, Joseph 45

Schwarzenegger, Arnold 89
Scott, Robert E. 72–3
Sewell, Thomas 92
Sing, Ajit 83
Singer, Fred 92, 95
Skidelsky, Robert 180–3
Skocpol, Theda 158–9
Slivinski, Stephen 121
Smith, Adam 35, 37, 40, 43, 45
Smith, Paul 120
Smith, Yves 182
Snow, John 41
Solis, Hilda 152
Spencer, Jack 98
Starr, Paul 2
Stern, Sir Nicholas 101
Stiglitz, Joseph 31, 148, 176
Summers, Larry 4, 22, 31, 156

Taylor, John 161, 162
Tett, Gillian 176
Tiersky, Amos 183
Toqueville, Alex de 115

Vigilante, Richard 161, 163, 166
Volker, Paul 31

Wallison, Peter 26, 161–2, 163
Warren, Dorian 152
Warren, Elizabeth 30, 139
Waxman, Henry 180
Winthrop, John 115
Wolf, Martin 39, 117, 143
Wright, Reverend Jeremiah 71

Subject Index

abortion 81
ACORN 165
adjustable rare mortgage (ARM) 166
Afghanistan 74
AFL-CLO 152
Africa 71
Al Qaeda 73
American Recovery and
Reinvestment Act 20, 25, 111
American superiority 114–19,
119–40
Answering Back 57, 174
anti-americanism 134
anti-poverty programs 151
anti-statism 47–8
Anton's Blindness 184
Apollo Alliance 109
Argentina 74
Asian financial crisis of 1997–8 82–3
auto industry 15, 21, 131–2

bailouts 14–15
bank bonuses, 15, 18–19, 53, 57,
144–5
banking system 24, 30–1, 170, 173–4
Bank of America 13, 18, 19, 175
bank regulation 22, 28, 150
bankruptcy 13, 14, 21, 24, 26, 29
Bear Stearns 13, 15, 174, 176
bipartisanship 1, 5, 32, 59, 141, 161
Blue-Dog Democrats 2–3
BP oil spill 91
Brazil 67, 77, 90, 127–8, 147

cap and trade 90, 97, 110, 112
capital controls 79
capital, impatient 132
capitalism 12, 77
carbon dioxide 90, 94, 95, 96, 99, 103,
104–5, 106, 112
Center for American Progress 109, 151
charity illusion 54
Cheney principle, the 113
Chicago School of Economics 180,
181, 182
Chief Executive Officers (CEOs) 18,
50, 78, 82, 151, 175
child care 151
child labor 86
China 66, 67, 72, 73, 74, 77, 79, 80, 82,
85, 87, 90, 97, 98, 194, 112, 127–8,
147–8, 177

Christian Right 8, 90
Chrysler 21
Citigroup 15, 18–19, 176
Citizens United 155
Clean Air Act, The 104, 110
clean coal technology 97, 98
climate change 91–2, 92–9, 99–100
collectivism 121
colonialism 76, 85
commercial paper 15
commons, tragedy of 107–8
communism 35, 37
Communist Manifesto, The 77
Community Reinvestment Act, The 160, 161
comparative advantage 61–2
Congressional Budget Office 20, 30
conservatives 1, 2, 5, 8, 11, 25–9, 41, 47–8, 51
Consumer Financial Protection Agency 19
consumer protection 49
consumers 37, 43, 54
contradictions 81, 108
Copenhagen 90–1
Countrywide Financial 13, 170, 175
Cowboy Capitalism 116, 121, 126
credit 12, 18, 70
credit crunch 12, 15, 29, 52, 160–78
credit ratings 174
crony capitalism 121, 156, 161

debt 70, 140, 143, 144–5, 146, 177
Declaration of Independence, The 115
deficits 27, 29
deflation 12
deindustrialization 71–2, 87–8, 145
democrats 2–3, 5, 6, 41, 119
Department of Commerce 87
Department of Housing and Urban Development (HUD) 149, 165, 168
Department of Labor 86, 149, 152
Department of Veteran Affairs 17
dependent development 75–6
deregulated markets 28, 145, 148
Dodd-Frank Wall Street reform and Consumer Protection Act, The 19, 142

Earned Income Tax Credits 151
economic growth 13, 19–20, 21
Economic Policy Institute 72, 109, 151–2
economic system 10
economy, U.S. 12, 15, 25, 27, 28, 116–17, 123–6
education 20, 128–9, 130
Efficient Market Hypothesis, The 163, 175, 180–8
empire 118, 135–7, 154
Employee Free Choice Act, The 152
employment 20, 25, 27, 31, 32, 70–1, 124
energy 88, 89, 97, 112
Enron 53
environmental degradation 108, 112
environmental standards 69, 87, 88, 89, 98, 111
Environment Protection Agency, The (EPA) 88, 90, 97, 104, 110, 111
Europe 40–1, 51, 56
European Union 105–7, 116, 118, 123, 124–5, 126–7, 128, 147
exceptionalism, American 115–16, 122
externalities 46–7

fair trade 86–7, 152–3
Federal Deposit Insurance Corporation (FDIC) 18, 165
Federal Housing Authority (FHA) 17, 26
Federal National Mortgage Association (Fannie Mae) 13–14, 16, 17, 26, 161–2, 165, 167–70
Federal National Mortgage Corporation (Freddie Mac) 13, 14, 17, 26, 161–2, 165, 167–70

Federal Reserve, The 12, 13–15, 19, 22, 26, 29, 40, 57, 162, 173
FIAT 21
financial crisis 12, 28, 52, 57–8
Financial Crisis Inquiry Commission 165, 174
financial institutions 4, 13, 14–15, 18–19, 30–1, 132–3, 142–3
financial instruments 176, 181
financialization 82, 143
financial regulation 4, 19, 68
Foreclosure, Home 9, 13, 15, 16–17, 23–4, 29, 30, 57–8, 138, 160
foreign direct investment 132
fossil fuel 97
Fox News 81
France 124
freedom 37, 46, 54–6, 67
free markets 13, 33, 34–41, 52
free trade 60–9, 85
full employment 49, 51, 52

G7/8, The 104, 133
G20, The 22, 133
Garn-St. Germain Act, The 171
General Motors (GM) 21, 41, 79
Germany 127, 147, 154, 177
Glass-Steagall Act, The 171, 172
global capitalism 15, 28, 77–8, 85
globalization 41, 67, 68, 85, 145
global warming 91, 93, 94, 96–7
global work force 78–9
GMAC 18
Goldman Sachs 19, 175, 176
Government National Mortgage Association (Ginnie Mae) 168
Gramm-Leach-Bliley Act 171, 172
Great Depression, The 12, 40, 52, 123, 163, 171
Great Society, The 159
greed 53, 175
green capitalism 108
green economy 89–113
greenhouse gases 95, 99, 103, 110
green politics 53
gridlock 5
GSEs 14, 16, 17–18, 26, 160

Hadley Centre, The 102
Hamilton Project , The 109
happiness, 55–6
health care 4, 6, 9, 50, 55, 56, 127, 138–9
health care reform 19–20
hedge funds 14, 19
Home Affordable Mortgage Program (HAMP) 16, 30
home ownership 27
house prices 13, 23, 25
housing 12, 13, 15, 16, 17, 18, 23, 24, 26, 29, 30, 31
housing crisis 16, 23, 26, 29, 30, 143
housing finance 29, 164, 167–70
housing policy 4, 26, 30, 149, 164–5, 168
Hurricane Katrina 57, 96

immigration 27, 64, 116
imperfect competition 44–5
imperial decline 137
imperialism 76, 132, 134–7
imperial over-reach 134–7, 154
import substitution industrialization (ISI) 66, 83
An Inconvenient Truth 95
India 67, 74, 77, 85, 90, 104, 112, 127–8, 147
Indonesia 67, 82
industrial militancy 121
industrial policy 49, 87–8, 153–4, 156
industrial training 49
inequality 46, 53, 55, 64, 67, 74–5, 138–9, 177
inflation 12, 24
information asymmetries 182–3
infrastructure 21, 49, 154
institutional strangulation 30
insurance companies 18
Intergovernmental Panel on Climate Change 93, 95, 101, 102–3, 105

International Labour Organization (ILO) 75
International Monetary Fund (IMF) 77, 78
international trade 62–3
investment houses 13, 15, 170, 171
invisible hand, the 43
irrationality 45–6, 175

Japan 67, 80, 82, 127, 154, 177
Jim Crow 121
JP Morgan Chase 13, 19

Keynesianism 40, 41, 48–9, 80, 135, 162, 182–8
Kyoto Accord 89, 97, 104

labor 121–2, 139–40, 144–5
labor markets 50–2, 53
labor productivity 124
labor rights 59, 69, 86, 87
laissez-faire 28
Latin-America 74, 75, 82
Lehman Brothers 13, 14, 176
libertarians 6, 9, 26–7, 28, 40
living standards 55
loans 13, 14–15, 17–18, 23, 24, 26, 30

Malaysia 82
managed trade 82–8
manufacturing, U.S. 15, 72, 77–8, 130–1, 145
market deregulation 35–42, 44, 47, 50, 58–9
Marshall Plan 65
Medicaid 138, 156
Medicare 8, 156–7
Mexico 83
military-industrial complex 135
military spending 134, 135–6, 154, 185
monetary policy 15, 167
money gluts 80–1
monopolies 46–7, 52
morality 38–9, 52–4
Morgan Stanley 19
mortgage-backed securities 14, 17
mortgages 13, 14, 15–18, 23, 24, 166
mutual fund industry 18

National Academy of Sciences 103, 130
Natural Resources Defense Council 109, 111
negative deindustrialization 72, 145
negative equity 13, 23, 25, 29, 30
negative freedom 54–5
neo classical economics 80, 175, 185–6
neo liberalism 76, 119
New Deal, The 23, 27–8, 33, 40, 122, 123, 158, 159
New Economic Foundation 74–5
New Zealand 96
North America Free Trade Agreement (NAFTA) 64, 72–3, 83
North, The 66, 67, 78, 84–8
North Carolina 79
Norway 96, 124, 125
nuclear power 97, 98

oil, drilling for 98
outsourcing of jobs 60, 66, 70, 85, 131–2

paradigm shift 58–9
perfect competition 43, 44, 45
Petersen Institute 65
Philanthropy, private 117
positive deindustrialization 72
positive freedom 54–5
poverty 53, 56–7, 74, 138–9, 151
productivity 52
progressives 31–3, 57, 149–54
property rights 82
protectionism 60, 63, 65, 69, 82, 84–8
Prudential Financial 18

rational expectations 45
regulation 4, 9, 39–40, 44, 47, 55, 58–9
research and development 130–1
Royal Bank of Scotland, The (RBS) 176

Russia 127–8

savings and loans 168, 169, 171
savings glut 80–1
Securities and Exchange Commission (SEC) 19, 172, 174
securitization 169
short termism 132
social compact 52, 78, 148
socialism 9, 42
Social Structures of Accumulation 187
solar power 112
South, The 66–7, 73–6, 78, 82–4
South Africa 90
South Korea 67, 82
state, types of 48–50
stealth imperialism 134
Stern Report, The 101
stimulus package 4, 9, 20, 111, 150–1
stock markets 49
stress 56
subprime lending 12, 164, 166, 170, 173
subsidies 121, 156
Supreme Court 90, 155
Switzerland 75, 125

tariffs 64–5, 82, 84, 86
Tea Party, the 5–6, 8–9, 10–11
terrorism 67, 73, 90
Thailand 74
toxic assets 14, 79, 170
trade barriers 62–3
trade deficit 66, 72–3, 80, 123–4, 131, 133, 135
trade policy 152–3
trade unions 51, 52, 116, 125, 151
training 128–9
triangulation 7
trickle down economics 59
Troubled Asset Relief Program (TARP) 16, 21, 25
Tyndall Centre, The 93

unequal exchange 53

values, American 10, 15–16, 120–1, 122, 136
Vietnam 83
voting 38, 49–50, 120

wages 52, 70–1, 152
Wall Street 4, 172, 173, 175, 180
Wal-Mart 57, 70–1, 72, 85
Waxman-Markey Bill, The 91
Wealth of Nations, The 35, 43
weapons of mass destruction 113, 134
welfare 10, 49, 59
welfare states 38, 41, 51, 126, 156
Wells Fargo 15, 19
wind power 112
women's movement 53
World Bank 14, 77
Worldcom 53
World Economic Forum 105, 125, 132
World Trade Organization (WTO) 66, 77, 82
World Wildlife Fund 101–2